A Music Journey Remembered

The Life and Times of Brad Evans, Musician

BRADLEY W. KUHNS

A MUSIC JOURNEY REMEMBERED

Printed in the United States of America

First Printing: 2012
Second Printing: 2013

ISBN:979-8-215-55057-7

Dedication

First, I dedicate this book to my beloved mother who bought my first musical instrument in my early elementary years. She wholehearted supported my decision to go into the entertainment business.

Second, to all of those musicians and vocalists over the years that worked in my musical group, The Encores.

To all of my entertainer show business friends with whom I had the privilege to work with throughout my career. It was a true experience.

With affection and gratitude to all,

Brad

Acknowledgements

I would like to acknowledge:

My agent, Mr. Jack Kurtze for representing my musical group and who booked "Brad Evans and his Encores" into some of the most popular night spots across the country and abroad and for his introduction to many celebrities that allowed me to work with them on my musical journey through my life.

A warm thanks goes to Elvis Presley and his father Vernon for their friendship and gifts over the years.

A special acknowledgement to the famous Rat Pack who gave me years of exciting experiences that will forever provide me with memories to last a lifetime.

Finally, to entertainers and celebrities- The Mills Brothers; Frankie Laine; Nat King Cole; Vikki Carr, Chuck Rio,(aka) Danny Flores "Mr. Tequila"; Cheryl Tiegs; Glen Campbell; Frank Gorshin; Tempest Storm; Herb Jefferies; Engelbert Humperdinck and others. THANK YOU, for your talent and friendship.

Contents

Introduction

This biographical story was written from the notes and journals of Brad Evans. It covers decades of his life up to the mid 1970s. The life of Brad began with him growing up in New York and then a small coal mining town in Pennsylvania. As a teen, his life moved forward as he relocated to the Pacific Northwest where in Portland, Oregon he begins his music career at the age of 17. He formed his own music group and toured and appeared with many well-known entertainers. When he joined the military he continued his music and played in the United States Marine Corp (U.S.M.C.) Band.

Following his military service, Brad formed his band, The Encores, and traveled around the country appearing on stage with some of the same well-known celebrities he worked with early in his music career. His musical talent allowed him to know and work with such notables as Frank Sinatra and the Rat Pack, Elvis, Frankie Laine, The Mills Brothers, Herb Jefferies, Lou Rawls, Savanna Churchill and many others. Brad enjoyed an interesting career while working as a musical sideman and band leader. For those that knew Brad in the 1950s through the 1970s and saw his group, The Encores, perform, these recollections will bring back memories of old.

About the Author

Brad Evans began his professional music career at age 17, playing saxophone in burlesque theatres, performing on a weekly radio show and touring the Pacific Northwest with a media-sponsored troupe, The Oregon Journal Juniors (O.J.J.) and Oregon Journal Seniors (O.J.S.). As a teen in Portland, Oregon, he formed his band, The Encores, and backed world-famous celebrities for 20 years.

While in the United States Marine Corp, he was assigned to the elite Marine Corp Band that performed across the nation. After military service, his musical group traveled the United States performing in casinos, hotels, nightclubs and dinner houses in small towns and large entertainment centers in Las Vegas, wowing audiences with their talent.

In 1973, he retired from the music entertainment business to pursue another career and in 1993, after retiring from the second career, he returned to the music scene performing as a one-man-band and doing recording work on music CDs. He officially retired from the music business in 2008.

Prelude

There must be of necessity of a certain interest in writing a story. The temptation of the author to walk down paths shaded by personal experience, to linger in some valley of happiness and excitement of his choosing, to climb high atop a hill and view his own particular swath of life is ever present. How much greater the achievement when the writer, without wandering from the main road, arrives successfully at the finish.

In the opening chapter, Brad Evans, Musician, takes the reader by the hand and introduces him to where his roots began. He then proceeds to his birth, his young life growing up in Long Island, New York and a small coal mining town in Pennsylvania and whose interest in music became evident at a very young age while in the second grade.

The biography continues as it follows Brad's introduction into the entertainment business during the fabulous '50s and '60s era where the long-forgotten days of old Las Vegas is remembered. Thus, Brad's biography lengthens with a list of entertainers, each of whom in their own way relates to their life and times in Brad's life.

01

Where It All Began

My Roots

My ancestor's footprints begin in Europe in Hungary. My maternal grandfather Joseph Basits, was born in Pecs, Hungary on March 16, 1875. He was a big man, stood 6'2" tall, had steely gray eyes and weighed 188 pounds. He married Mary, in 1897 and they had a male child named Edmond while living in Pecs. Joseph and his family later immigrated to Germany. They spent time in Hamburg where my mother, Mary, was born on December 12, 1899. She was the second child of six.

Joseph then emigrated from Bremen, Germany with his wife and three children on September 18, 1902 aboard the ship Chemnitz and arrived at the port of Baltimore, Maryland on October 2, 1902 with only $6 to his name. Mom was three years old when the family arrived on the shores of the U.S.A.

Joseph became a United States citizen on November 2, 1908 when he was 33 years old. The family settled in with some relatives in the small coal mining town of Heidelberg, Pennsylvania located near Pittsburg. The relatives were the sponsors for my grandfather's family into the United States. Joseph worked as a coal miner in towns in the southwestern part of Pennsylvania and it wasn't long until Joseph became settled in their new country. He told his family that they were to learn English and speak English now that they were in America. Joseph was teased, made fun of and called names by his co-workers in the mines for the first couple of years because he didn't speak English very well. He was called a 'hunky', a 'square head' and a 'kraut'. He made it a point to learn English as quickly as possible.

Joseph saved his money, bought a small farm and made all of his kids work the place; Mom only got to go to school through the third grade. She says her dad was very strict and expected all the girls to help around the house. He told my mother and her sisters that they had to earn their keep and learn to cook and clean house because that was their place in life. He also told them that when they were old enough to make money, they should work outside of the house. The farm had cows, chickens and other farm animals and when mom was seven years old she had to help her mother milk the cows and make butter and cottage cheese. She would churn butter for hours and her mother would form the butter into one-pound blocks. Mom was then sent into the nearby town of Brownsville, Pennsylvania where she and her brother and sisters sold the fresh butter and cheese to the rich Jewish families that lived in town.

Joseph was injured in the coal mine when a large slab of slate rock fell and landed on him. After he was hurt he couldn't do heavy lifting and he couldn't dig or shovel coal anymore. After the injury, Joseph became angry, grouchy and even more strict. He found fault with most everything that happened around the farm.

One day, Joseph and his wife were talking to the vegetable and fruit man that delivered to the houses in the area and the man asked if Joseph knew of anyone to help his wife around the house and take care of his children. He told the man that he had a daughter that was trained to take care of children. He indicated my mom, Mary, helped raise her sister and brothers and she also knew how to clean house. At this time mom was 14 years old when Joseph told mom it was time for her to earn her keep.

Brad's mothers grandsparents.

Theresa (Mangold Basits) and Joseph Basits, Sr.

Brad's mothers parents-Mary and Joseph

Brad's mothers family arriving in the U.S., in 1902. Brad's mother is the little blonde, far right, first row, sitting on white fur rug. Behind her is her grandmother and in center, at table, is her parents.

UNITED STATES DEPARTMENT OF JUSTICE

IMMIGRATION AND NATURALIZATION SERVICE

300 NORTH LOS ANGELES STREET

LOS ANGELES, CALIFORNIA 90012

C# 63263E

December 27, 1978

Mr. Bradley Kuhns
P. O. Box 1514
Ontario, CA 91762

RE: Jozef Basits (AKA: Jozsef)

Dear Mr. Kuhns:

We are happy to inform you that we have located some records
on the above named person; per your two G-641 requests submitted last year.

According to those records: He was born in Pecs Baranja,
Hungary, on March 16, 1875. He emigrated from Bremen,
Germany on the vessel "Chemnitz", and arrived at our port
in Baltimore, Maryland on or about October 2, 1902.

He listed his wife as Mary, age 39 in his naturalization
petition dated July 7, 1915. He also listed six children:
Edmund, born September 27, 1898 at Pecs Baranja, Hungary;
Mary, born December 12, 1899 at Hamborn, Germany; Joseph,
born June 26, 1901 at Pecs Baranja, Hungary; Alexander,
born October 15, 1907 in Braznell, Penna.; Helen, born
July 1, 1909 in Elkhorn, Penna.; and Theresa, born October
27, 1911 also in Elkhorn, Penna. Their residence was in
Grindstone, Penna., and his occupation was a coal miner.

He declared his intention to become a citizen in the
Western District of Pennsylvania Court on November 2, 1908,
at the age of 33. This paper remained in his possession
until about March 16, 1912, when his home was destroyed
by fire. He then requested a duplicate copy of it, and
was issued one on June 24, 1915.

He petitioned for naturalization (see date above) in the
Common Pleas Court at Fayette County, Penna., and took
his oath in Uniontown, Penna. on December 3, 1915. He
was issued a certificate number 632638.

Sincerely,

E. Bressickello
Privacy/FOIA Clerk

Brad's mother, Mary , 2 years old.

Mom was sent to a prominent Jewish family and was told her duties were to clean the house, wash dishes and care for the family's children. She went to work as a live-in servant and was paid $3.50 a week. She received $.50 a week and her father took the rest. She worked that first job for about three months and then worked other small jobs which included working as a cook in a small restaurant. A couple years later, Joseph told mom to come back home and help take care of the family on the farm. Being the dutiful daughter she was, she went back home and did most of the chores around the house.

In 1917, my grandfather became so mean and demanding that mom's brother, my Uncle Edmond, ran away and joined the Army. Edmond had a hatred for his dad because of the way he was treated growing up and he couldn't take his dad's bullshit anymore. When Edmond was in the Army he never wrote one letter to his dad, though he did write to mom, they were a very close brother and sister. They tried to look out after one another when their dad went off on one of his rampages. Once Edmond left the family, Joseph began to pick on mom. He told mom and the other girls that he didn't want any lazy loafers sitting around the house and they had better get out of the house and get a job.

Joseph began having his drinking buddies over to the house. Nick, owned two or three drug stores nearby and wanted to marry mom even though he was 22 years older than her. Nick told Joseph that he wanted to get married, raise a family, have someone that could help him in the business and he had his eye on mom. Joseph tried to keep mom at home on the poker and drinking nights so she would be around when Nick was there. Nick told Joseph that if he would let him marry mom he would give granddad a large chunk of money. That seemed to be a deal granddad couldn't pass up, so he was going to arrange that mom marry Nick.

Mom Marries Conrad Gaisbauer

During the drinking and gambling at granddads, mom would go outside to get away from the action. Sometime she would meet her brother's friend Conrad, who she called Connie. He lived nearby and would often come over to say hi to mom. He and Edmond had been friends for years so she felt that she could talk to him. One night she told Connie about her father's plan to marry her off to a much older man. Connie told her they'd figure something out and they sure did. They decided to run off and get married before she could be sold off to Nick, the druggist. Conrad gave mom $20 to buy a new dress—that was a lot of money in 1917. Conrad worked in the coal mines as a motorman. The two of them planned to run away on the night she was supposed to be delivered by her father to Nick. Her father was planning to take her into Brownsville to meet Nick who was going to take her·to a movie and then, following the movie, propose to her.

Mom and Connie laid out the plan that she would meet Connie at the train station and near train time she would excuse herself from her dad saying that she had to go to the restroom. Connie would be waiting for her by the train that was leaving for Pittsburg. He already had the tickets and luggage and was waiting for mom to come into the station. Mom went into town with a brown bag with a few things in it so her dad and Nick wouldn't get wise to what she was planning. Mom boarded the train with Conrad, they got to Pittsburg and married on September 17, 1917. Mom was only 17 years old.

They stayed in Pittsburg for a week because they were afraid to go back home. Conrad did go back and talked to Joseph and Mary, telling them he married mom. Granddad chewed out Conrad and said that since there was nothing he could do to change the situation he would have to live with it. He told Conrad, "Okay, you got her, you keep her. She can't come

Brad's mother, Mary at 17 years old with her first husband, Conrad Gaisbauer.

Grace Gaisbauer. first child of Mary Brad's half sister.

home." Joseph told Conrad that he and Nick stood outside the train station waiting for mom for over an hour.

Mom and Conrad settled in the small coal mining town of Orient, Pennsylvania where Conrad took a job in the coal mines. Meanwhile, Joseph bought some vacant land in Grindstone, Pennsylvania and built a movie theatre. As there was no movie theatre around for miles, Joseph thought he could draw a lot of people from the surrounding coal mining towns. Joseph built the family's living quarters above the movie theatre and made room in the theatre for a candy store. The small concession stand also sold cigarettes, soft drinks and ice cream. Grandmother and mom's sisters helped out at the movie theatre. The films shown at the theatre were all silent movies since "talkies" hadn't come to the movie industry yet. It looked like Joseph made a smart move because the theatre did a very brisk business.

A few years later, June 16, 1921, mom and Conrad had a daughter and named her Grace. Mom and Conrad then moved back to Grindstone where he got a job in the coal mine as a motorman. Mom would take Grace, my half-sister to the movie theatre when my mother's husband Conrad was too tired to go out. Because mom's mother, Mary, worked every night at the theatre selling tickets, my mother began to relieve her mother, giving her a break. While mom was working at the theatre she met a regular customer named Cook and began having an affair with him. He worked as a miner in the Grindstone coal mine. My mother's marriage with Conrad was coming apart and she decided to end it so she moved out of the house leaving Conrad alone. My mother took her daughter, Grace, to her mother's house and made arrangements for her mother to care for her. My mom told her mother that she was going to go to Pittsburg and get a job cooking. As the story goes, when my mother's husband Conrad came home from work, she was gone. No one other than my mom's mother knew where she went. My mom's mother kept Grace, my half-sister, at her house. My mother paid room and board for Grace's care.

The day after my mother arrived in Pittsburg she landed a cooking job at a tuberculosis sanitarium that was operated by the City of Pittsburg. Mom would also return to Grindstone to help out at the theatre whenever she could. This is where my dad, William Bradley Kuhns, came into the picture. Mom was back in Grindstone selling tickets at the theatre when a very handsome, tall, smooth-talking man walked up to the ticket booth and bought a ticket. He returned to the movie theatre three nights in a row buying a ticket for the same film each night. His name was Bill, short for William and he hung around the ticket booth and talked to mom between customers. He asked her out and my mom went out with him one time before she had to return to Pittsburg and her other job. About the same time of this meeting with Bill, my mother was still continuing her affair with Cook, better known as Cookie to his friends. While all of this was going on my mother's divorce with Conrad was becoming final. My mother was conflicted as to which man she wanted to be with. Was it Bill Kuhns or Cookie? She knew Cook was a steady, stable person and a hard worker but my dad, Bill, had somewhat of a wild streak in him.

Shortly after my dad came into the picture my mom's lover, Cookie, relocated to Akron, Ohio. He told my mother that he was getting away from the coal mines and was going to get a job working in one of the many rubber factories in Akron. Akron was a rubber capitol. The city was turning out tires for the auto industry by the millions. Once Cook was in Akron he wrote my mom telling her Akron was a boom city and opportunities abound.

Mom Marries Dad

By June, 1924, mom had moved to Akron, Ohio. My mother bought a small 200 seat restaurant there in 1925 and the restaurant did a tremendous business. My soon-to-be father followed her to Akron from Pennsylvania. He took a job as a barber, but after a couple of weeks he was fired from the job. They lived together living off mom's earnings. On June 26, 1926 they went to city hall and were married. Mom sold her restaurant and, with the money from the sale, bought a small farm near Pittsburg, Pennsylvania.

Mom and dad were married for four years when Ramona was born on April 26, 1930. The night before Mona's birth, mom told dad that she didn't feel good, but he was drunk and told mom he didn't believe her. The next morning mom again told dad that she was feeling sick and wanted him to stay home from work to be with her, but her pleas fell on deaf ears. His reply was, "You'll be telling me the same thing when I come home from work tonight," and he walked out of the door on his way to work in the coal mine.

At about 5:30 in the morning, after dad left for work, mom experienced some labor pains. She decided to walk to a phone booth near a small grocery store to call the doctor. During her walk up the hill she experienced more pains, but after about half an hour she made it to the phone booth and called the doctor. He told her he was on his way. Mom told the doctor that she would walk back home and he should look for her along the road; however, she made it back home before the doctor got there. She was alone and afraid, but had enough sense to leave the front door open so when the doctor got there he could walk right in. Ten minutes after mom got home, the doctor arrived and about 20 minutes later Ramona was born.

I'm Born

On January 24, 1936 mom was 36 years old. She and dad were sitting in the kitchen across the table from one another drinking coffee when he looked at mom and said, "Let's fight." He threw his heavy coffee mug at mom but missed then he got up and grabbed a hot stove poker from the nearby coal stove and went after her. This act was nothing new for dad because he'd used a hot poker on mom in the past. From all accounts, dad was a mean man especially when he drank booze; he was abusive to mom on a regular basis. One time he pressed the hot stove poker against her breasts and burnt them. He caught mom and began slapping and punching her. He hit mom in the stomach with his fists then knocked her to the floor and kicked her.

Following that beating, and on dad's birthday, January 27, 1936, mom went into labor. It was freezing cold in the dead of winter and Dr. Harrington walked two miles from the trolley line to our farmhouse because his car couldn't get through the five and six foot high snowdrifts. He stayed at the farmhouse for those three days until he and my mother could bring me into this world. On January 27 the doctor asked mom, "Do you feel the baby moving?"

Mom said, "No, all I feel is pain."

The doctor put a wooden apple box at the bottom of the bed by mom's feet and said, "When the pain gets bad, brace yourself by pushing against the box."

On the 28th the labor pains became further and further apart and the doctor became worried because of mom's worn out condition. Mom was no longer having contractions and the doctor said if mom was to have some pain; it would help with the delivery so he sent Mrs. Richardson, a neighbor who was staying in the house downstairs, to go get dad. Dad took one

Allison, PA-on Brad's parents farm, circa-1920's. Brad's mother and father, Mary and William "Bill".

Brad at 10 months.

arm and Dr. Harrington took the other. In order to shock mom and cause pain, he proceeded to pull out mom's wisdom teeth one by one without anesthetic.

On the third day, January 30, Dr. Harrington felt as if the baby might be dead. He told dad that he was going to give mom some medication to throw her into convulsions so she would react and that would help with the delivery. Again, dad held one arm, the doctor the other, while he administered the medicine to cause mom to go into convulsions. Nothing happened and Dr. Harrington made the decision to use forceps to make the delivery. A couple of hours later I came into the world. I was what they called a 'blue baby' back in those days. The doctor held me in the palm of his hand. I was so small my feet were at the doctor's fingertips and my head was at his wrist. The bones in my skull weren't completely closed, my ears were like little celluloid disks about the size of a nickel. Dr. Harrington turned to my father and said, "Your son weighs only 14 ounces, which one do you want me to save?"

My dad's reply, "My wife."

Mrs. Richardson, the neighbor, continued to stay at the house. She was told by the doctor that there was little hope for my survival, but if there was any chance at all she was to get a basin, fill it with warm water and submerge my small body into the water leaving the face above the water. The doctor showed Mrs. Richardson how to dip me into the basin of warm water and if I began to turn blue or black, he showed her how to blow into my mouth when I would quit breathing. Dr. Harrington slept on the floor by my mother's bed for the entire three days of delivery. When I would stop breathing the doctor or neighbor would breathe into my mouth and then work my little arms and legs like an accordion until I regained a pinkish complexion. They didn't dress me for weeks because I was constantly being submerged into the basin of warm water.

Dr. Harrington prescribed a feeding regimen for me. I was to be fed with an eyedropper that contained three drops of breast milk and one drop of whiskey every hour. The doctor explained to mom, dad and Mrs. Richardson that the whiskey was for the sole purpose of keeping my heart beating. When I cried after the birth it was only a little squeak like a bird chirping. I was three weeks old before I could nurse from mom's breast and then only for one and two minutes at a time. During this time they continued to give me artificial respiration and work my arms and legs. It was a struggle for the first eight weeks according to mom and notes from her journal. When I was three months old I weighed only three pounds.

Dr. Harrington came by every day. He'd walk the two miles from the trolley to the farmhouse through the snow, stop in the doorway and ask mom, "Is he still with us?"

Mom replied, "Yes."

He said, "That's good, because for every hour we can keep this baby alive it will give him an extra day to live."

Mom told me that when I did nurse I would drink only about a thimble full of milk a day. She wrote in her journal that if it wasn't for the care of Dr. Harrington and Mrs. Richardson, she and I might have died. Mom went on to say in her writings that dad cared less about the delivery and birth. He would come into the room once a day, but would quickly leave and resume his drinking sprees.

Mom Runs Away from Dad

My mother had thoughts of leaving dad many times. He was a drunk and an abusive husband who left her pregnant and barefoot without any money. When it came to money, dad would only dole out enough for mom to buy the needed groceries. She knew she needed money to run away and when dad was out on one of his drunken binges mom got her chance. She dug up an old Prudential Insurance policy that her mother took out for her when she married dad. Her mother paid $.05 a week for the policy. With me 18 months old, Mom walked to the schoolhouse and took Mona out of her first grade class. Mom walked to the nearby grocery store and called a taxicab.

When the cab came to pick us up Mom asked the taxi driver if he would take a few chickens in exchange for the fare. The driver agreed. He took us back to the farm, gathered up a few chickens and took us downtown. Mom walked in to the insurance office and cashed out her policy for which she received $33. With that and the little cash she scraped together at the house, she had $60 to her name for her and two kids to live on. She had no idea where she would run to when she got to the bus depot, but decided to buy a ticket for New York City, even though she knew no one in that city. Ramona and I were so young we rode for free on the bus. We left for New York City before dad got home from work in the coal mine. We were on the bus 24 hours and the first thing mom did was buy us some food in the bus terminal as soon as we arrived in New York City.

Surviving in New York City

Mom changed her name using the alias Margaret Wilson. She got work as a chef in a number of major hotels and was living from hand to mouth to support us. Close to a year after arriving in New York City in 1937, mom became ill and was hospitalized. Mom's hospitalization came about when she was walking home from work. Mom stepped off of the curb to cross the street, she began to bleed and passed out in the street. The police and ambulance came to the scene and transported mom to the hospital. She was taken to Saint Luke's hospital on Morningside Drive. It was a private hospital for patients who could afford to pay but even though my mother wasn't someone who could pay for private care, the ambulance was required to take patients to the nearest hospital. My mom, Mary, suffered serious complications during my birth.

After the difficult birth on the Pennsylvania farm doctor Harrington told mom and my dad that as soon as my mother could get out of bed she and I should both be followed up in a hospital but according to my mother my dad refused to let mom go to the hospital.

One of my mother's medical problems following my birth was that she would have bouts of profuse bleeding. She used Turkish face towels to stop the bleeding because regular sanitary napkins were not adequate. When my mother told me this story she said following my birth it was like having a continuous period. The internal bleeding was a by-product of my birth.

On arrival at the hospital my mother was unconscious and in a coma. She underwent three blood transfusions. While at Saint Luke's she went under the knife. The doctors performed a hysterectomy. After a few weeks at Saint Luke's mom was transferred to a convalescent hospital. Weeks into her stay there she had a repeat bout of severe bleeding. The doctors at the convalescent hospital rushed her back to Saint Luke's Hospital by ambulance. My mother experienced partial paralysis in her legs and her vision was impaired. Mom's sight was so blurry she couldn't read books, papers or signs. The doctors immediately reopened mom's old incision for another surgery to determine what was causing the excessive bleeding. The doctors found that the ties they used in mom's first surgery had broken loose.

During all those months my mother was in the hospital my sister, Ramona and I were cared for by Catholic Charities. While mom was in the hospital her sister, Helen, who lived in Clarksville, Pennsylvania, wrote her and asked for $50. Helen was in some sort of accident and thought mom was making a lot of money working in New York City. That was far from the truth, Mom was struggling, but she told her sister that if she'd watch my sister and me, she would pay Helen $60 a month for our room and board. Helen agreed and mom saved some money to get the fare to go back to Pennsylvania where she gave us over to her sister. Helen and her husband Bill Byrnes had two children, a son Billie Byrnes, about my sister's age and a daughter, Patti Ann, close to my age.

Mom returned to New York City and buckled down to earn money. She began to take every job she could find in hotels as a chef. Besides working as a chef in major hotels like the famed Essex House and the Aberdeen Hotel, she began to fashion model to make extra money. She began living with a guy named Vanderbilt who was a watchmaker by profession. They got a nice apartment in Flushing Queens on Long Island. Now that mom was making more money and living in a fairly large apartment, she made the decision to bring us kids back to live with her. It was 1940 and things were really going good for everyone in New York City and all over the country.

Living in Clarksville, Pennsylvania

Ramona was eight years old and I was two years old when we were sent to live with Aunt Helen and Uncle Bill. Clarksville was a small town of a few thousand people and most of the residents worked in the coal mines. Aunt Helen and Uncle Bill's house was a wood-framed three bedroom with an outhouse instead of a bathroom. While living with the Byrnes family, when I was in first grade, I had to help dig out a cellar beneath the house. Uncle Bill, my cousins Billy, Patti Ann and my sister, Mona, also worked on this project. This was really hard work, I recall carrying out buckets of red and blue clay from underneath the house as the cellar was built.

My cousin, Billy, who was about seven years older than me was a mean, sneaky, conniving kid. Billy would do bad things and break house rules and blame it on me or my sister; we were the ones that got punished for his mischievous and harmful acts. My sister and I got the brunt of the beatings and punishment. Billy was so mean that he told me what to eat before meals. When we were out of earshot of his parents, he told me what I could eat during meals and how many servings I could have. He would say such things as, "You can't have any corn, string beans or dessert tonight and you can have only one slice of bread. If I tried to eat more than what he told me, he would kick me under the table to warn me not to reach for a certain food. If I didn't obey, he would get me alone after the meals and beat on me. One time he was playing with matches in the garage and burned down the garage, but when his parents asked him how the garage burned he immediately told them I was playing with matches and burned the garage to the ground.

Mom came in from New York for a visit and while sitting on the porch, she saw Billy hit and kick a four-year-old neighbor girl to the ground and then run back into the house. When the girl's parents complained to Aunt Helen, Billy denied the incident and Aunt Helen took Billy's side. Mom also saw Billy kick me until I cried and saw him tie my wrists with wire and hit me. That was the last straw for mom, she told Helen that this trip was to retrieve us and take us back to New York City, not only because she missed us, but that no one was going to abuse her children like she saw Billy do to me. After four years with the Byrnes family in Clarksville, I had finished the first grade, and my sister and I were again living with mom in New York City. I never saw the Byrnes family again.

Vanderbilt began to quarrel and argue with mom about us

kids. Mom got mad and told him if he didn't want to accept her children in their relationship then the relationship was over, and it was. She told him to leave and get out of the apartment. This meant that she had to pay the apartment rent by herself, but she was working two jobs and managed to make the rent and feed us. When mom went out on her own and ran away from my dad, she became a very independent woman; she was a woman that stuck up for herself and her kids.

Dad Shoots Girlfriend

While mom, my sister and I were living in New York, mom received news from Pennsylvania that on September 11, 1940 my father shot and killed a teacher with whom he was having an affair. The newspaper report said that dad went into the schoolhouse in the small town of Royal, Pennsylvania and shot Carolyn Bellama. Like mom she got tired of his abusive behavior and him seeing other women and refused to see him again. Apparently, he couldn't take the rejection or decided that if he couldn't have the lady no one else could. He went to the school, knocked on the classroom door and when Carolyn opened the door, he shot her. She fell dead on the floor. Then he shot himself and fell atop Carolyn's body.

The children in the class began jumping out of the windows of the little schoolhouse. Other teachers ran to the scene and called an ambulance. Carolyn lay dead, but dad was not dead, he survived his wound. He was hauled off to the hospital and then jail. People in the surrounding communities became very angry and some said that if they could get their hands on him they'd kill him. Once he was in the custody of the cops, no one could get at him.

Mom came in from New York City to attend Carolyn's funeral. There were hundreds of people attending the service to pay their respects to this beloved teacher. After the service, Carolyn's parents came over to mom, put their arms around her and hugged her. They said to mom, "I guess you left this man in time, but our daughter waited too long to get away from him." This murder case was big news in New York City with headlines screaming 'Lover Shoots Teacher in Presence of Children'. Mom returned to Pennsylvania to meet with authorities. After the court sentenced dad to die for his crime, they provided mom with the paperwork to divorce him. Instead of the death sentence originally sought, Judge S.J. Morrow sentenced dad to life in prison. The life sentence was ironic for mom because she had often told dad, "Bill, if I ever live long enough, I'll see you rot in prison." Judge S. John Morrow sentenced my father, William B. Kuhns to life in prison. The sentence was to begin on December 4, 1940. My father was taken to the Western State Penitentiary where he served a total of 21 years, 2 months, and 11 days. He was paroled by the Pennsylvania authorities and allowed to relocate to Florida under the supervision of the Florida Parole agency so he could work in a gas station which was owned by one of his brothers.

As far as I know from second hand accounts my father continued working at his brothers service station. My father died at the age of 69-years old on October 15, 1972, from a heart attack in the city of Hallandale, Florida.

Early New York City Experiences

Living on Long Island was a good time for me in the early 1940s. It was 1943 and I was 7-years old.

My sister and I did a lot of neat things together with mom. Mona would take me by the hand and we'd jump on the subway and go all over the city. She took me to Time Square to parks and Astoria, Rockaway and Jones Beaches, we went to Radio

City Hall to see the movies and the famed dance team, the Rockettes. When mom had time between her many different jobs we would take the subway to Central Park for the day. Mom would also take me shopping at the Woolworth's, about a block from our apartment, where she bought me all kinds of toys–cap guns, toy soldiers all kinds of little doodads. We'd sit at the counter and enjoy hotdogs and ice cream sodas. She and I would go the museum. We'd step off the subway at a museum where there were large windows depicting an African scene with lions, tigers and elephants. I remember other displays of dinosaurs and birds. The New York City Museum was a fantastic place; I never got tired of going there.

My mother, my sister, Mona and I had a fairly comfortable life. We were not rich by any stretch of the imagination. I would say we were middle class comfortable. My mom was working multiple jobs to support us two kids. She worked in some major hotels throughout New York City as a chef, she worked in small restaurants to make extra money, she cooked for large banquets and mom did her fashion modeling. It wasn't uncommon for mom to come home from one job ,change clothes, and go off to another job.

It was a nice life living with mom in New York. We did spend a lot of time as a family. All the time we lived on Long Island we never, ever went to a restaurant to eat. We ate all of our meals at home. Mom always found the time to cook and we would sit around the table eating together. That gave us a lot of quality time as a family. My mother managed to keep my sister and I fed and clothed. It was only because of mom working her butt off as a single mom that allowed us to have the basics and enjoy a ten cent movie or a day at Radio City Music Hall or a chocolate shake and hot dog at the counter at Woolworth's Five and Dime. My mother was a hard worker and to this day I don't know how she did all that.

The apartment we lived in was large and we had an aquarium full of tropical fish. Mom loved the tropical fish and was always adding fish to the tank, they were her pets. We had a large Philco Console Radio where I would lie on the floor and listen to radio programs like the Lone Ranger, Tom Mix and Gangbusters. Reading was one of my favorite pastimes and I had a good supply of comics and magazines. Though I played outside with the other kids on the block, I hung around the apartment a lot because of run-ins with the street bullies and street gangs.

In 1942, Mom enrolled me in the second grade on Long Island at P.S. #152. My desk was in the rear of the classroom and after a few weeks the teacher suspected I had trouble seeing the blackboard clearly from my seat. Mom took me to the optometrist and sure enough I needed glasses. Once I was fitted with glasses I could see the blackboard clearly and do my work. While in second grade, I was only 4'11", small for my age, and I was constantly picked on by the bigger kids. These bullies would take my lunch money and my jackets, hats and sweaters.

In the early 1940s, the school sold war bonds to help out the war effort. Parents gave their kids change to buy stamps, for war bonds, that were placed in a book and when the book was full we'd get a war bond. Mom would give me a quarter to buy stamps, but bullies would steal my quarter and I'd come home crying. My sister tried to look out for me, she would walk about a half a block behind me and when the bigger boys jumped me, she came running to my rescue. She was six years older than me and capable of beating up the bullies; they were afraid of her.

Many of these New York gang bullies, who attended my school, made fun of me because I came from a small town in Pennsylvania. They even blackmailed me, told me to bring

Brad's father, William, "Bill."-1940.
Bill's mug shot after his arrest.

Brad's dad, William, "Bill". Circa early 1940's.

Brad and his sister Ramona, 1941. His 5th. Birthday,

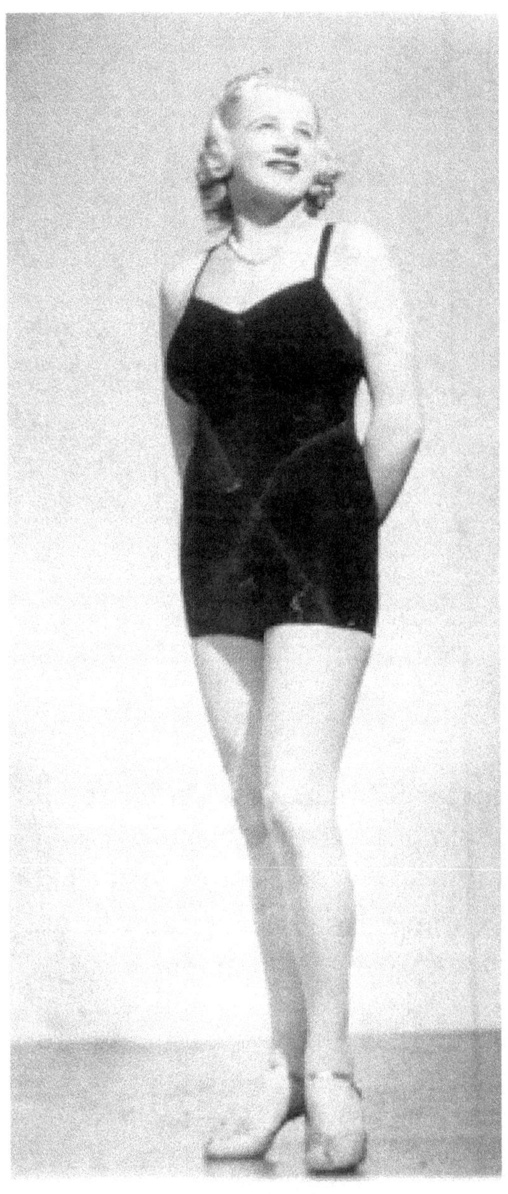

Brad's mother, Mary (aka) (Margaret Wilson), fashion modeling in New York City, in the 1940's. She was 42 years old at time of photo.

Brad's mom-Earlier years-Fashion Model Chef Business owner; Later in life, in her sunset years she went bach to school and was the oldest student at Chaffey College. She was attending classes a! 80 years old. Mary was a great lady, Article- appeared in the Ontario, California newspaper.

money to school or they would beat me up. Mona couldn't follow me to school every day, so many times I really got whipped by these gangs. Mom was working 16 to 18 hours a day, working her butt off to provide for us and she couldn't do too much to watch me on my way to and from school.

Besides taking care of us, mom had some problems of her own. One evening walking home from work mom got mugged. She was hit from behind with what was described by police as a metal pipe. The assailant tried to assault her, but mom started screaming bloody murder. That scared off the attacker, but mom was hit in the head so hard that the impact broke her denture plate. She was treated at the hospital and released. Following the attack, newspaper reporters came around to the apartment in an attempt to interview mom, but Mona told them to go away and leave mom alone.

It took a while for mom to get back to work after the assault. After the incident, she wouldn't walk on the sidewalk after dark. When she would walk home, she'd walk in the street whenever she could. She said that she was afraid that someone might try to spring out of an alley or from inside a doorway, so she preferred to walk in the street. Even after the attack, mom still tried to do what she could to look out for my well being at the school. She made arrangements with the owner of a small diner across the street from the school. Mom told me to go there each day and the man would fix me a hot meal, sometimes it was a burger, pie and milk. That helped a lot. I was now eating lunch where before the bullies stole my money. After a while mom found out that the guy at the diner was cheating her and charging money for meals that I didn't eat. She caught on to the scam and told him and his diner to take a hike.

Mom made me a plastic nameplate with my name and address and she put it on a string for me to wear around my neck. She told me that if I ever got lost or got into trouble while walking to school, I was supposed to stop a policeman and show him my nameplate. In the 1940s there was a policeman on just about every corner. The cops walked a beat in those days and we looked up to the policemen. They'd always say hello to us as we walked to and from school.

While I was in the second grade, I talked mom into letting me take violin lessons. She bought me a cheap violin and set up some music lessons, but it didn't take too long for me to find out that I didn't like playing the violin. I quickly lost interest, wouldn't practice and after a few months I gave it up completely.

02

Growing Up in Pennsylvania

Sent to Live with Aunt and Uncle

Because of the gangs and bullies I was exposed to on Long Island and at school, mom decided to send me to live with her other sister, Tres Hager, who lived in Pitt Gas, Pennsylvania, a small coal mining town a few miles from Clarksville. My sister, Ramona stayed in New York with mom.

Pitt Gas was also referred to as a coal mining patch where only a couple of hundred houses made up the community. The roads were dirt and covered with red dog, a crushed red rock that resembled the crushed rock you might see in a desert landscape or on a mobile home lot. Once a year the state would send a truck around to spray oil all over the red rock so it would pad down on the road.

The move back Pennsylvania caused me a bit of anguish and dismay. I missed mother and my sister. It seemed like two different worlds. I missed going to the movies, parks, museums and beaches with mom or my sister, Mona. I wondered how I would adjust to my new living arrangements with my aunt, uncle and their three kids.

Most everyone living in Pitt Gas worked in the coal mines. The coal town is surrounded by creeks, woods, hills and slate dumps that were created by coal being mined there. Pitt Gas had one general store, which was owned by the coal companies, where miners could buy their food and supplies. The store owners would carry many families on credit from payday to payday and when the miners collected their pay the store owner would collect what was owed on their bill. This was what the coal miners called the "company store."

To a large degree Pitt Gas was segregated with black and white housing areas. Each group basically stayed to themselves; although black and white children attended the same school. The coal patch had one school with grades from one to eight. Once a student finished the eighth grade they attended high school in Jefferson, Pennsylvania. The coal town had two churches, one for the white residents and the other for the blacks. Every Sunday when we walked to church, we passed the black church and could hear them inside singing all that great gospel music. I often thought I'd like to go into their church and take part in the music and singing. It appeared that the black folks were having a great time during their Sunday service compared to our church service. In our church the minister gave the sermon, the congregation sang a few hymns and a person passed a collection plate. Once the sermon and collection was over, some families stayed for Sunday school classes. Because of the times, there was no chance I would be able to walk into the black church.

Our House

Our house was a wood-framed and tar-shingled with two bedrooms and a cellar that ran the length of the house as did the front and back porches. There were no bathrooms in the Hager's house, we had a two-seat outhouse. Our toilet paper was newspaper and Sears and Montgomery Ward catalogues. Other than when I was with mom in New York and at school, I used outhouses for a bathroom until I was 15 years old. Since there were no bathrooms in the house, after we were in bed for the night, we used a pee pot, sometimes called a chamber pot or a thunder pot. We kept one under each bed in the house.

The weather in Pennsylvania was sometimes so bad that

during the winter it was difficult to walk outside through the snow to use the outhouse. When a person had to pee or poop the pot under the bed did the job. My cousins and I had to empty all the pots from under the beds every morning. We'd take turns carrying the pots to the outhouse and dump them. Taking turns made sure none of us were stuck with the toilet job all the time. The outhouse was emptied every few years when a truck came to the coal patch to every house and hauled away all the waste. The men that emptied the outhouses were called 'honey drippers' by us kids.

Since we didn't have a bathroom in the house, there was no such thing as a shower. When we had to bathe, we would place a large round metal tub in the middle of the kitchen floor and fill it with hot water that was heated in pots and kettles on the kitchen stove. We'd pour the hot water into the tub and cool it down to the point where we could step into the water. Each one of us kids would take our turn at a bath in the same warm water. We often fought over which one of us would go first so we could enjoy the clean water. Aunt Tres and Uncle Louis finally set up a schedule where each of us would have a turn to bathe first. We took our weekly baths on Sunday or Monday night, sometimes it would be on Saturday before we went to the movies. After each weekly bath we had to stand for inspection in front of Aunt Tress or Uncle Louis so they could see that we washed behind our ears and everywhere else. From 1945, when I went to live with the Hager family until 1951 when I left Pennsylvania to live with mom in Oregon, I continued to bathe in that round metal tub.

Sleeping arrangements were simple, my cousins and I all slept in the same bed in one bedroom. After living with the Hager's for a couple of years, Uncle Louis turned our attic into a bedroom for us kids, but we still had only one bed. My three cousins, Bobby, Louis Henry and Dickie, were all about my same

Clarksville, Pennsylvania-Brad, 6 years old. Living with his aunt Helen Byrne's family. In first grade-1942.

Pitt Gas, PA: The Hager house where Brad was living in the 1940's. Pitt Gas was a small coal mining town near Clarksville, Pennsylvania.

Brad, 13 years old. With one of Hager families coon dogs.

Pill Gas, PA; 1948-The Hager home where Brad lived while growing up in Pennsylvania

Brad, (left) Louis Henry Hager (Right).
Pitt Gas, Pennsylvania, at the Hager Home-
1940's.

Brad-At Hager residence, Pitt Gas,
PA. In band uniform, Freshman year at Jefferson H.S.

Pitt Gas, Pennsylvania at the Hager residence.
Brad , 12 years old with his Hager cousins.
Left to Right: Bobby Eager, some other Eager relative,
Dickie Eager, Louis Henry Eager, neighbor kid,
Brad, (far right, wearing glasses).

Pitt Gas, PA: Christmas holidays at the Eager
home. Brad, 10 years old, with mother. Mary, who
came to Pennsylvania to visit-1946.

Brad, 14 years old, with sister Ramona at the Eager residence, Pitt Gas, PA.-1950.

age, there was only a couple years between each of us. When I began living with the Hager family mom provided for all of my needs. Besides the monthly money she would send Aunt Tres for my room and board, she'd send a large package once a month with clothes for me and my cousins. The package would also include candy and gum for us boys and things for Aunt Tres to use around the house. When it came time for me to learn to ride a bicycle, mom sent me a bicycle from New York City. She also sent all of my cousins a bicycle at the same time. Mom was like that. If she sent me a shirt for school she also sent three other shirts for my cousins. If it was pants, shoes or toys, the same thing occurred. Whatever I got, my cousins got also. In reality, mom was buying four of everything. My cousins and I would look forward to the packages from mom. The nearest post office was in Clarksville and we would all walk to the post office to pick up mom's package and then take turns carrying it back home. I missed mom, but on holidays like Christmas she'd come to Pennsylvania for a short visit. I really looked forward to those visits. I was proud of mom because she was a fashion model in New York City and she always looked and dressed great. She looked like a movie star when she came for a visit.

Chores

Like all of the Hager children, I was expected to share the chores with the rest of the family and I was soon helping to clean the house, make the beds, wash the dishes, cut the grass, feed the animals and a lot more. Aunt Tres and Uncle Louis treated me like I was one of their own kids. The family had a typical structure. Uncle Louis worked in the coal mine every day and Aunt Tres was a housewife who took care of the house and cooked and cleaned, did the sewing, ironing and the laundry. In the Hager household there was a time for work and a time for play.

I didn't think of us as poor, but looking back on it, we were poor. Our family always had full bellies and a roof over our head because we provided for ourselves with our own meats and produce. Most of the food we ate was caught or grown by us. My cousins and I would gather blackberries, walnuts and fruits in season and Aunt Tres would can them, making jams and jellies. The same was done with vegetables, we'd pick them in season and Aunt Tres would can them. Uncle Louis made his own wine in our cellar from the blackberries and elderberries we brought home. Aunt Tres and Uncle Louis would also go to nearby farms and buy apples, pears and other fruit by the bushel basket and we'd store them in the cellar so we would have an apple or a piece of fruit to put in our school lunch bag each morning. Uncle Louis also had a piece of fruit in his dinner bucket for lunch break in the coal mine.

Our breads and pastries were all baked at home by Aunt Tres. She baked on Wednesday for the entire week, there were always fresh loaves of bread and rolls and desserts were fantastic. She made apple, berry, rhubarb, raisin, peach and graham cracker crust cream pies. Aunt Tres assigned one day of the week for specific chores. Monday was her wash day, Tuesday was ironing day, Wednesday was baking day and so on.

When we came home from school we'd change out of our school clothes into our work-around-the-house clothes. We had chores like cleaning and scrubbing the cellar floor or the porch, feed the dogs and chickens and we'd slop the hogs by throwing garbage into their pen for them to eat. In the winter we shoveled coal into the cellar for our furnace and shoveled snow from around the house exits. After breakfast, lunch or dinner, my cousins and I cleaned the table and washed all the dishes. After a meal Aunt Tres and Uncle Louis would get up from the table, go into the living room or out on the porch and sit in the swing and talk while we finished up.

Before school our morning breakfast usually consisted of a bowl of cold cereal or a piece of jelly bread and a cup of half coffee and half milk. Aunt Tres would also cook us a hot breakfast of pancakes or scrambled eggs. Once we finished breakfast we had to wash the dishes, put them away in the cupboards and then change into our school clothes. On the way out the door we'd pick up our bag lunch that Aunt Tres made for us. Lunches were usually a bologna, cheese or peanut butter and jelly sandwich and a piece of fruit.

We kids were also expected to do a once a year spring cleaning of the house. We literally tore down the house to its bare bones, we carried out all the furniture and set it in the front yard while we scrubbed all of the walls and floors. We beat all of the rugs on an outside clothesline using a rug beater device. Beating those rugs was a chore, it was heavy-duty work. My arms felt like they were going to fall off by the time we got the rugs clean. The same procedure went for the cellar. We emptied out everything in the cellar and carried it into the yard and then scrubbed the cement cellar floors with bleach, soap and water. After we said we were done, Aunt Tres and Uncle Louis would inspect our work to see if it met their satisfaction. If it did, we could then return all the furniture, rugs and boxes to the house and cellar.

On their monthly trip into town for household supplies and food items they always brought back a large bag of candy for us kids and if we did all of our chores each day like we should, Aunt Tress or Uncle Louis would give us two or three pieces of candy after dinner from a bag that was kept in the kitchen cupboard. We couldn't get into the candy bag ourselves; my aunt and uncle handed out the candy to us.

When we were finished with our chores and before bedtime, I remember lying on the living room floor with my cousins in front of a large Philco console radio. We listened to radio shows like The Fat Man, Mr. Keen, Tracer of Lost Persons and Amos and Andy. During the winter when we were snowed in and couldn't go outside to play, the radio was our entertainment. We always had a good supply of comic books because when it was good weather we walked through the coal patch and traded comics with other kids. Another pastime during the snow days was playing board games. We sat around the kitchen table or on the living room floor for hours playing Monopoly. When the winter weather was okay for us to go out, we bundled up in heavy clothes and coats, wearing gloves, hats and earmuffs and we went sledding in the snow. There was a steep hill directly above our house and a lot of the neighbor kids joined us. When we didn't have a sled to use, we used old refrigerator doors or anything else that was flat enough to slide through the ice and snow. We stayed out romping in the snow until Aunt Tres or Uncle Louis yelled to us to come in the house for bedtime.

All in all, my cousins and I didn't fight among ourselves. If we ever did start to get physical with one another, Uncle Louis would take us into the cellar, put us into a pair of boxing gloves and tell us to duke it out. No one ever got hurt, the boxing gloves were so soft, the worst that ever happened was that one of us would walk away with a bloody nose. On the other hand, no stranger could pick on any one of us. We stuck together, if anyone fought with one of us, they had to take on all three of us.

During the summers if my cousins and I were caught up on our chores, Aunt Tres and Uncle Louis would sometimes send us to their friends' farms to help them with their chores, such as bringing in the hay for the farmers' livestock. We didn't get paid much for the work, after a week or two on the job the farmer would give each of us two or three dollars. That was extra money we were allowed to spend as we saw fit. We usually spent our earnings by ordering things through the

Sears Roebuck and Montgomery Ward mail order catalogues. We bought things like BB guns, pocket knives and toys. After my first summer of helping the friends and my aunt and uncle, when I was 14 or 15, I filed for and received my first social security card in the event summer jobs were going to be a regular thing.

During the summer my cousins and I very seldom wore shoes anywhere around the coal patch, the bottoms of our feet were like leather. We walked and ran on the roads and through the hills and creeks all summer barefoot. The only time we wore shoes during the summer was when we went to church or to the movies on Saturday night.

School

I attended Pitt Gas Elementary starting in the fourth grade. It wasn't long before I told Aunt Tres I wanted to study clarinet and she let me enroll in the music program at the elementary school. Mr. Small, the music teacher, loaned me an old clarinet to practice. I continued my music studies on the clarinet all through elementary school and graduated from the eighth grade in 1950. I put up with a lot of teasing from my cousins and friends because I played clarinet. When they were outside in the yard playing, I was in the house practicing and the kids would call the sound of my clarinet a 'fish horn'. I missed out on a lot of play time with friends, but I enjoyed learning music so I took all the teasing in stride.

In elementary school I began to smoke cigarettes when I was 12 years old. Like kids do, some of the boys brought cigarettes to school that they stole from their parents. After I began smoking, I too would sneak a cigarette from Uncle Louis' pack of smokes. My cousins Bobby and Louis Henry also smoked on the down low. We were the typical kids, we smoked a cigarette walking home from school and stomped it out a few hundred yards from the house. Uncle Louis or Aunt Tres never did suspect or find out us kids were smoking.

As a freshman in high school at Jefferson High, I played clarinet in the band. Our school colors were orange and black and I was given a band uniform that Aunt Tres had to take in quite a bit because I was so small. At age 14, I was only 4'11" tall. I completed my freshman year at Jefferson before relocating to Oregon to live with mom.

Mom Marries Again

In 1948, a year or two before I graduated from elementary school, mom married again. I came home from school one day and Aunt Tres sat me down before dinner and told me about mom's marriage. Mom left Long Island and moved to Oregon. She married a man named Don Rolund on July 1, 1948 in Coos Bay, Oregon. My sister, who was 18- years old, stayed in New York when mom left for Oregon. Three years later on April 7, 1951, my sister Mona married a man named Alphonse Paul Kiselius and they moved to Brooklyn. Mona later had two children with this man.

A year or two later when I was living with mom, she told me she met Don at dance marathons she used to frequent. Mom was a dancing fool, it was her passion. Once she ran away from my abusive drunken father William B. Kuhns and started a new life in New York City, she became a woman that began enjoying life. Even when I was living with mom on Long Island when I was in the second grade, she went to ballroom and marathon dancing on her days off. My sister would look after me on mom's night out. In the 1940s, especially in New York City, dance marathons became the rage. It was the thing to do and mom entered quite a lot of marathon contests.

During the 1940s, mom, a single divorced woman on her own, had an affair with the cowboy movie star Hop-a-Long Cassidy. His real name was William Boyd. They met while he was riding in a parade in New York City. His car stopped beside where mom was standing on the curb watching the parade. He sent an aide over to mom and asked her out. She accepted the invite and the affair began. Being a high-fashion model and a beautiful lady, it wasn't hard for mom to turn a guy's head.

Her beauty also got her noticed by mob boss Mickey Cohen. She had an affair with him as he commuted between the east and west coasts. That affair lasted quite a long time. Mickey gave mom furs and diamonds and wined and dined her at some of the most exclusive spots in New York City. She loved the way he looked after her and said he treated her like a queen. Even after they went their own ways and hadn't seen each other for years, Mickey helped mom out when they were both living in California.

Apparently, mom was having a problem with some businesspeople and was threatened by them, so she contacted Mickey and like magic, the problem went away and mom never was bothered again by those people. Mom had a very interesting life and she put a lot of her experiences in a journal. Following her death, in 1989, her recollections and journal notes were published and can be found under the title of *Life Experiences and Recollections of Mary Basits Kuhns.*

Discipline

If my cousins and I failed to do the chores properly or fought with one another about who did what, all Aunt Tres had to say was, "Wait until Louis gets home." That usually got our attention because we didn't want that. When we did get disciplined we always knew why it was being handed out. Uncle Louis had two belts he would whip our butts with.

One was a leather pit belt he wore into the coal mine with little metal buckles on it. Wow, those buckles hurt when they landed on your butt. The other belt was a cat-o-nine tail with a wooden handle that had nine leather strips attached to it. The strips looked like a cat's tail. He kept this hanging on the wall on a nail in the kitchen. Just looking at the belt hanging there made us boys tow the line. When the cat-o-nine tail was used, those leather tails would wrap around our butt and sting something awful. There were times when Uncle Louis didn't know who deserved the whipping because we wouldn't fess up to the wrong doing. When that happened, Uncle Louis would tell us all to go down to the cellar and take down our pants for a whipping. After all of us got our butts whipped, the ones that got whipped for nothing usually punched out the guy that didn't face the music and confess to Uncle Louis.

There were times when Uncle Louis and Aunt Tres would be sitting in the swing on the porch having coffee or a cigarette or just talking while we played in the yard. Like kids, we fought among ourselves, argued or even sassed back at my aunt and uncle. When that happened, Uncle Louis told the offending kid to go across the road to the woods and bring back a switch from one of the tree limbs. He'd also tell us to make sure that the switch was green so it wouldn't break. He let us know that if he had to get up and get his own switch for the whipping, it would be worse. Oh, boy, what a feeling that was to have to go and cut your own whipping switch from a tree and know that when you brought it back you were really going to get it. When he did whip us, whether with a belt, cat-o-nine tail or a tree switch, he'd tell us not to jump around or he might miss our butt and hit our legs, so we'd always stand still and take it like a man on the butt. The discipline handed out by Uncle Louis was standard treatment by most households in Pitt Gas in the 40's. Most kids in the coal patch were spanked and whipped on the

Hop-A-Long Cassidy (William Boyd), western movie
star and his horse Topper. Brad's mother had a
lengthly affair with Hoppy in 1940's.
They met when he was riding in a parade in New York
City. He saw Brad's mom standing in crowd and
asked her out. Circa-1940's.

Hop-A-Long Cassidy (William Boyd): Popular
movie star in the 1940's. He had an affair with
Brad's mom for quite some time.

Brad's mother-Mary. fashion model.Dating;
mobster, Mickey Cohen (a gansters moll?) and
movie star Hop-A-Long Cassidy in the 1940.

Mickey Cohen-Reknown Mob Boss.- Brad's mom
continued a lengthly affair with Mickey. Mary, said he
treated her like a queen.

Brad's mother, Mary, leaving Long Island, New York
to marry Don Rolund in Myrtle Point, Oregon- 1949.

butt. The discipline taught me the meaning of right and wrong, taught me manners, discipline, order, structure, fair play and respect for others. The butt whippings were never meant to be abusive. It was only dispensed when we kids did wrong and we all knew why the whippings were being done.

Aunt Tres would whip us on occasion, but it was usually up to Uncle Louis to hand out the punishment. Whenever Aunt Tres would tell Uncle Louis that one of us did wrong and deserved a whipping, he would do the honors. If he scheduled a time to whip us, we knew we'd get the whipping and it always happened at the time he said it would. Sometimes he would say that after dinner you'll get you whipping. Sure enough, after dinner the one to be whipped had to march downstairs to the cellar, drop their pants and get whacked. There was no forgiving or turning back, we always knew why we were being punished.

We had other punishments too. We'd have to stand in the corner facing the wall or our privileges of listening to the radio were taken away. That was a biggie because there were a lot of radio shows we liked to listen to in the evening before shuttling off to bed. Then there was the punishment of being grounded and not allowed outside to play with other kids. Another punishment was when the wrong-doer would have to do someone else's chores while the other kids were allowed to go out and play.

We only received discipline when we deserved it such as disobeying, talking back or neglecting to do our chores. There was never a slap in the face or a hit on the head, just the old-fashioned whipped butt. Getting whipped wasn't an everyday occurrence, it was done only when needed and all in all most of the memories I have of my childhood are happy ones.

Our Meals Growing Up in Pennsylvania

Ours was a very self-sufficient household. We rarely bought store meats, vegetables and bread and if we did that was a real treat. Uncle Louis had us plant rows of corn in a field down below our house. We also had a second vegetable garden in the yard by the side of the house where we grew radishes, onions, lettuce, cucumbers, carrots, potatoes, green peppers, peas and green beans and a host of other veggies that we used on our dining room table each day.

We had chickens and we kept a couple of hogs in a pen below our house, our meat came from what we killed or butchered. Every winter after they were fattened up we would butcher one of the hogs. Uncle Louis would invite some friends and relatives over to help butcher. Next to the hog pen we had a large vat of scalding water sitting atop a fire pit. Uncle Louis would then shoot one of the hogs and he and his friends would immediately lift the dead hog up and drop it into a big vat of scalding water. After a short while, the hog would be removed from the scalding vat and us kids would then scrape all of the hair from the hog's entire body. Once the hog was scraped clean, it was dressed out and cut up into pieces which were divided between all of the people that helped Uncle Louis butcher the animal. In the cellar Uncle Louis would make hot and mild homemade sausage from the hog. He would also smoke different cuts of the hog and hang it in the cellar so we could eat all year long. Besides the hogs and chickens we ate, Uncle Louis took us kids hunting and fishing for food. We fished for large bass, catfish, bluegill and crappie. Other meat we would hunt and eat were squirrel, rabbit, groundhog and raccoon.

Hunting and Fishing

When Uncle Louis took us kids with him on fishing and

hunting trips in the woods, there were times that our coon dogs would tree an opossum. We'd catch it and sell it to the colored folk in the coal patch for a dollar or two. The colored folks loved opossum, they knew how to cook it and make a tasty meal from it. We didn't eat opossum because Uncle Louis told us they were a scavenger critter. He knew a lot about hunting and fishing. He was good at it and taught us how to go about it. On fishing nights we would sit for hours with a lantern beside us waiting to catch a string of catfish or bass. If we caught carp, sometimes called mud suckers, we sold them to the blacks for $.50 each. To our family, the mud suckers had too many bones, but the colored people knew how to prepare them for a good meal.

There were many nights we'd go hunting and sit in the dark for hours on end waiting to shoot a deer. On other hunting excursions we'd take the coon dogs and have them search for raccoons. Once the dogs treed the raccoon we'd shoot them out of the tree. We used the dogs for hunting groundhogs too. The dog would sniff out where the groundhog was hiding in the ground and we'd send the dog in to pull it out. Uncle Louis taught us how to skin and dress all of the wild game we killed. That was our job once we got all the critters back home. When we skinned out the raccoons or squirrels we'd keep their furry tails to attach to our bicycle handlebars.

Aunt Tres could make all of that wild game taste like gourmet food. In fact, all of the women in our family were outstanding cooks. Our meals were simple fare at the Hager household, but it was wholesome good food. Many times our meals in Pitt Gas would only consist of a large platter of fish that we caught. Aunt Tres would fry them up, place them on a large platter and then set them on the table and that was our supper. Other days it could be just a large platter of fresh corn on the cob or a large bowl of butterbeans and ham hocks. Many times just a large kettle of chili and some fresh baked bread were set on the table. Other times it was just a large kettle of vegetable soup made from the veggies in our garden. Aunt Tress would sometimes put a large soup bone in the soup for us. That too was a treat.

On one of Uncle Louis' hunting trips, he and some friends went rabbit hunting and during the hunt one of his friends accidentally shot him in the face. Uncle Louis lost an eye as a result of that accident. I remember the day he was shot. Aunt Tres received a call from the hospital where Uncle Louis was taken for treatment. Talk about someone being upset, she was. She told my cousin Bobby, the oldest, to look out for us kids as she ran to the garage at the top of the yard. She got in the car and sped away like a demon. When they brought Uncle Louis back home he was laid up for a week or two. He quickly returned to work in the coal mines, minus one eye, and continued to work in the mines for the rest of his life.

Later in his life, like most coal miners, Uncle Louis eventually contracted black lung disease. The hazard of working down in the bowels of the earth, breathing coal dust into your lungs, was a given for any coal miner. Uncle Louis worked decades in those coal mines. After he retired and contracted black lung, his health began to deteriorate more and more as the years went by. As his health got worse, I can only assume he gave up on life and on October 10, 1988 he committed suicide. He shot himself. He was 75 years old when he died.

I could only imagine what affect Uncle Louis' death had on the Hager family. I know Aunt Tres took it very hard. Uncle Louis and Aunt Tres were together for decades and they were a loving, caring couple. They were like my second parents. I felt a loss too and mourned his passing. The Hager family had always treated me as one of their own kids. Following Uncle Louis death I believe Bobby, the eldest Hager son took his mother under his wing and looked out after her.

During our dinners we drank a lot of homemade Kool-Aid, lemonade, iced tea and just plain old water. For breakfast we'd drink powered milk and if we could con Aunt Tres or Uncle Louis, they'd occasionally let us kids have a cup of coffee with about three-quarters of it being milk. A treat was having the coffee diluted with milk, and tearing a slice of bread into pieces and dropping it into the coffee and eating it.

In the 1940s, there was a war going on and food was being rationed across the country. We couldn't afford to buy some essentials like butter or milk so the majority of the time we drank powdered milk and ate powdered eggs. The same went for butter. We couldn't afford to buy real butter so we ate oleo. The oleo was a big white blob of margarine in a sealed plastic bag with an orange vegetable capsule inside the bag. To make the oleo look like butter, you had to squeeze the orange capsule in the bag until it burst open. Then you squeezed the bag until all of the orange color mixed with the white blob and it turned into a yellow color making it look like butter. When we did get a glass of real milk or had a taste of real butter that was really something we appreciated.

Sunday Dinner

Our Sunday dinners were a different story; we ate like royalty on Sunday. The dinners were mostly fried chicken. Aunt Tres would tell us kids to go kill two or three chickens. We'd catch them, wring their necks and cut their heads off and dress them out so Aunt Tres could get them in the frying pan. We also peeled potatoes and picked veggies from the garden for our salad and made the lemonade or ice tea. Our Sunday eats were always a nine-course meal, the whole nine yards. First we began with homemade soup, then the homemade salad. After that the main course of fresh fried chicken with mashed potatoes, vegetables and gravy. Following the main course we also had dessert, which was generally home-baked pies and cakes.

On Sundays our table was always full with other relatives who came to visit. One of the frequent visitors was my half-sister Grace and her family. Grace, her husband Alden Mills and their daughter Lana would drive in from nearby Belle Vernon, Pennsylvania for the Sunday dinners. My half-niece Lana, who was seven years younger than me would follow my cousins and I around like a little puppy dog but we didn't mind, she was fun and me and my cousins would look out after her. Whenever we had these large meals and visitors over, we kids had our own table or were told to take our plates into the living room to eat. If we wanted seconds, we had to go back to the table and say please and after receiving the plate, we had to say thank you. The kids were to be seen and not heard and we had to behave ourselves. If we sassed back you could be sure that once the company left we'd get our butt whipped.

Holidays in Pitt Gas

Christmas was a big occasion in our house. Every Christmas Uncle Louis would go out into the woods and cut down a fresh tree. Aunt Tres would lay out all of the decorations and we kids would have the job of decorating the tree. Our tree always had four or five Lionel electric trains set up and running around it. Aunt Tres baked up a storm and made candies and fudge. She made a candy called divinity with walnuts which was one of our favorites. Again, my half-sister Grace, her husband Alden and their family who lived in the small town of Belle Vernon, always joined us for Christmas. After we opened our gifts and had dinner at our house, we drove to Grace and Alden's house and opened presents there.

Holiday meals were a lot like our Sunday dinners, except instead of two or three chickens we had six or seven. We also had large hams to accompany the chicken. On Thanksgiving we had turkey, chicken and ham as the main course, plus all the trimmings and desserts. During our Christmas holidays we had more presents than we actually could use. Gifts were plentiful and we had more than enough toys, clothes and shoes to go around. Mom would often show up on the holidays to see me.

When she couldn't make it she would always send a large gift box for us on holidays. She made sure all of us boys had clothes, school supplies and toys. Every Easter mom would send me a new suit to wear to church on Sunday. She would also include a new outfit for the rest of my cousins. We had our special go-to-Sunday-school clothes, but had to change out of them as soon as we got home from church. Even though Aunt Tres and Uncle Louis made us kids go to church every Sunday and attend Sunday school, they didn't go themselves. They told us we had to go because attending church was part of growing up and doing the right thing. They said that when we were adults we could make up our own mind as to whether we wanted to continue to attend church. As long as I lived with Aunt Tres and Uncle Louis, my cousins and I went to church every Sunday.

Games and Play

If my cousins and I were good and we did all of our chores, we were allowed to go to the movies every Saturday night in Clarksville. We walked a couple of miles from Pitt Gas to the movie house. We'd meet other kids from school along the way because most of the kids in the patch that we went to school with also walked to the Saturday night movie. Just before going into the movie, we would go into Julio's, a candy store where we were allowed to spend a nickel each on candy to take into the movie theatre.

Before going to the movie, we would each have to take a bath and be inspected by Aunt Tres. When we were ready to leave the house, she gave Bobby, my oldest cousin, $.40 to pay for us to get into the movie. That's $0.10 a piece. Then she would give him a nickel for each of us to buy candy. She also made it a point that we should all walk together to and from the movie. The Saturday night movies were something we looked forward to because at the end of the movie they would run a short film of a serial which would end with a cliffhanger about the hero being caught up in a dire situation, leaving the audience wondering how he would survive until the next week's episode.

One night after leaving the movie we were walking home along the side of the road and a car came by, swerved off of the road and hit me but missed my cousins. The blow knocked me unconscious and I had a cut on the side of my left temple. The car stopped and two women and a man got out, the driver was drunk. When I came to, the people in the car looked at us and then got back in their car and drove off. Bobby and my other cousins walked me back home. When Aunt Tres saw me and was told what had happened she was upset and mad at Bobby because he didn't get a license number or any information. My head hurt for a few days and, eventually, the cut on my temple healed. Aunt Tres called mom in New York and told her about the incident and she also was upset that Bobby didn't get any information from the drunk driver. We never did find out who the drunk driver was.

Though my cousins and I always looked forward to going to the movie on Saturday night, Uncle Louis and Aunt Tres very seldom went to a movie. They were mostly stay-at-home people and did things together around the house. Our family was always a together-type family. We kids were never alone that often, except when Aunt Tres and Uncle Louis would visit neighbors or go shopping in town for household items. Aunt Tres and Uncle Louis had card playing nights with neighbors and friends. They regularly played Pinochle and Hearts. On those nights there was a lot of beer, pretzels, chips and cigarettes set out on a table in the kitchen. On the nights that Uncle Louis didn't have to get up to go to work the next day the card games would go late into the night. It was taboo for us kids to go into the kitchen and disturb the card game, it was for adults only. We were told to play outside, in the cellar or in the living room until it was time for bed. I lived with Aunt Tres and Uncle Louis for six years, from 1945 through 1951 and I have to say they were some of the most memorable years of my life.

We also had our swimming hole. It had a rope hanging from a tree so we could swing out over the water and drop. We also had a rubber tire tied to a tree limb so we could jump into the water from the tire. Our swimming hole was so popular that once or twice a year the Baptist ministers would come to Pitt Gas and baptize people there.

Visit to New York City

The summer when I was 11 years old and still living in Pitt Gas Mom asked Aunt Tres if me and my cousins could come to New York for a visit for a couple of weeks when school let out for summer vacation. Aunt Tres and Uncle Louis thought it was a good idea, so mom sent us the Greyhound bus tickets and we were off to New York City. On one of our outings around the city, my sister Ramona took us to Astoria Beach for the day. We laid and played on the beach all day, but unfortunately I fell asleep and after a few hours I was as red as a lobster.

By the time we got back to the apartment I was throwing up and the slightest touch on my skin caused me to grimace and cry out in pain. Large blisters were forming on my back and legs. Mom laid me down on the mattress on the living room floor that was for me and my cousins to sleep on while we were visiting, and rubbed salve on my back and legs. Over the next few days mom and Mona carefully peeled the loose skin from my body little by little and I didn't leave the apartment for a few days. Mom and Mona watched me closely for the rest of my vacation. Even with the severe sunburn I was glad I was back with mom. I didn't want to go back to Pennsylvania, but I knew I had to because mom had to go back to work and I had to finish school. Even though I was treated very well by Uncle Louis and Aunt Tres, I always hoped that mom would bring me back to New York to live with her.

03

Move to Oregon

Leave Pitt Gas

During my freshman year at Jefferson High School, my mother was living in Myrtle Point, Oregon with her husband Donald Rolund. Don's grandparents received a 172 acre homestead piece of property from the government in the mid-1800s near Myrtle Point, Oregon. The ranch was filled with large Oregon timber that was logged occasionally for money. Don didn't work the ranch and it was quite rundown. The property and the original 1850 structure that was now falling apart, was owned by Don's mother, she was elderly and the two of them lived there for many years.

To me, Don Rolund seemed an unlikely choice for my mother. They met while Don was serving in the Merchant Marines and while on leave in New York City he met mom at a dance. Mom was 20-years older than Don and the only thing I could figure out was the attraction on Don's part was that here was a hard-working New York City fashion model, entrepreneur, business woman who looked twenty years younger than her real age and possibly a woman that could take care of him. From mom's point of view I would guess it was the physical attraction. But here it was a non-working rural Oregon guy and a smart, vibrant, beautiful woman that knew her way around.

Mom called Aunt Tres and suggested that my cousins and I come out to Oregon and help her and Don build a new ranch house. Aunt Tres agreed. Dickie, my youngest cousin, didn't go with us, he stayed in Pennsylvania. Mom sent us the Greyhound bus tickets and Bobby, Louis Henry and I, were on our way to Oregon in the summer of 1951. Bobby was 17, I was 15 and Louis Henry was 13.

Mom bought and operated the Dillard Steakhouse, in Dillard, Oregon for a couple of years. Previously, she owned a small grocery store, tavern and cabins in a small blip in the road called Gravel Ford, about two miles from the ranch house in Myrtle Point. Don came to the Greyhound Station in Roseburg to pick us up. He drove us a few miles to the Dillard Steakhouse where mom was cooking and working the place. Mom and Don had living quarters above the restaurant and my cousins and I slept in a back room and ate at the restaurant. We killed time by swimming in the Umpqua River which ran directly behind the steakhouse. It sure felt good to be back with mom.

The Ranch Property

Mom broke free from her duties at the steakhouse and she and Don drove us out to the ranch in Myrtle Point so we could get started building the new place. We stayed in the old rundown dilapidated house and slept on the living room floor. There was no water line to the ranch, the only water we had to use or drink was from a water well, which we had to hand pump every day. For cooking, mom had an old 1900 wood stove. She lifted the round metal covers and filled it with wood in order to cook. The old house had electricity and the kitchen had one light bulb hanging from the ceiling on a cord. There was a rickety barn a few yards from the main house, but it was rundown and the roof was falling apart. The ranch had two or three cows and a few chickens and that was it. The house sat on a small hill overlooking large meadows that stretched out below. Across the meadow was thick forest and woods.

Mom went back to the steakhouse and Don stayed at the

ranch with us boys. Don had no money of his own, Mom gave Don all the money to build the new house. The money came from mom's restaurant earnings and the savings she accumulated over the years. My mother had always been a thrifty person and always saved some of her earning for a rainy day. That was a result of early life living with an abusive husband that kept her barefoot and pregnant and not letting her have any money of her own. My mother always impressed upon my sister, Mona and me, the value of saving. She always told us to save at least ten cents out of every dollar.

Until mom came along, Don lived in the old broken down ranch house with his mother for years until he went into the Merchant Marines. He occasionally worked in the woods and sold timber off of the ranch but he was just scraping by. When he married mom, it was her money that she saved over the years that bought all of the businesses they acquired throughout their marriage. By this time my mother had been married four times. There was Gaisbauer, my father William B. Kuhns, then there was a two week marriage that she had annulled to a man named Grannel in about 1946 and now her fourth marriage to Don Rolund. From what mom told me, the Grannel marriage was annulled after she found out he lied to her about his occupation. The fact was the guy wasn't working. His intention was to stay at home and let mom work. When mom found out about this, she wasn't having any of it and told him to take a hike.

The old house on the ranch had no bathroom, only an outhouse. It had no modern appliances and the rooms were separated by only a curtain hanging between each room. It was just like houses in old western movies. Mom had all of the lumber, supplies and appliances delivered to the ranch and we started cutting lumber and building the new place. She drove from Dillard as often as she could and fixed breakfast and dinner for Don, me and my cousins. Other than the two or three days we spent at the Dillard Steakhouse, the rest of the summer was spent working on the ranch.

As we were building the new house we also took breaks to help Don bale hay from the lower field to feed the cattle. Occasionally we explored the 172 acres but we would go only as far as we could walk because we didn't want to get lost. Sometimes Don would take us to Coos Bay, Oregon to see a movie.

We built the ranch house without any plans. I never built any structure like this before in my life and neither did my cousins. Don would show us kids where to cut the 2x4's and other lumber and then he would show us how to nail the pieces together. The house went up in pieces. First one wall, then another, and so on.

I Stay in Oregon

The summer came to an end and the new ranch house was finished other than for a few touchups s and some inside work. It was time to get back to Pennsylvania so we could get ready for another school year. When it came close to the time to leave, I took mom aside and told her I wanted to stay in Oregon with her.

I reminded her that there wasn't much of a future for me in Pennsylvania and I didn't want to wind up going to work in the coal mines. I also told her that if she put me on the Greyhound to return to Pennsylvania, I would get off the bus before it arrived in Pennsylvania and run away. Mom listened to what I had to say, told me I made a lot of sense and that she didn't want to see me graduate from high school and then work in a coal mine for the rest of my life. She talked the situation over with Don and he had no objections to me remaining in Oregon.

When we put Bobby and Louis Henry on the bus to return home to Pennsylvania, that was the last time I saw my two cousins for 26 years.

That summer of 1951, mom enrolled me as a high school sophomore in Myrtle Point, Oregon. To get to school each morning I walked two miles down the road from our ranch to the Gravel Ford Store to catch the school bus. The Gravel Ford Store, Tavern and Cabins were owned by mom a few years earlier, but the place caught fire and burned. Mom rebuilt it, sold it and bought the Dillard Steakhouse.

It was about this time, when I was 15, that I began driving a car. During trips with mom from the ranch to the steakhouse, she'd sometimes let me drive our 1951 Ford. Mom taught me to drive on that run through the mountains between the Dillard Steak House and Myrtle Point and I thought I handled the car pretty good. During all of those years throughout her life, mom didn't have a driver's license and was never stopped by a police officer. In 1957, when she arrived in California, she got a license because there were a large number of cars on the highway. That California license was her first driver's license ever. It is amazing that she got away with not having a license for all those years.

Mom Sold the Steakhouse

During my sophomore, year mom sold the Dillard Steakhouse and spent a lot of time at the ranch cooking and cleaning. Don's mother, Doris, was also living with us in the new house. Doris never liked mom, they didn't get along at all. Doris didn't want her son to get married, her vision was that she would live with her son on the ranch and he would take care of her. Doris refused to help mom with any of the chores in the house. She sat in her room and only come out when mom called us to breakfast or dinner, she would eat and then go back to her room, her sanctuary. She was always trying to talk Don into leaving mom.

One afternoon I overheard an argument she had with mom where she said that because mom was 20 years older than Don, it was a bad marriage and it shouldn't have happened.

Now that mom didn't have the steakhouse to take up her time she began to upgrade the ranch. She purchased more milking cows and calves, she bought loads of chickens and ducks and she also bought three or four dozen turkeys. Mom and I built pens for the chickens, turkeys and ducks so the wolves and cougars couldn't get at them. Mom could just stand on the porch and call the turkeys and ducks and they'd come running to her, she even named some of them. Many of the turkeys followed her when she would walk around the ranch. She was like the pied piper of the ducks and turkeys. She called them her pets, but had no problem selling them after they reached maturity or butchering them for dinner.

Don began staying away from the ranch more and more. He went into town, met his buddies and ran around. It was no secret that he was cheating on mom, but mom tried hard to save their marriage. She provided Don with a new house, the restaurants and taverns and she worked hard, often by herself. Don promised to help out in the businesses but he would quickly tire of the work, slack off and eventually quit showing up so all the work fell on mom's shoulders. Don chose to run around with his friends and drink rather than buckle down and work.

I had my chores at the ranch and to do my part I brought the cows in from the fields and mom and I would milk them. Don rarely helped with ranch chores. It was my job to clean out the barn after each milking and get rid of the cows' waste. Cleaning the chicken coup was another of my chores. I didn't have that many jobs to do so it wasn't a hard life for me, in fact, it was an easy existence. I had a lot of time to fish in the river that ran through one of our meadows. It was a great place to fish, especially during salmon season.

Oregon has always had a salmon run on the Umpqua River, it's been going on decade after decade. I would take some chicken wire and stretch it across where the river narrowed to only a few feet. I'd wait for the salmon to run and their gills would get caught in the chicken wire, all I had to do was pick them off the wire. I would wade through the salmon as they were running up stream to get them off the wire. The salmon run was so thick I could literally walk across their backs where the river narrowed to a few feet. Some of the salmon weighed 30-40 pounds apiece. In less than 20 minutes I would have 15-20 salmon. I'd carry them up from the meadow and mom and I would clean and dress them. She cut the fish into large salmon steaks and froze them. A lot of people ate the salmon eggs, considering them a delicacy, I used them as fish bait. Mom had a large floor cabinet freezer in a separate side room attached to the house where we kept the salmon, venison and venison liver along with the other fish and animals we butchered.

Oregon was the place where I ate my first beef steak at 15 years old. Throughout my early years while living with Aunt Tres and Uncle Louis, a steak was a luxury that I had never tasted. If and when a steak was bought it was for Uncle Louis' meal only. I was used to eating squirrel, raccoon, rabbits and groundhog, wild fish and other wild game. Mom, being the excellent cook she was and after being a chef in all those hotels in New York City, knew how to fix a beef steak. They were yummy. I didn't know what I'd been missing all those years. Our venison steak dinners at the ranch were nothing to turn our noses up at either, mom made those steaks taste great too. We ate quite well living on the ranch all year long and had everything for an exceptional meal at any time. We had fresh beef, any cut you could think of. We had fresh fish–salmon, trout and bass. We ate fresh chicken, duck and turkey and had fresh milk from the cows. Mom even baked our desserts with fresh chicken and duck eggs from our own flocks. I wandered all over the ranch picking apples and some of the biggest blackberries anyone could ever imagine. The smallest berries were the size of a person's thumb and the big ones were gigantic. I'd take a large bucket of these berries to mom and she'd make berry pies and freeze the rest.

As I roamed around the ranch or walked the road on the way back from school, I could hear cougars in the trees, a cougar sounds like a baby crying when it growls. And then there were snakes. I hate snakes, always have. Sometimes I walked the two miles from the bus to the ranch and would see a snake or two lying in the middle of the road. I'd stand back a few feet waiting for them to move and would even yell and throw rocks at them. Eventually they'd slither off and I'd go on my way.

I liked Oregon, it was always green and beautiful. We got a lot of rain and in my sophomore year it rained so hard and long that the meadows beneath the house were completely flooded. The rain came down four days straight and the water was 15-20 feet deep. We couldn't see or get to our road leading from the house to the main road, so I couldn't go to school; we had to wait for the water to recede. Oregon gets lots of rain, and for anyone living there they soon get accustomed to it and learn to live with it.

Summer Visiting Relatives

I finished my sophomore year at Myrtle Point and during the summer, Don and mom took me to Don's sister's family, Jesse and Esther Coleman, in Klamath Falls, Oregon. They had two children, Carlene who was about my age and a son named Ronald, who was a few years older than me. Jesse worked for a dairy in town, delivering milk door to door. Esther was a typical housewife, tending to household chores and duties. I stayed the summer with them while mom and Don went on vacation in Mexico and planned to drive deep into the interior. They saw Acapulco, Mazatlan and all the little villages in between.

The Coleman's son, Ron, played piano as a hobby so I took my clarinet with me and we played together while I was there. I also got a small part-time job at the local newspaper so I could make extra money for the summer. I could work when I wanted to inserting the ads from advertisers into the main body of the paper. It paid a nickel an insert, the faster I worked, and more inserts I placed in the paper, the more money I made. I made $12 to $15 dollars a week, movie and spending money for me while I was in Klamath Falls for the summer. I saved the rest for a rainy day like mom taught me to do.

The Coleman kids and I hit it off from the start and on the weekends went to the movies. On Jesse's day off he took Ron and me fishing on Klamath Lake. I was smoking on the sly and a block or two from the newspaper office there was a vendor selling candy, newspapers and cigarettes from a small outside stand. The vendor was blind so it was easy for me to walk up to the stand and buy my Chesterfield cigarettes on my own. I would try to deepen my voice when I asked for the cigarettes and dropped my money into a plastic tray in front of him. I don't know if he suspected I was a 16 year old kid, but I always got my cigarettes. After a few weeks I had my suspicions that he knew I was a teenager, but we had become friends and he'd always say hello and hand me a pack of Chesterfield's as soon as I said hello, he knew what I wanted before I even asked for it. I would always light up and smoke while walking home from the newspaper office.

I felt sorry for the blind guy and was glad to buy something from him every time I left work. I always wondered if people tried to cheat him out of money when they dropped the coins or bills into his tray. I wondered if anyone helped themselves to a pack of gum or candy bar without him knowing it. I wouldn't even think about cheating the guy because he was blind and probably struggling to make a living. It always amazed me that this blind man could pick up a coin or bill from the tray in front of him and knew what change to give back to the customer. He never missed as far as I could see.

After that first summer I had occasion to visit the Coleman family off and on and during the winter Don and I would go back to the Coleman's house in Klamath Falls to duck hunt. During duck hunting season we would get up at 2:00 a.m., have breakfast and then Don, me, Jesse and Ron would drive to Klamath Lake where we would sit in a duck blind, sometimes for hours on end waiting for the ducks and geese to fly over. Once the ducks and geese showed up we would shoot our limit, take them home, dress them out and have Esther cook up the game for us. The feasts were awesome, we had platters of duck and geese with baked and mashed potatoes and gravy and always followed by homemade dessert. I did those hunts two winters in a row.

Mom's Sick

On that first stay with the Coleman family in the summer of 1952, my visit was cut short after a few weeks, Mom and Don came back to Klamath Falls, picked me up and we returned to the ranch. Mom was really sick, she got checked out at the hospital in Klamath Falls, but the doctors couldn't find anything causing her ailment and she was released. As we drove back to the ranch, a few hours away, mom was complaining of stomach cramps and pain. We stopped a number of times along the way so she could vomit. Seeing her in this condition and not knowing why she was sick upset me to no end. When we returned to the ranch, besides mom's stomach problems she was also complaining about having trouble walking. She went to see a number of doctors in Myrtle Point and Coos Bay and even drove to Portland, which was a few hours drive from home, but those doctors couldn't tell her what was causing her illness either.

In September I had to return to high school and mom was still attempting to find out why she was so sick. At this point she could hardly sit up straight in a chair and experienced profuse sweating bouts. Finally the friend of a neighbor told her to see a doctor that she used for one of her ailments. The lady told mom that if anyone could find the cause of her problem, it would be this doctor. Mom then went back to Coos Bay and saw Dr. Kaiser, who later became one of the founders of the famed Kaiser Health Plan System. Mom told me later that within 10 minutes of her visit with Dr. Kaiser, he told her she had a severe kidney infection and didn't know how she even had the strength to walk.

Within a few hours of her visit with Dr. Kaiser, she was operated on. She lost one of her kidneys during the operation, according to Dr. Kaiser there was no way to save it. Following the operation, she stayed in the hospital for a couple weeks. During that time I refused to go to school. I skipped school and hung out at the hospital. I slept in the hallways and while my mother was recovering I wouldn't leave the hospital. At one point, following her operation, a priest was called in and they were going to administer last rites. It was a tough time for mom and I was scared out of my wits. The doctor and nurses tried to look out for me while I was there and even suggested I go back to school but gave up on that when they saw there was no chance in hell I was going to leave mom in the hospital alone.

Dr. Kaiser later told mom that her infection was due to the food and water she consumed in Mexico. Mom only ate salads while in Mexico, but Dr. Kaiser explained that the salad was contaminated with filth from the irrigation used on the produce in Mexico. He said the bad water and tainted salad she ate caused the growing and severe infection that deteriorated and shut down her kidneys. He emphasized that if she'd waited any longer before coming to his office when she did, she would have died in a very short time.

To top it off, her Mexico vacation hit her with a double whammy. When she and Don were on a shopping trip in Mexico City, she was robbed, and her purse was picked. The thief opened her purse and stole a few hundred dollars in U.S. currency and a diamond ring. When they reported it to the authorities, they were told there would be no chance of recovering her property. The officers told mom that most of the people in Mexico were poor and the thieves are very skilled at picking someone's pocket or purse; the police refused to even look for the culprit. Hell, $200-$300 in American currency in Mexico in the 50s would make the thief a very rich person and the diamond ring would sell for hundreds of dollars. The crook sure made out. I say Mom's Mexico vacation was rated as one of the worst experiences of her life.

Once mom was out of the hospital and recuperating at the ranch, I went back to school. She was a fighter and tough little cookie, she didn't let much get her down. After a few months she was back on her feet and told Don she was tired of him running around and not working around the ranch. Don never did work the ranch to generate any income for the family. Mom went on to tell him she would buy another business well away from the ranch and his drinking buddies. She laid the law down and told him she expected him to work alongside her in running the business. We drove to different cities in Oregon, California and even Nevada where they looked at restaurants, taverns and nightclubs but nothing struck their fancy. In Hawthorne, Nevada, they considered buying a small casino/restaurant business that had everything inside ready to go. The El Capitan casino was the only one in town and the owners wanted $50,000 for the place—that was a lot of money in the 50s. Even though mom thought the place had potential, there was no way she could come up with their asking price, so that prospective deal fell by the wayside.

Myrtle Point,Oregon: A ranch house built in the 1800's that sat on 172 acres and homesteaded by Don Rolund's family. Brad lived in this house from 1951 through 1953 while he helped his step-dad Don and his mother Mary build a new ranch house on the property. The house had a well and pump for water, no toilet, just an outhouse.

The new ranch house Brad helped build in Myrtle Point, Oregon-1951, when he was 15 years old.

At the Myrtle Point Ranch-1951. Brad's mom, Mary, age 51 and his stepfather Don who was 20 years younger than Mary.

Gravel Ford, Oregon. Early 1950's. Brad's mom owned the Gravel Ford store and Tavern. It was located about 2 miles from the family ranch in Myrtle Point, Oregon.

04

Living in Portland

The Harmony Café and Tavern

In late 1952, mom and Don bought the Harmony Café and Tavern in Portland, Oregon. It was located on Wino Alley, the slum streets of Portland on Madison Avenue and First Street where the bums and homeless found refuge. The building was built in the mid-1800s, it had a poker room with a few green felt poker tables and brass spittoons on the floor by the tables, booths and bar stools. The back bar was hand carved from floor to ceiling with a large mirror running the full length of the bar. The tavern had a bar section and a small counter of five or six stools for food service.

Behind the bar there was a large floor safe which probably weighed a couple thousand pounds and on the large door the name of the safe company was painted in gold lettering. It looked like a large Wells Fargo safe from an old western movie. The place itself could have been a movie set for an old cowboy movie. When mom looked at the place it was filthy with dust, dirt and grime everywhere. Old bums were sitting at the poker tables sleeping and not buying any booze.

She asked why those old coots were sitting at the tables nodding off and not buying drinks. The owner replied that the old geezers were regulars that hung out here every day. Mom bought the place and hit the ground running. The first thing she did was kick out all the old regulars sitting around the poker tables and not spending money on beer. She re-varnished the old wooden booths and installed a large Wurlitzer jukebox and shuffleboard. She added a Shoot the Bear machine where you could put a quarter in the machine and use a rifle with a light source to shoot at the bear. When they hit the bear on target it would stand up on its hind legs and growl. The customers really liked it and would challenge mom to a shoot-off.

The person to hit the bear the most times won the game and the loser had to buy the beers. Mom had it down and won most of the time, but when she lost the customers loved it because they knew they got drinks on the house. It was a great hook to get the winos and bums to spend their money.

Mom was selling beer at $0.10 a glass, like there was no tomorrow and the place was booming. In fact, it went so well she paid the place off within a year. The customers at the tavern were mostly white folks and Native Americans. Oregon had a large population of Native Americans and members of almost every tribe hung out in this part of Portland. Even though it was the slum area, the Native American Indians made it home and chose mom's tavern to hang out in and spent a lot of money drinking there. Most of the Native Americans in Oregon received checks from the government just because they were Native Americans. Once a year they got a super big check and bought large ticket items like cars, trucks and even airplanes. They went through their government money like melted butter, spending big chunks of it on beer and wine in mom's tavern and café.

Business became so good that mom cleaned up the restaurant section of the tavern and began offering homemade chili, stew and sandwiches to the Native Americans and winos. When mom bought the tavern it was licensed to only sell beer, but she soon got a license to sell wine, and business exploded. These drunken Indians loved their cheap $2.00 Thunderbird wine and would buy bottle after bottle. When their money was gone they would have one their friends cough up the money until their next check.

The jukebox in the place brought in so much revenue that it nearly paid the monthly rent on the place. The jukebox man would come by to change records and divvy up the cut with mom and would tell her the jukebox in her tavern made four times the money than jukeboxes in other taverns on the block. Mom was a good businesswoman and she kept the music going from 6:00 in the morning until she closed at 2:00 a.m.

It wasn't long, after buying the place, that mom wound up doing all the work again. Don was bartending at the tavern for a couple weeks, but decided to leave, go back to the ranch to live with his mother, run around with his friends and hang out at his sister's place in Klamath Falls. He really didn't like to work and mom was stuck with making money for the family. She put in many 16-18 hour days at the tavern. When Don did come back to Portland to get money and stay at our apartment, I heard them argue that he needed to buckle down and work but mom's pleas fell on deaf ears repeatedly. Instead, Don would run back to the ranch to his mother and lay around.

Shortly after we became somewhat settled in Portland, mom hired a temporary bartender to stand in for her and she, Don and I spent some family time together and went out to eat. This was a real treat for me because until we moved to Portland, I'd never eaten in a dinner house or restaurant. When I was a little guy in Clarksville with Aunt Helen and Uncle Bill, we ate all our meals at home. In New York we never went to eat in a restaurant, we always had our meals together around the table in the apartment. While I was living with Aunt Tres and Uncle Louis in Pennsylvania, we never went out to eat, all our meals were at our house where we sat around the table as a family. In all of my early life, mealtime was family time. I had no idea there were restaurants that a family could go to and have a meal. When I moved to Oregon, mom prepared all the meals for us at the ranch. We never once walked into a restaurant where we sat down and had a family meal together. So for the first 17 years of my life I only knew of meals at home with family. Other than steaks that mom cooked at home, I didn't know what a restaurant steak was.

One of the first meals we had together as a family in a full-blown restaurant was in Portland at the Red Barn, home of the 72-ounce steak. At this restaurant, if a person could eat the 72-ounce steak with all the trimmings; it was free. If you couldn't eat the entire steak you had to pay for it and in 1953, a 72-ounce steak cost $10—that was a lot of money for a steak. The 8 and 16-ounce steaks went for $3 to $5. There were pictures on the wall of people who had eaten the large steak over the years, but mom, Don and I settled for the 8 and 16-ounce steaks which were served on a sizzling hot silver platter with a baked potato or steak fries and a veggie. It was so tender the steak would practically melt in your mouth. That became a regular place for us to have an evening out together enjoying a meal.

It was at the Red Barn that I let mom and Don know I smoked. After finishing our meal and relaxing with a cup of coffee Don lit up a cigarette. I reached in my pocket, pulled out a cigarette and lit up as well and they both had a surprised look on their face, but all mom said was, "I see you're smoking now." Don just asked what brand I smoked. They both told me they were happy I smoked in front of them rather than sneak around behind their backs to have a cigarette. There were never any other comments about me smoking. Mom never smoked a day in her life even though she worked in restaurants, hotels and bars throughout her career. Now that I had the experience of eating out in restaurants I always looked forward to our outings. Mom liked Chinese food so we often went to China Town to have some of our family dinners.

Police Protection

Owning a tavern and bar in Portland also came with some baggage—police protection. There were three shifts of cops walking the beat and every day, during each shift, mom gave each cop a carton of cigarettes. She gave six cartons a day to the cops. Then came the day, the cops began asking for cases of beer. There were times when they came in and stood next to the bar and told mom their patrol car trunk was open and she should have a case of beer for each cop put in the trunk. Mom would motion for the wino that swept the floors for a few dollars and beer to carry two or three cases to the cop's car. He would put it in the trunk and close the lid and the cops would drive off. For these payoffs, the cops turned a blind eye to me being under age and in the tavern eating and they ignored fights, arguments and violations.

The payoffs didn't stop there though, on holidays like Christmas, Thanksgiving and Easter, each shift cop would come into the tavern and collect cash. It wasn't long after the payoffs began that the cops suggested to mom that rather than cigarettes and beer they would rather have the cash. Cash payments became the norm, but the cigarettes and beer payoffs also continued. The cops rationalized the payoffs as birthday and Christmas presents and she was expected to give them money as a gift. These cops had a real racket for themselves. The upside of the payoffs was that if mom needed help at the tavern at any time, for any reason, she could call the station and ask for a cop by name who would then come down to the tavern to handle the matter. She often called them to standby when she closed in the wee hours of the morning. They kept an eye on her until she got in her car with her nightly receipts and headed for home.

Boosters

Another fringe benefit of owning the tavern for mom was that many customers boosted items and brought them into the tavern and sold them to her. They brought in name brand clothes, shoes, coats, jackets and jewelry stolen from department stores. My mom even bought a 1½ carat diamond ring set in white gold and platinum from one of her customers who boosted it from a jewelry store. She paid pennies on the dollar to these thieves for the boosted items.

Mom brought the ring home and gave it to me. I wore it for about a year until one day I took it off in a restaurant bathroom, laid it on the counter while washing my hands and walked out without it. As quickly as I left the bathroom I returned to retrieve it but there was no ring because someone had already walked off with it.

Another deal mom got was in 1954, when she bought a 1954 Pontiac for $250, which had only 2,000 miles on the odometer and was in great shape. The Native American that owned it decided to buy another car with the money from his annual payment from the government. We kept the car for about a year and mom let me drive it even though I didn't have a driver's license.

One day I was driving some musician friends around in the Pontiac and cops pulled me over for running a stop sign. They told me to park the car on the side of the street and called a cab for me and my friends to get home. They didn't give me a ticket when they found out I was mom's son because they were taking her payoffs. Mom sent a part-time bartender over to pick up the car and bring it back to the tavern. She had really made the tavern a hot spot in the slums and was doing very well.

In 1956 she bought a nice toy for herself, a brand new four-door baby blue Lincoln Premier. Ford had just released it to the public that year, it had all the bells and whistles and was a car ahead of its time. She loved that car.

One afternoon I dropped by the tavern to grab something to eat but mom wasn't there. A substitute bartender said mom was taken to the hospital. I called the hospital and was told that mom was treated, released and taken home in a cab. I hurried back to the apartment and mom was lying on her bed with her hand bandaged in gauze and tape. I asked her what happened and she said she was closing the door to the safe, someone called her name and when she looked up the door closed on her hand and cut off her middle finger. She blacked out temporarily from the pain and became sick to her stomach, but she had the wherewithal to call a nearby bartender and a cab to take her to the hospital. She was a tough critter. I sat on the edge of the bed looking at her with her forehead and eyes covered with a wet cloth. I knew she had a severe headache and was still sick to her stomach, I felt bad for her, yet there was nothing I could do to help the pain go away. I didn't want to bother her too much so I kissed her on the cheek, told her to get some rest and if she needed anything I'd be in the living room. When the doctors removed the bandage from her hand, all that was left of her middle finger was a small stub, the finger was three-quarters gone.

I Start High School

Mom enrolled me in Lincoln High School where I began my junior year. I was in the high school band playing clarinet and during band practice I struck up a friendship with trumpet player, Ernie Carson, and a drummer, Bennie Miller. Before the music instructor came into class, the three of us jammed around and played jazzy songs. At pep rallies and games we also jammed it up with swinging jazz tunes and it wasn't long before word got around school and the rest of the high school band that the three of us were playing some good music. We gained a fairly good reputation and I told mom I also wanted to play saxophone so she took me to the local music store and I picked out a sax. The only thing she said was that if she bought the instrument, I had better use it. I promised her I would and Ernie, Benny and I started playing music after school and on holidays just for the fun of playing.

At Christmas it wasn't unusual to see the three of us on the main drag of Portland in front of the Whistling Pig Restaurant or The Nut House on the back of a flatbed truck playing Christmas carols and Dixieland jazz music throughout the holidays. A store or business would pay us a few bucks to play in front of their establishment so it would gather a crowd. I can still smell the aroma of those roasting hot nuts coming from The Nut House as we stood outside wailing away.

My Professional Music Career Begins

It wasn't long until the three of us decided to go to the musician's union and audition to become professional musicians. Here we were three teenagers walking into the union hall and asking to become professional musicians. In the 1950s, anyone that wanted to join the musician's union and play professionally had to demonstrate their music skill by auditioning before other professional musicians. That's not the case today, if a person has the money to pay the dues, they can join the union whether they're a good or bad musician. All three of us auditioned and passed. We were given union cards and were off to the races. In the musicians member directory I chose the professional name of Brad Evans. I chose the name of Evans because I didn't think my real name, Brad Kuhns would look too good on the marquees and Evans seemed easy for people to remember. For tax purposes the musician's union retained my real name on file. Now at 17-years old, I was one of many entertainers that used a stage name. Ernie immediately went to work playing with Monte Ballou Castle Jazz Band at the

Diamond Horseshoe Club in downtown Portland. Bennie got a temporary job with a local western band and I lined up two other musicians from the union and took them into the Third and Fourth Avenue burlesque theaters. We played backup for the striptease artists appearing in the theaters.

The high school had a policy to allow teenagers to get out of school early and work, but it soon became a big story when some of the parents found out that a teenager was working in a burlesque theater. It hit the local papers and there were people on both sides of the argument, but eventually it was old news and my working in a burlesque theater faded into the background of the everyday Portland news cycle. I was sure popular at school though, a lot of students wanted me to get them in to see the strippers but there was no way I could do that even if I wanted to. Burlesque was an adults only game in the 1950s. The burlesque circuit had all the major strippers of the day coming through Portland and during my stint at the theaters, I played backup for ladies like the world famous Tempest Storm and the lady with the million dollar legs, Debbie Rae, along with many others.

Debbie was a good looking lady, a cute redhead and a great exotic dancer. Of all the women at the theater, if I had my pick of the litter she would have been it. Debbie was appearing on the same bill as the energetic Tempest Storm. Deb was strictly business, she came on stage, did her thing, and went her own way. She was always courteous to the band, told us what she wanted us to play for her act and never complained. She had her routine down pat. A lot of the men that came to the burlesque shows came just to see her dance.

After I finished up at the Fourth Avenue Theater it was 10 years before I would see Debbie again. In the entertainment business you can never tell when you'll run across someone that you've worked with early in your career and Debbie was one of those

ON GARDEN HOMESHOW
"Brad" Kuhns will perform
with the OJJ-OJS talent troupe
at Garden Home grade school
March 24 and 27 at 8 p.m.

Brad, 17 Years old–
Travels with O. J. J. S. J., 1953
Talent Troupe. Out of Portland,
OR

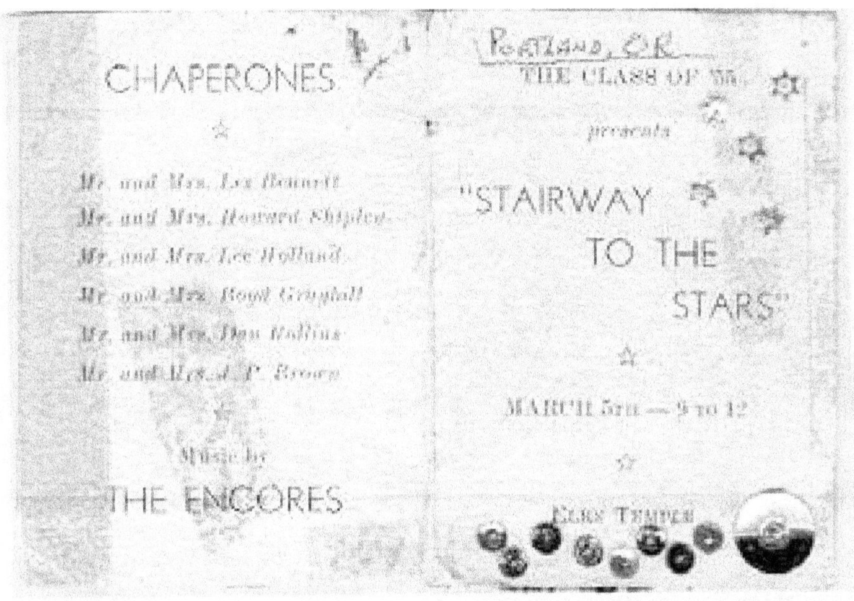

Brad and his "Encores" played for Class of 1955, Portland, Oregon.

The Diamond Horshoe Club, Portland, Oregon Left to Right: Benny Miller,(Drums), Brad Evans, (Sax), Ernie Carson, (Piano and Trumpet).

Three high school chums that began their professional music career in 1953.

4th. Ave. Burlesque theater, Portland, Oregon-Between 1953 and 1955

Brad had the house band and Debbie was one of the exotic dancers that often performed there.

Tempest Storm- the fiesty reknown
exotic dancer worked with Brad at the
4th. Avenue burlesque theater, Portland,
Oregon frequently between 1953 and
1955. She later married singer/actor Herb
Jefferies.

cases. It was 1964 , I was living in Southern California and I was on the town with a few of my friends and one of the stops that evening was The Body Shop on the Sunset strip in Hollywood. It was a well known strip club and had a reputation of hiring some of the best-looking exotic dancers around. My friends and I went in, sat down at a table and were enjoying the show when the emcee (Master of Ceremony) introduced a dancer, the fabulous Ms. Debbie Rae, the lady with the million dollar legs. I looked up on stage and to my surprise there she was. It was Debbie, the stripper I'd worked with 10 years earlier in Portland, Oregon and wow did she look great! Ten years hadn't hurt this lady in any way whatsoever. She still had a fantastic smooth curve, lean body and her routine was as good as ever. I called the waitress over and handed her a note to give to Debbie, which read, 'Do you remember the Fourth Avenue burlesque theater in Portland, Oregon, and the 1954 bandleader Brad Evans?'

When she finished her routine and was in her dressing room, she sent a note to me, 'Yes, see me back stage.' I excused myself from my friends and went to see her. It seemed like 10 years never happened, it was like yesterday and she looked just as luscious as ever. I only stayed a few minutes because she had to change and go on stage and I had a table full of friends waiting.

I said to her, "Meet me at the coffee shop down the block tomorrow when you get off work."

And she said, "Okay I will."

The next evening we had a bite to eat and talked about old times in Portland. She knew my band was on tour, I was on my way back to Las Vegas in a few days and she would be moving on to another club. She told me if I ever needed an exotic dancer to appear with the band I should give her first crack at the job. I promised her I would. Leaving the coffee shop we kissed and then went our separate ways. I haven't seen her since. I always did wonder how she was doing. My guess is she hung around Hollywood and continued dancing.

My First Affair

I was a 17 year old saxophone player playing for good looking strippers. They would tease me and my band on occasion when they'd dance over to the edge of the stage in front of the band and they would sometimes quickly flash us by pulling their G-string back or pulling the pasties and tassels off their nipples to expose themselves to us. Since we were sitting in the band pit below the stage we could see everything. I think they enjoyed teasing me because I was the only teenager in the group. Many of the strippers were anywhere from 8 to 13 years older than me. The one I wish would had shown interest in me was Debbie Rae, the cute redhead, but she always seemed too busy to give me a tumble. Other than an occasional coffee break at a coffee shop with her and the other women, there was nothing much happening. Even though nothing worked out with Debbie, there was one afternoon at the Fourth Avenue Theater that I'll always remember.

I met Misty, one of the headliners at the theater, in her dressing room to discuss the songs we were to play for her performance the following week. When I got to the theater to meet with her no one else had arrived yet. Inside her dressing room was the makeup mirror and table, wardrobe closet along with a couch and chair. I knocked on the door and she invited me in. She was sitting in front of the mirror putting on her makeup, wearing her G-string and a flimsy pink see-through negligee. Misty was a beautiful lady with dark piercing eyes and long brown hair that dropped down to the middle of her back. If I had to guess I'd say she was pushing 30. On stage she sure knew how to impress the men in the audience and she was one of my favorites.

After discussing her music she asked, "How old are you?" and smiled.

"Seventeen," I told her.

She said, "You're cute," as she saw me looking at her. She asked, "Do you like what you see?"

I blushed and nodded yes.

She stood up from the makeup table, walked to the door and turned the lock. As she sat on the couch, she said, "Brad have you ever been with a woman?"

"No," I told her.

She asked me to come over and sit beside her as she patted the couch seat. I wouldn't say she forced herself on me, but she leaned over and kissed me. Her kiss got my attention and my automatic reflex was to run my hand down her back causing her to arch against me.

In a blink of an eye I was out of my pants. I guess my young teenage hormones kicked in. "Oh God," I moaned, prolonging the moment and then I began to move, undone by her fire, torn in shreds by the extreme passion she ripped out of me. The groans and moans tore out of me from deep within my chest as my release surged through me, throwing me briefly into a place full of light colors and sound, before leaving me gasping and gathering her close, trembling and shaking. After that experience with Misty in her dressing room and the things she taught me that day about sex; I guess I became a man. We continued with the hidden relationship for the remaining few weeks she was in town. We secretly met at her apartment or inside the theater when no one else was there. My music career was getting off to a great start.

I Worked With the Famed Mills Brothers

After I finished my contract with the burlesque theaters I checked in with my best friend Ernie, to see if we could get a group together, but he was still working with the Castle Jazz

Brad and his music group first backed the Mills Brothers in 1953 at Amato's Supper Club, Portland, Oregon. After that, over the years Brad worked with them in I Hawaii and Las Vegas, Nevada.

Band. There was no way I could play with that band because they already had Jack Moffett, a super good clarinet player, who had been with the band for years and there was no hint that he intended to leave the group, so I moved on to form my own band and play around town. I named my band The Encores, sometimes the newspapers referred to it as Brad and his Encores. We played a lot of the well-known local clubs in town such as The Zombie Zulu, Tropics Club and Amato's Supper Club. Some of those clubs expected the band to back the entertainers the club brought into town.

One of the first groups I had the pleasure of playing backup music for was the famous Mills Brothers, who were appearing at Amato's Supper Club, the finest club in the city and known for hiring well-known entertainers of the time. My band had the opportunity to back this famous music group for a few weeks. These guys recorded records that were known worldwide and had also appeared in movies. In their early music career they had a gimmick of mimicking musical instruments as they sang, but in the early 1950s they dropped that routine in favor of using a real live band to back up their great vocal stylings. John Mills, Sr. headed up the group, but was getting ready to retire and leave the group to perform as a trio with brothers Harry and Herb running the show.

After John, Sr. retired the group had a big comeback in 1959 with the record 'Yellow Bird' and then the public began having other music style interests and the group faded again. In 1968 they hit it big again with their vocal stylings and recordings of 'Cab Driver', followed by 'My Shy Violet'. These songs were received extremely well, even with the music charts showing that people were getting into soul and psychedelic sounds. By the time the men in the group were in their mid-50s, John, Sr. didn't get a chance to see the group's revival because he died in 1967.

Over the years every time the Mills Brothers returned to Portland for an engagement they called me to use my band for their backup. After the Mills Brothers closed their Portland engagement, I received a call from the group again and they asked me to work with them at The Flamingo Hotel in Las Vegas. Between 1953 and 1955, I worked off and on with the group in Vegas. That was the place to appear in the 50s, so I jumped at the chance. Then again in 1955, the Mills Brothers were going to appear at the Laui Chi's Supper Club in Honolulu, Hawaii for one week and wanted my band to work with them again. A chance to play in Hawaii, you bet! I considered that a big break for my band so off I went. When I got to Hawaii I hired a few musicians who I knew could work with me and follow the arrangements I had for the Mills Brothers Show. To quote French author George Sand, *'There's only one happiness in life, to love and be loved.'*

Regardless how love is manifested it's truly a powerful force. From the day we are born it is our parent's love that keeps us alive. We grow up, learn the ways of the world and consider ourselves happy when we're surrounded by things we truly love, like family, friends, career, or hobbies. In a flash I traveled my road through life, those different chapters attempting to give the definition of love. My life's many encounters have taken love and friendship beyond the personal and considered it from a universal perspective. My love of life, personal association, friends and music have been more than satisfying; I couldn't ask for more.

Working With Other Entertainment Greats

During some of my engagements in Portland, from 1954 to 1956, I had the pleasure to back Frankie Laine, a nightclub singer, recording artist and movie star who was great to work

Spade Cooley-King of Western Swing. Brad played sax
with his band in Las Vegas, Nevda at the Golden Nugget
Hotel/Casino in the late 1950's.

Article on Spade Cooley's wife's murder.
The Los Angeles Mirror. Brad played sax in his band
in the 1950's.

Brad played sax with Nat King Cole between 1953 and 1955 in Portland, Oregon. The "Encores" later worked with Nat on various tour dates.

Frankie Laine-Brad's group the "Encores" First worked with Frankie in 1953 in Portland, Oregon. Then again in Las Vegas, Nevada through the years.

January 9, 2002

Dear Brad,

It's good to hear from you. Yes, we have a lot of great memories, don't we?

In 1993 I lost my precious Nan. Since then, I have married my companion, Marcia Kline, a lovely lady. She takes good care of me.

Hope you have a happy and healthy 2002!

God bless,

Frankie

Frankie Laine & Brad were friends since 1953. They worked together on stage over the years.

Brad, 18 years old. His group appears at the Tioga Hotel, Coos Bay, Oregon while on tour through the state. In its day, the Tioga Hotel was a popular nite spot.

1954-Tioga Hotel, Coos Bay, Oregon. Brad's group played in the Pirates Den

with. We became good friends and remained so until the day he died. After our first engagement together he decided to use me and my band to back his show each time he came through town. Then, in the late 1950s through 1970s, I worked with Frankie in Las Vegas where we had many appearances at the Fremont Hotel which was one of his favorite places to perform. We also did a lot of engagements and benefits in southern California. Frankie was big on charity and benefits, he always said he liked to give back to the people that made him. He was a gracious, kind and down to earth person. Frankie, and his wife Nan, always kept in touch over the years. I could always depend on an annual Christmas card if nothing else. Nan died in 1993 and that took a big toll on Frankie, but he continued to plow on. Frankie eventually married his longtime companion, Marcia.

The last time I saw Frankie he was in his 90s and came to Las Vegas to perform at the Orleans Hotel. He called and said he'd be in town to do an engagement and wondered if I would like to drop by and say hello. I told him I'd be there. At 92 years old Frankie still had his pipes, he belted out all his songs and had the audience yelling for more. At intermission we sat and talked, schmoozed and reminisced about the old days and good times we had in Portland. I'll always have good memories of Frankie. Marcia sent me a card when he died in 2007 at 94 years old. Frankie recorded one of the greatest hits 'That's My Desire' in 1946 and after that he had a straight 14 year run of hit after hit, not to mention his movies.

In the 50s Portland, Oregon was a major city on the entertainment circuit and it was good days for me and my band. I worked with the late, great Nat King Cole, a talent that could sing just about any style of song. He was an accomplished jazz pianist himself but he always appreciated other musicians' work. Like some of the other well-known personalities that toured through Portland in the 50s, he promised that each time he came into town he would hire me as his backup group. Over the years we continued our friendship by exchanging Christmas cards and an occasional phone call. In 1956 Nat got his first television show, which was only 15 minutes long, but during that era it was very hard for blacks in this country, and he was one of the first to land his own television show, a tremendous feat in the 1950s. At the time, Nat had everything going for him, he was a handsome guy, an impeccable dresser and like so many other entertainers of the era, he had class. He was a very popular star and looked great on television. The sad part was that his show began to lose television ratings. I personally believe the only reason his ratings dropped was because blacks in television those days weren't fully accepted. His show was great but I'm just a musician that saw another musician doing their thing.

While I was in the Marine Corp I received cards and notes from him and he said he was trying everything to make his show a success. He told me he took his show seriously and was trying to oversee the entire production and format of the show on his own terms. It must have worked out because in 1957 he presented his show to the network execs and they gave him a full 30-minute show, which was really something, a black man with his own 30-minute television show. However, the same year his show was okayed by the network, it began losing ratings and continued to tumble. He said the network people called him in and advised him that television wasn't ready for a black entertainer to have their own show and with that the network pulled the plug on his show. I was still in the Marine Corp when he told me his show was being terminated. He took it hard. I told him I was getting out of the Corp in 1958 and was looking forward to seeing and working with him again, but we never did. We lost touch after 1957.

Remembering those early years playing music in Portland, I

was at the Tropics Club and in the audience was bandleader and western country music star, Spade Cooley. He was on tour with his band in Oregon. He sent a waitress up to the bandstand with a note and a $10 bill folded inside. The note was a music request for the song 'Vaya Con Dios' and a blurb, asking me to join him and his party during the next intermission. A $10 bill was a big tip in the 50s. I played the song and then announced a break. I walked to his table, shook hands and he made the introduction of his agent and some band members. He complimented my playing and said he liked the sound of the band. We sat, chatted and bantered about music, his tour and then I excused myself to get back on stage. As I was leaving he told me, "I'm always looking for good musicians for my band, if you ever want a job, look me up." Little did I know we would meet again.

A few years later I was working a gig at the Fremont Hotel in Las Vegas and Spade Cooley's band was directly across the street at The Golden Nugget. On one of my breaks I went over to catch his show. During intermission I introduced myself to him and asked if he remembered playing Portland, Oregon. When he said yes, I reminded him of our conversation at the Tropics Club. He had to think for a minute but told me he recalled our visit. I told him I was playing across the street at the Fremont Hotel. Over the next few days we saw each other performing and had dinner together. During our dinner conversation he asked if I would like to play sax in his band. I told him my gig was up at the Fremont at the end of the week and I would be available. When my band closed at the Fremont Hotel, I sent my men back to California and took the job playing sax in Spade's band. He was known as Spade Cooley, King of Western Swing and his band was popular during the 50s and 60s. He had one of the few western bands that used brass and horns, his band was ahead of its time.

I worked with him for a few weeks at The Golden Nugget

and a few other times over the years. Noel Boggs, an excellent steel guitar player, was a regular with his band. About this time Spade and his band were recording with Columbia Records. His biggest hit was 'Shame on You' and that song was the essence of his contract with Columbia. He also was a stand-in for Roy Rogers in the movies in the 30s and 40s. Spade was a clothes hound who loved to dress in $500 and $600 handmade western suits with string ties, white Stetson hats and expensive western boots. He had a lot of money from his movies and recordings, he bought a lot of real estate and briefly went into the real estate business. He credited his success to one of his business agents, Bobbie Bennet. Spade told me she played one of the biggest parts in him becoming a larger than life entertainer. I continued to work with Spade whenever I had time off from my own group.

As the 60s rang in I was surprised to hear that Spade got himself into a mess of trouble. In 1961 he was living in San Fernando Valley near Mojave and apparently went off the deep end, flew into a rage and attacked his young wife, Ella Mae. The marriage was one of those May-December things, Ella was about 20 years old and Spade was 48. He filed for divorce from Ella Mae and won custody of his 14-year old daughter Melody and Donnell, his 12-year old son. Even after he filed for divorce that wasn't enough, he lost it and kicked Ella Mae to death while his daughter Melody watched. According to Melody, Spade grabbed Ella Mae in the shower and dragged her naked by the hair into the den. He banged Ella Mae's head on the floor a few times and called her a slut. Ella Mae was unconscious and he leaned over and said, "We'll see if you're dead." He then proceeded to stomp her in the stomach with his boots and then took a cigarette he had been smoking and burned her twice.

The trial was held in Bakersfield, California and was a sensation as far as celebrity trials go. Like the rest of the band members, I followed the trial on radio, TV and in the newspapers trying to understand why. Spade's defense was that he went into a rage when his young squeeze told him she was involved in a sex cult. He described in lurid detail specific acts of sodomy, different sex acts and sex-capades, but when it was all said and done the jury didn't buy his story. On August 19, 1961, Spade was found guilty of murder in the first degree. On August 22, 1961, he withdrew his insanity plea and Judge William Bradshaw sentenced him to life in prison. He and his attorneys appealed the verdict, but it was an exercise in futility. What a waste of talent, Spade had everything going for him.

Spade kept his nose clean while doing his time and was granted a leave from Vacaville Prison, so he could take part in a benefit concert in Oakland, California. He was well received at the benefit, the audience raved about his performance, but his life, luck and whatever else makes the world go around stopped for Spade. He walked off stage after the performance, keeled over and suffered a fatal heart attack right on the spot. He was only 59 years old when he died.

My Friend Ernie and I Team Up

I finished up some of my contracts in Portland in the early 50s and my friend Ernie also got a break from the Castle Jazz band, so we decided to team up as a duo playing small towns in Oregon. We took a job at the Tioga Hotel in Coos Bay, Oregon. It was one of the plush spots for city nightlife. We didn't plan ahead and book a place to stay, but one of his relatives owned an apartment house in North Bend, Oregon, which was near Coos Bay. He got us the okay to stay there while we were in town. What I didn't know was that the apartment housed a bunch of girls that worked as prostitutes. How good is that? Here we were, a couple of teenagers living in a whorehouse. We saw the girls come and go but neither Ernie nor I had sex with any of them. It's not that we didn't think or talk about it, but it was the girls who stopped us, they thought we were too young to have sex with pros. I was approaching 18 and Ernie was 16. The girls would smile and wave at us as they came and went, but we had no physical interaction.

Things changed though, when the high school girls around town found out we were professional musicians, we had our choice of girls. In a sleepy lumber town where the streets roll up at 9:00 or 10:00 p.m., the only thing the girls had to look forward to was a night out to a local movie with their boyfriends. It was no contest, those girls wanted to date the two of us. Maybe it was because they wanted to show off or make their boyfriends jealous. That was okay with us. Ernie and I chose one or two to be with on a steady basis while we were in town. Donna, the young thing I spent most of my time with in Coos Bay, was a knockout for her age. Eventually the time came when we finished our gig and I told her I was leaving town and heading back to Portland. She cried and made me promise to write to her. A crying female really gets to me so I promised I would write, but never did. That's the last time I saw Donna.

Years later, in 1962, I received a phone call at my residence from her. When she told me who she was I asked how she got my phone number. She told me she was a telephone operator and explained that all telephone operators try to locate friends and relatives around the country when they have a slow night at work. She told me she was married, had put on a lot of weight, and wondered what I looked like. I was courteous and polite but I told her I was on my way out the door to my job and suggested that, since she was a married woman, she shouldn't be trying to renew an old relationship. I think she took the hint, because I never heard from her again. I felt uneasy at her calling after all those years but I was glad she didn't call me again. It was a little spooky getting a call out of the past like that.

I Play Ice Capades

In 1955, when I got the call from the Mills Brothers to be musical backup for their singing group in Hawaii, the Pacific Island life sounded good to me. Hawaii wasn't even a state in 1955. En route to Hawaii I stopped in Los Angeles for about a week to check on a few musicians and see if I wanted them to work with my band. I was also on the lookout for costumes the band could wear on stage in Hawaii. I made the rounds to the costume shops and found Jack's of Hollywood that catered to the movie star clientele. I called ahead for an appointment and when I arrived Jack was fitting movie actress, Alexis Smith. She and I began talking and I found her to be pleasant and polite. In between our conversation, Jack came and went as he showed her other costumes. Eventually Jack joined in the conversation and we all decided to break for lunch.

During lunch Jack mentioned that he was in charge of costuming the Los Angeles Ice Capades cast members. The Ice Capades was going to be performing for the next few days and Alexis looked at me and suggested that since I was a bandleader and musician I should play in the Ice Capades. Jack chimed in and thought it was a good idea. He said, "I'm in charge of all the costumes and I'm sure I could talk to some of the people there into allowing your band to play."

Yikes, the game was on! Alexis and Jack both left the table to make some phone calls.

Alexis came back to the table smiling and said, "See, I told you I could do it."

Then Jack sauntered up to the table and said, "Everything is all arranged, you have a slot on the show to perform. It's only one number, but it's something."

I believe the only reason I got in to play for the Ice Capades was because actress Alexis Smith requested it and at that time she was very popular. Later that afternoon I signed on to play the engagement. Jack fitted my band with stage clothes for our appearance and it went well, the band received a lot of applause. That was my one and only appearance at an ice arena, a fun time for me.

Jack was gay and I think he offered to get the performance for me because he had some idea that he could get to me. He was hitting on me at lunch but I tried to ignore his advances by directing most of my conversation to Alexis. He wrote his phone number on a piece of paper and slid it across the table, asking that I call him so we could go to dinner in the near future. I let him know that I was straight and thanked him for the offer.

Alexis began laughing and said, "Jack, why don't you stop hitting on every young man in Hollywood?"

He said, "You can't blame me for trying."

As we were leaving I reminded Jack that I was in town for only a few more days before flying to Hawaii. I thanked him for arranging the band's costumes and said my goodbyes. I boarded a Pan Am flight to Hawaii two days later.

My Engagement in Hawaii

I touched down in Hawaii and checked into the hotel that the Mills Brothers had arranged for me to stay at while working with them. The Mills Brother show did a bang up job every night, they had the audience's ear on every performance. I spent my days lying around the beach all day and ate many of my meals at the open air restaurant a few feet from the ocean. Hawaii's weather was outstanding, it took me only two days to look as dark as a Hawaii native. While I was on stage working with the Mills Brothers, a lot of entertainers on the island dropped by to see the show on their nights off. Herb Jefferies, a movie star and very good singer who made the song 'Flamingo' famous, and Savannah Churchill, a fantastic gospel, blues and jazz singer stopped by. At intermission we talked shop.

Brad, 19 years. Finished engagement at the
Tropics Club, in Portland. Oregon and leaving for
a music tour in Hawaii - 1955-

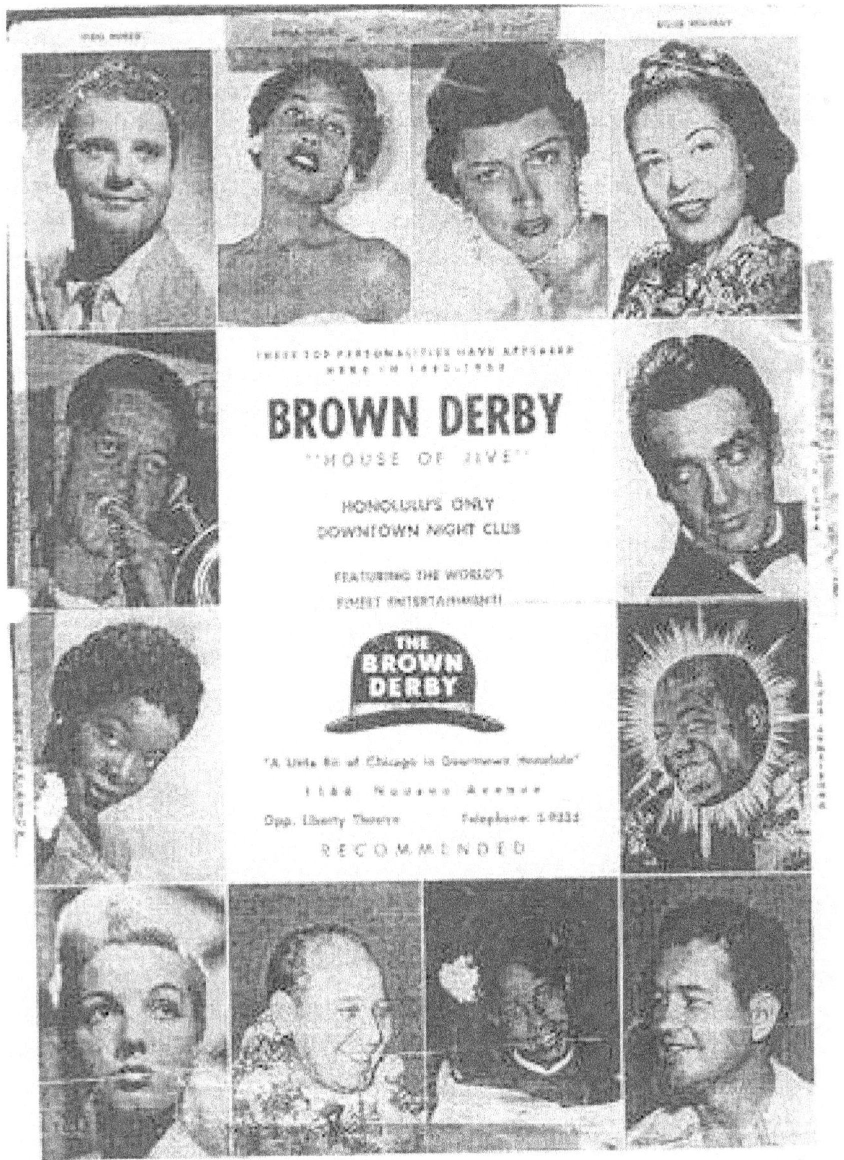

Brown Derby, Honolulu, Hawaii,1955
Brad, his band and other celebrities jammed here.

Herb Jefferies- Last surviving member of the Duke Ellington Band-Herb was first black movie star. Brad and he worked together in Honolulu, Hawaii at the Cloud Room in 1955.

HOTEL GUESTS OF THE WEEK. When singer Herb Jeffries arrived at a Jim Crow western city hotel for a two-week engagement, the manager greeted him cordially: "Your room is all arranged here," he said, "and it's in the white section. You see, when we have Negro performers like yourself appearing here, we usually keep rooms for them in a special section." Jeffries nodded. "That's just fine." The manager continued: "However, you understand, of course, that the gentleman traveling with you, your piano accompanist, Mr. Dick Hazzard, will have to stay in the Negro quarters." Answered Jeffries, "I do, if he does." An hour or so later when Hazzard put in his initial appearance at the hotel, the manager found himself in a very embarrassing situation. Hazzard turned out to be white.

Herb Jeffries

Singer Herb Jeffries Hotel Experience - Jet Magazine. May 28. 1953

Singer Herb Jeffries Hotel Experience - Jet Magazine. May 28. 1953

Herb Jefferies, who made the song "Flamingo" famous and earned Herb the nick name of Mr. Flamingo

1955-The Blue Note--
The after hours club in Honolulu, Hawaii where
Brad and musicians would jam until the wee
hours of the morning.

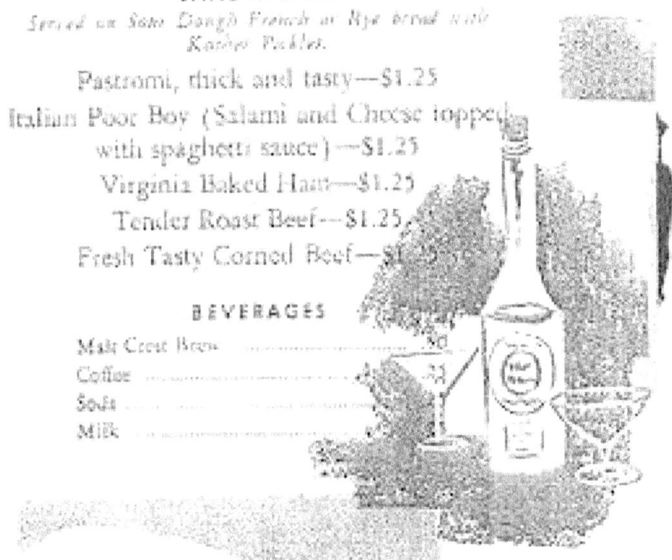

1955-Blue Note After Hours Club Prices of food
items at the place in 1955.

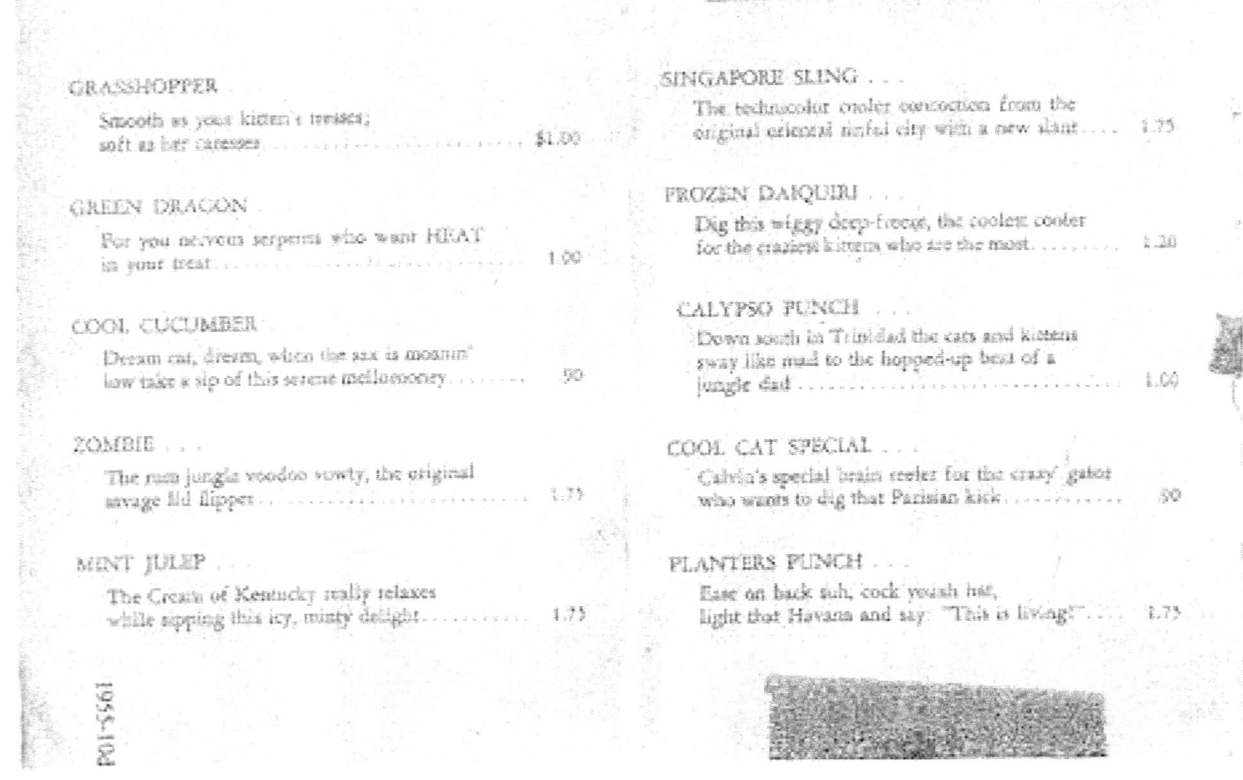

1955-BIuer Note Club-Drink Prices

One evening I told Herb that our engagement was coming to a close in a few days and he offered me a job playing sax with his trio at the Cloud Room, a popular dinner house where he was packing the tourists in. It was a nice small intimate club above some shops and I took him up on his offer. In the afternoons on our days off, Herb, Savannah and I, along with other musicians and entertainers, held jam sessions at an open air club that sat on the oceanfront with the ocean waves lapping against the stilts below the restaurant. The jam sessions were free to all the customers and the tourists got to hear all the headliners while hanging out at the beach. Once the sun went down, these same tourists paid big bucks to see us perform in clubs around the island. The tourists saw Savannah walk through the audience clapping her hands singing one of her gospel blues signature songs 'Shake a Hand' and they'd go wild screaming for more.

Louie Bellson

A drummer that frequently showed up for the jam sessions and made the crowds stomp and holler was world renowned Louis "Louie" Bellson. While I was on the island we worked together at the Blue Note Club and The Brown Derby, two popular after hour joints in downtown Honolulu. During the 1940s and up until 1955, the Blue Note and The Brown Derby presented stars like drummer, Gene Krupa, vocalist Ella Fitzgerald, Anita O'Day, Louis Armstrong, the Dorsey Brothers and many others. It became a regular routine that when my group finished up for the night in the high rent district, we went to after-hours clubs and jammed. There was no alcohol served at the after-hours clubs, but the customers listened to music performed by major artists and enjoyed coffee, soft drinks, and super good beef dip and pastrami sandwiches.

Lou and I became fast friends and stayed in touch after the engagements on the island. He was married to famed singer, Pearl Bailey, since 1952 and she also appeared at the Blue Note.

Like most entertainer friends we communicated for years with hello and holiday cards. I received a card when his daughter, Dee Dee, was born in 1960. Other than that occasional card I didn't see him in person again until 1970, when he called and asked me to come down to catch his band that was playing at Disneyland in Anaheim, California. It wasn't far from where I lived so I made the trip and it was worth it, people loved his performance. It had been 15 years since our 1959 Hawaii gig and now his daughter was also singing with his band. She pulled off a great performance that night; she was an excellent addition to his band. We caught up during intermission. When he went back on stage I left and it would be another 20 years until I heard from Louie again. In 1990 he was living in Lake Havasu, Arizona and he called me to let me know that his wife, famed singer Pearl Bailey, had died in Philadelphia at Thomas Jefferson Hospital from coronary heart disease. The next thing I heard about Louie was when he died on Valentine's Day in 2009. Shortly, after that, five months later, his daughter, Dee Dee, passed on. Wow!

A Leper Colony

On my 1955 tour in Hawaii, the state officials hired my band to entertain at the leper colony that was located in the Hawaiian Islands. That was really an experience. I had never seen a leper before and there were certainly a lot of them in the colony. At the time, Henry J. Kaiser, an eccentric automaker, owned a lot of property in Hawaii and he had a substantial affiliation and involvement with the leper colony. His little Henry J. Kaiser cars were fast selling items in the 50s with a lot of them on the islands at the time. He was well-respected as a businessman and everyone that was anyone wanted to be seen with and to hang out with him. He had his quirks though, but I guess with his many millions he could afford to be a little looney tunes and

The Leper Colony on Molokai, Hawaii.
Brad and his "Encores" and the Mills Brothers were invited to appear on the island to perform a show for the lepers in 1955.
The only way to get on the island was by invitation only." It was an experience and an honor to appear on the island."- Brad

The Leper Colony on Molokai island, Hawaii. Brad and his band, the "Encores" had the pleasure to perform for the residents of the leper colony in 1955. Other entertainers that also performed with Brad was Herb Jefferies, the Mills Brothers and Savannah Churchill-

Savannah Churchill-
Queen of R&B. Worked
with Brad's band , the
"Encores" in Honolulu.
Hawaii in 1955. She
also sang with Brad's
group performing at
the Leper Colony on
Molokai, Hawaii the
same year. Sanannah
was an exceptional
talent.

no one called him on it. One of the things was that he liked the color pink, so many of his properties throughout the islands were painted a bright pink and in fact, most everything on the leper colony was the color pink, as was one of the bestselling models of his car.

I spent four months appearing in Hawaii and it wasn't too long after my arrival that I began connecting with the ladies. At first I was dating a cute, well-built spitfire, stripper, named Rita, who was appearing in downtown Honolulu. When her engagement was up she returned stateside so I hooked up with June, a 29 year old 5' tall luscious blonde. She was a few years older than me, but the 10 years difference didn't bother me at all. June was visiting the island while her husband, George, a well-known professional wrestler, was wrestling on tour in Japan. She was supposed to meet up with him in Hawaii when he finished his tour, but she had no idea when he was going to show up. He told her when his tour was finished he'd jump over to Hawaii and meet her there. That was unsettling to me, but not enough for me to stop jumping her bones. Not knowing when he would show up on the island presented an edgy situation, so I was like a cat on a hot tin roof when I was with June. I could imagine what a professional wrestler could do to me when he found out I was balling his wife. He'd probably rip my arms off and throw me to the sharks.

When June told me he had an extended tour, that worked out to my advantage because I left my little sweetie June, to return stateside, before he showed up. While she and I were romping around the islands, she had her new 1955 green and cream-colored Oldsmobile shipped to the islands before she arrived so it would be there on her arrival. We toured all around the island in that car. She was very attractive, but a little loopy for my taste. One day she would tell me that she was going to divorce her wrestling husband and next day she would say that she loved him with all her heart and she didn't know why she wanted to run around behind his back and have sex with other men. She was a bit strange, but a very good sex partner.

June and I spent our days on the beach enjoying the sand, sun and good food. Herb and I went on stage at 9:00 p.m., so he and I spent a lot of daytime hours with our ladies at the beach. We all lived in our swimsuits for the four months we were in Hawaii. Herb hung out at the beach but he didn't want to stay in the sun too long, so he wore a large plantation type hat and stayed covered with a shirt. If he was exposed to the sun too long he would turn black in a matter of minutes. Herb was a black man that looked as white as me, but he was afraid the sun would do a number on him.

Herb Jefferies

Herb was an interesting guy. One of his first gigs in showbiz was when he was only 19-years old, appearing in one of Al Capone's clubs in Chicago, the Savoy Dance Hall. He brought his orchestra in to play at the club and in 1931 he was hired to sing with Earl (Father) Hines Band. He put up with a lot of segregation when his band was touring in the south. Because he was black, but looked white, he was shouted at, spit on and called every name in the book. He re-located to Los Angeles and began singing with the Cab Calloway Band and worked for the Duke Ellington Band for about 10 years. Herb was a 6'3" tall, good looking, mustachioed, blue eyed, light complexioned man who had a charismatic, matinee type Latin look. He was a prime candidate for the (Sepia) movie pictures that only played in the ghettos and segregated theaters which were advertised with an all-black cast. Herb made his first movie as a crooning cowboy in the 1937 film 'Harlem On the Prairie', which was considered the first black western following the introduction of talkie films.

While appearing in this black cowboy film, dark makeup was applied to his light skin to make him look like the black man he really was. In the numerous western cowboy movies he made over the years he almost never took off his white Stetson cowboy hat because it would have revealed that he had naturally brown hair. While Herb was making movies in the 30s he continued to show off his vocal talent and impress people as a very good singer. In 1947, while singing with the Duke Ellington Band, he recorded his signature song 'Flamingo', which earned him the title of Mr. Flamingo. After that, during the 50s, Herb mostly worked in Europe which I believe was because Europeans were more tolerant of black men, entertainers in particular. He was well received in Europe and eventually bought a nightclub, The Parisian, where he held court and sang every night. Herb wound up owning two successful night clubs in Paris.

The 50s were good to Herb and in 1957 he starred in the movie 'Calypso Joe', which co-starred Angie Dickinson. Herb also appeared in episodes of "I Dream of Jeannie", "The Virginian" and "Hawaii Five-O" with Jack Lord. Without a doubt Herb could have passed himself off as white anytime and anywhere, but he told me he was very proud of his heritage and made no bones about it to anyone. He always identified himself as black. In the 90's western movies came back in style and he recorded a revival album titled 'The Bronze Buckaroo Rides Again' for Warner westerns. Herb was a true ladies man. He was married four times, once to the much talked about stripper, Tempest Storm, who I worked with in Portland in 1953/55'.

When he and I finished our gig in Hawaii in 1955, we talked by phone or mail on an infrequent basis. The last time I saw Herb was when we sat and talked in 1985 at a Denny's Restaurant on Ventura Boulevard in Sherman Oaks, California. We met for a cup of coffee and caught up on old times in Hawaii when we were entertaining and sharing the same women. He shared my

June and I shared his Susan. During our meeting he told me he cut back on his singing and touring, but he was still married to Tempest and she was as notorious as ever. Tempest was one of the biggest mistakes I ever made, he said. He knew I worked with her in Portland in the early 50s and he said he would give her my best. Tempest was the most famous exotic dancer ever, except maybe, Gypsy Rose Lee. Herb didn't change that much in the 30 years I've known him. He was still wearing one of his straw hats like one wears when vacationing in the South Sea's and he still had the scar down his face, which was like a trademark that I always thought gave him character. That character scar was received in an airplane crash in the early 1940's. Herb suffered such severe injuries from the plane crash that he went to study with Paramahansa Yogananda, the Indian spiritual guru who founded the Self Realization Fellowship where this guru taught yoga and healing practices. Herb told me that the training he received helped him handle the pain. I once told Herb someone should make a movie of his interesting life. My opinion, it would be a winner.

Herb was married four times, once to Rose Bowl princess Betty Allensworth, and he admits to five children, seven grand-children and eight great-grand kids. The man was such a talent that in June 2010, President Bill Clinton proclaimed him a National treasure. Herb is now living a comfortable life in a cozy mountain view home above Palm Springs, California with his business partner and significant other, Savannah Shippen, 45-years his junior. His home has the ever present pink Flamingo figurine at his living room window. Herb, now in his late 90's, is active in the music business. Now sporting a beard I think Herb resembles the late actor Vincent Price.

05

The United States Marine Corp

Join the Marine Corp

It's the mid-50s Ernie, Benny and I were draft age. None of us wanted to be drafted so we joined the military service to get our military obligation out of the way. Every man had to register for the draft in those days when they turned 18 years old; there was no volunteer Army in those days. We had two choices, one was to get drafted into the Army and the other was to join one of the other military branches of service. We tossed around the pluses and minuses of each branch of the military and made the decision to select the Marine Corp. None of our parents had any objections to us joining the military, so when I was 20 years old, we went to the recruiting office and signed up for the entrance exam. All three of us passed and we were told we would be leaving for San Diego, California after we were sworn in. The recruiter tried to get us to sign up for a six year hitch, promising all kinds of training schools as incentives. We told him we would go for the two-year enlistment program and if we liked it we would re-enlist for a longer term later.

Marine Corp Boot Camp-Basic Training

A few days after being sworn in, we left Portland on our way to the San Diego Marine Corp Training Depot. A Marine Corp bus picked us up at the San Diego Airport and took us to the Marine Corp Training Center. Our first introduction to Marine Corp life was a true awakening. When the bus stopped on the base, the drill instructor told us to line up in front of the bus.

Then he asked everyone from New York and Texas to take one-step forward. After those recruits stepped to the front, the drill instructor walked up to each of them and punched them in the stomach or in the face with all his might. He yelled at us and said, "No matter where you're from or how big and bad you think you are, that means nothing in the Marine Corp."

He waited for all of us to respond with a loud, "Yes, sir.

When some didn't answer he again yelled louder, "Do you understand?"

And then we all yelled back, "Yes, sir."

That was our introduction to the Marine Corp.

During basic training some of us were sent to other units. Benny, my drummer that joined with Ernie and I, was sent to another unit. Ernie and I were assigned to the 1st Marine Division headquarters company. Boot camp was a toughie, they had us running, jumping and working out everyday. The guys that were overweight, when we arrived, began losing weight and the recruits that were skinny and thin began putting on the pounds. Basic training was 16 weeks long and we were not allowed to leave the base. During basic training we couldn't eat candy or snacks such as chips, pretzels, cookies and peanuts. The Corp called candy and snacks 'poggie-bait' and no Marine recruit was allowed poggie-bait. The drill instructors opened and inspected every package and piece of mail that was sent to us before they allowed us to have it.

If a Marine recruit's family sent poggie-bait to them in a parcel, the drill instructor kept it for themselves. When a package arrived for a recruit, the drill instructor called the Marine to the duty hut and asked if he had any objections if the sergeant kept the goodies for themselves. Occasionally a recruit said yes, the wrong answer, which resulted in being punched or beaten up. Mom used to send me a few cartons of cigarettes and the drill instructors would call me to their duty hut, give me a few packs and keep the rest for themselves. This was standard practice in the Marine Corp during boot camp training.

While going through basic training a couple recruits couldn't take the rigor of training and committed suicide. It was tough training to be a Marine in the 50s, but we did it without question. Recruits that couldn't keep up with the rest were put at the end of the line when we marched anywhere and ate the dust the rest of us stirred up during the march. Our company did a required 13-mile march from San Diego over mountains and woods on the way to one of our gun ranges. We were rationed water during the 13 miles and some of the men dropped out of formation and passed out saying they couldn't go on. Those recruits were picked up and trucked back to San Diego where they were later disciplined. I was one of many other Marines that completed the march successfully. My mindset regarding these long marches was to tune into the idea that I was going to be a Marine and a Marine can face all obstacles. At the same time that I and my fellow Marines were doing these extended marches, we were lucky. About this same time we were going through training at Camp Pendleton, across the country at the Marine Corp base, Camp Lejeune, in North Carolina, Marine Corp drill instructors marched their recruits into the swamps of North Carolina and approximately 29 men died on that training march into the swamps.

At the gun range we were ordered to disassemble our M-1 rifles. We had to take them apart and reassemble them blindfolded, by feeling each part. One recruit lost one of the parts to his rifle in the dirt and couldn't find it. The drill instructor made our entire company break down their rifle and bury the parts in the dirt and leave them there overnight. The next day he ordered us to dig up the parts we had buried the night before, telling us we had better find all the parts or pay the consequences. We all found every part, cleaned the parts and reassemble the rifles.

If any one Marine recruit fouled up in some way in a competition or on a maneuver, the drill instructor woke the entire company up at 2:00 or 3:00 in the morning and ordered all of us to duck walk back and forth holding our heavy footlockers in front of us. I didn't know what duck walking was until the Marine Corp. We Marines had to squat down with our butts as low to the ground as possible and then we had to walk. As we walked in that squatting position us Marines looked like a bunch of ducks walking. To make the duck walk more aggressive and punishing the drill instructors would order us to hold and carry our footlockers in front of us as we duck walked. That was tough because those large, wood, foot lockers which held our gear weighed close to 100 pounds each. The same discipline occurred when we didn't salute the company mascot, a bulldog that wore sergeant stripes on his dog collar. In the scheme of things, recruits were ranked lower in standing than the bulldog mascot. We had to treat the dog with the same respect we gave a non-commissioned officer. If the dog walked past any of us we had to stop, salute the dog and say, "By your leave, sir." If the drill instructor saw that we didn't salute the dog when he walked by, we were called to the duty hut where we were punched and hit. Sometimes the drill instructor took it out on the entire company and made us run, at double time, around the tarmac. Or he took away our smoking privileges and let the men in the company know which one of us caused the rest of them to be punished. Marine Corp boot camp was tough but I made it though by sheer determination, will power, and strength of character.

Some of My Punishment

I was disciplined a few times. One morning I tried to get by without shaving. When we were standing for inspection, the drill instructor noticed small stubble on my chin. He told me to go into my footlocker and return with a razor and a new blade. He stood me in front of all the other Marines in the company and said he was going to teach us a lesson so we'd learn to shave every morning. He put the new blade in the razor and handed it back to me. He then ordered me to shave with the razor, without shaving cream, just a new razor blade against my skin. As I was shaving he ordered me to run in place and continue shaving. Within a few minutes my face was chopped up with nicks and bleeding. When he ordered me to stop, I was told to stand in front of the rest of the men so they could see the result of not following orders. There was never a day after that discipline that I didn't shave.

Another time I was caught smoking a cigarette without permission and again the drill instructor made an example of me for the entire company. He had all the Marines fall out from their barracks and line up at attention to witness my punishment. The D.I. (drill instructor) asked me to fetch an empty bucket and blanket from my bunk. I sat the items in front of him and stood at attention. He asked me to light a cigarette and told me to smoke it. After a few puffs he asked me if I was enjoying the smoke. I shouted back, "Yes, sir."

Then he told me to light another cigarette and put it in my mouth with the first one. After that he told me to light a third cigarette and put it in my mouth with the other two and continue to smoke all three cigarettes.

With the three cigarettes in my mouth and my puffing on them, one of the drill instructors picked up the bucket and blanket. One D.I. put the bucket upside down over my head and face, while the other D.I. threw the blanket over my head covering up the bucket, while at the same time ordering me to continue puffing and smoking the three cigarettes. About two minutes into smoking the cigarettes with the bucket and blanket on my head, I became deathly ill. The D.I.s removed the blanket and bucket from my head and told the rest of the men in the company that this is what would happen to them if they ever smoked a cigarette without permission. They told us the next time it would be a half a pack instead of just three cigarettes. One of the drill instructors turned to me and gave me permission to run to the 'head', Marine Corp talk for the bathroom.

When I began to leave, the other D.I. shouted double time, meaning I should run twice as fast. He shouted, "If you throw up before you get to the head you'll be punished again." When I returned to my quonset hut, which is a light-weight prefabricated structure made of corrugated, galvanized steel that the Marines used as barracks, a number of Marines told me they wouldn't be caught dead smoking without permission after seeing what happened to me. I never again smoked a cigarette during basic training without a D.I.'s permission. Some people have to learn the hard way and I did, but a lesson learned is one that stays with you forever.

Some Recruits Can't Take It

During our basic training there were a few recruits that couldn't take the pressure of discipline that's required to be a Marine and some of those recruits went absent without leave (AWOL) and ran away from the training center. In most cases they were quickly caught, brought back to the base and returned to their unit. There were consequences for going AWOL and that was being beaten by the M.Ps (Military Police) or D.I.s. The ones that were brought back to the company and suffered those consequences never ran away again, as far as I know. We also had those recruits that wanted out of the Marine Corp so bad that they faked being crazy, hoping to be sent home with a medical or dishonorable discharge.

I recall one recruit that cried in his bunk at night and told us that he wanted to go home because he was homesick. He tried to go over the fence once or twice, but was brought back by the M.P.s. After being beat a few times for running away, he swore he would find a way to get out of the Marine Corp. He came up with a novel idea, or so I thought. One day while we were eating at the mess hall he squirreled away some peanut butter and corn kernels off his mess tray. Then one morning while some of us were cleaning the head and scrubbing the sinks and toilet bowls he placed some of the peanut butter and corn mixture inside the rim of the toilet bowl. When the D.I. walked in to inspect our work, the recruit was sitting on the floor in front of the toilet. He looked up at the drill instructor and scooped up some of the mixture from under the toilet bowl rim, put it in his mouth and said, "Sir, look at me, I'm eating shit." Then he reached under the toilet bowl rim again and put the rest of it in his mouth and swallowed. The rest of us just stood there in amazement. The D.I. had a surprised look on his face as he watched the recruit eating from the toilet bowl. The recruit was ordered to be taken to the duty hut where he was briefly knocked around by the drill instructors and from there he was taken to the shrinks for evaluation.

The rest of us never knew what happened to the guy, he was never returned to our company. I've always wondered if he got what he wanted, a Section 8, which means a crazy discharge and booted from the Marine Corp. Some people will go to great lengths to get what they want but I thought this guy's act was over the top.

A Marine is Indispensable

There was an incident that occurred in boot camp that brought the point home that a Marine is a Marine. Our company mascot,

Sgt. Bailey, was always brought along with our company almost anywhere we went. One recruit was usually assigned to watch over the mascot and one morning our company had to march to the firing range for firearms practice and the mascot and his handler accompanied us to the range. Sgt. Bailey was put on a leash nearby while the Marines were firing at targets. We were laying in the dirt with our M-1 rifles, shooting at targets down range. For some reason Sgt. Bailey broke off his leash, maybe frightened by the gunfire, or maybe he saw a rabbit to chase. Whatever the reason, he started to run down the range in front of the targets we were firing at. When we saw the dog running in front of our targets we stopped firing and someone yelled, "Stop shooting, there's Sgt. Bailey."

Our drill instructor yelled, "I didn't order anyone to cease, fire." He walked up behind a couple Marines lying in the dirt and slapped them on their helmets and kicked their asses shouting, "You pussies, continue to fire. You assholes had better resume firing now!" An order is an order in the Marine Corp, so we began firing at the targets again.

Our mascot, Sgt. Bailey, was fatally struck by a bullet from one of our weapons. When the firing practice was over, the drill instructor ordered two of the recruits with the lowest shooting score to retrieve Sgt. Bailey's carcass and bury him in a spot near the shooting range. As we were preparing to leave the range, we were ordered to stand at attention and the drill instructor stood before us and said, "A lesson has to be learned here today. That lesson is that a Marine is indispensable and that included Sgt. Bailey." When we returned to the barracks, the Marine that was assigned to look after Sgt. Bailey was called to the duty hut and was worked over by the D.I.s. He was told that he shouldn't have allowed Sgt. Bailey to break off his leash. Two weeks passed and the D.I.s brought another bulldog to our company named Sergeant Murphy.

The punishment in the Corp may have seemed harsh but the Marine Corp was always know for it rigorous training. As I look back on those Marine Corp training days I can say that it did build my character, self-discipline, self-reliance and helped develop my values and judgment for years to come.

My Sister Visited Me During Basic Training

While going through boot camp we all had to take turns working in the mess hall serving food, washing dishes and peeling potatoes. One afternoon while I was assigned to mess duty and in a small room peeling potatoes, my Sergeant came by and said that I was to report to the front gate. When I asked him why, he said my sister, from New York, was at the front gate to see me. He had talked to her and her husband and he was authorizing me to go off base with them for a two-hour visit. He told me I was not to be gone more than the two hours and I should report back to him after the visit.

I went to the front gate and met my sister, Ramona, and her husband Al. I hadn't seen Ramona since I was 14 years old and I had never met her husband. We drove to a nearby restaurant and stopped to eat and talk. Ramona said she and Al were on vacation, they drove out to the west coast to see mom in Oregon and then decided to come to California to see me. They asked the base commander if they could see me before they returned to New York and he ordered my Sergeant to let me off base for the two-hour visit. When Al got up to use the restroom, Mona told me that she was going to divorce him. She wanted to come to the west coast and asked if I could help her out until she got on her feet and settled in California. I really didn't know her that well but she was my sister so I told her I would do what I could.

At the time I had one-half of my monthly Marine Corp salary withheld and sent directly to mom under the Marine

Corp Allotment Program. During basic training my salary was only $73 a month, but because I was getting a place to eat and sleep I didn't need the entire paycheck. I told Mona I'd write to mom and let her know that I would stop sending the allotment to her, but instead give it to Ramona when she came out west. Al and Mona dropped me back on base within my two-hour window and went on their way back to New York. As ordered, I reported to my Sergeant so he could verify my return and then it was back to mess hall duty.

A few months following Mona's visit to Camp Pendleton, she wrote me and said she was coming to California and would live in Los Angeles and try to find a job. She again asked if I could provide her with some money for her living expenses until she got on her feet so I began giving her my allotment money. She eventually got an apartment and shared it with two other girls. After I completed my boot camp basic training, me and my Marine Corp band buddies would often go to Los Angeles to play music and while I was there I visited Mona.

Marines Complete Boot Camp

During our boot camp basic training each of us Marines were called to the administration office so we could make a request for duties we would like to have after we graduated. It was just a formality, nothing was set in stone, because the Marine Corp gave us the assignments they wanted us to work at. At my interview I told them I wanted to be in the United States Marine Corp Band and play clarinet and they told me I had to audition. My friend, Ernie, also requested to be put in the band. One day I was called to the duty hut and my drill instructor told me to report to a certain barracks on base. On arrival there were two Corporals and two Sergeants sitting in the room. They pointed me to a clarinet on a small table nearby, then picked up some music and told me to play. I played all the music they put in front of me and after five or six pieces they told me to stop and go back to my unit. They didn't say one way or the other if I'd passed the audition. The next day my buddy, Ernie, went to audition and when he returned to the barracks he said he also had to wait for word as to whether he passed the audition.

At boot camp graduation the drill instructors handed each of us an envelope with orders for the job we would be assigned while in the Marine Corp. That's a scary moment because many Marines don't get the jobs they want, they have to take the assignment and go where the Marine Corp orders them to be. Ernie opened his orders first and he was accepted to play in the 1st Marine Division Band at Camp Pendleton, California. I was happy for him and congratulated him and then I tore open my orders. I took a deep breath and looked down at the piece of paper. I was also accepted to play in the Marine Corp Band at Camp Pendleton. My stress levels fell like a rock, I was elated. Ernie and I reported to the 1st Marine Corp Division Headquarter Band barracks and were looking forward to the rest of our military service.

Mom Relocated to California

It's 1957 I was plugging away in the Marine Corp. During mail call I received a letter from mom, she was getting a divorce from Don Rolund and wanted to visit California and possibly stay. Her marriage with Don had lasted nine years and I was guessing she had her fill of supporting the guy and doing all the work and heavy lifting in their marriage. I wrote back saying I'd love to see her and thought it was a good idea for her to come to California. Mom knew Ramona was living in Los Angeles and since Camp Pendleton was only an hour down the road, I told mom I'd meet her and Mona at Clifton's Cafeteria, in Los Angeles, a well-known landmark. During lunch I convinced her to stay in California and I returned to base. Over the next week or two she began looking around the communities outside Los Angeles for a house to buy. She found a big roomy ranch-style house that she liked in Lynwood, California, a suburb of Los Angeles.

At the time Lynwood was known as California's All American City. It was a nice quiet middle-class city close to anywhere you wanted to go in southern California. There were trolley cars running from Lynwood and Compton to all over downtown Los Angeles. On my days off from Camp Pendleton I went to Lynwood to visit mom. She quickly found a job and began working as a clerk at the Compton Music Store. Her house became a hangout for me and my Marine Corp buddies. When we had leave, off base, we had a place to stay and to rehearse. Mom kept her job at the music store for about a year and then quit and began a job at a local donut shop where she made and sold donuts.

Out of Basic Training

Ernie and I quickly became very popular when the rest of the Marine Corp Band members found out we played professionally before joining the Corp. The Marine Corp Band had its own barracks and each morning the band marched to the drill field and played while the American flag was raised. Ernie and another trumpet player played reveille each morning to wake up the base. Once the flag was raised, the band stayed on the field and practiced marching formations and played songs. When the United States Marine Corp band returned from the drill field to the barracks they rehearsed every day and those rehearsals made it the best military band over and above all the other military bands in the service. The band traveled around the country and marched in parades for all occasions. We traveled to places like Cheyenne, Wyoming to celebrate Cheyenne Day, to Reno, Nevada for celebrations and we even played concerts at the Greek Theatre in Los Angeles.

The Marine Corp Band was transported to each city in California in one of the Marine Corp buses. If the trip was a few states away the Marine Corp flew us in on military transport planes. We stayed in each city for only one to three days and then were taken back to Camp Pendleton. Following a parade in San Diego, I met Karen, an insurance executive that lived in La Jolla, California. She took me aside and told me how much she liked the Marine Corp Band. I thought nothing of it at the time, but on our next three engagements throughout California she showed up every time. She followed the band from city to city and state to state. She drove her Mercedes SL to our location and after we finished our parade or concert she took me to dinner and run me around town to different events. I didn't know if she had the hots for me or if she just liked guys in uniform. Who follows a military band around the country?

One of our engagements was to march in a parade in Reno, Nevada. As our bus pulled up in front of Harrah's Club, I looked out the window and Karen was standing there waving to me. Some of the guys in the band began teasing me when they saw her outside the bus waving at me. I was wondering if I had a groupie, not sure what her story was. Before we got off the bus, a Harrah's Club representative boarded and gave each of us band members a $10 chip and a book of comps for free meals and shows. We were also given rooms at the hotel for the three days we were playing in town, courtesy of Harrah's Club. Two band members were assigned to each hotel room. When I got off the bus I asked Karen what she was doing in Reno. She said she drove up from La Jolla to see me. That's when I knew she wanted to hook up with me and now I knew why she was following the band everywhere we performed. She said she had a present for me and asked me to go with her back to her motel. I told her I had to check in to the hotel and would be busy for the next few hours with band business, but she could pick me up in front of the hotel at 10:00 p.m. that evening and she agreed.

After check-in, most of the band members changed into civilian clothes and went downstairs to the casino and gambled for a few hours. I walked out front at 10:00 p.m. and sure enough, she was waiting for me in her car. We drove to her motel, where she poured us a cup of coffee and handed me a gift box.

"This is for you," she said.

"What's the occasion," I asked?

"No reason, I just wanted to buy you something."

I smiled and opened the box. Inside was an expensive watch. I removed the cheap Timex watch from my wrist, removed the watch from the box and slid it on my wrist. After her buying me a few dinners in California, driving me around in her sports car and now the watch, I thought it was time to get sexually involved.

"Thanks, honey, it's a great present," I said. As we stood by the bed I reached down and pulled her close and kissed her. At the same time, I gently laid her back onto the bed. When my lips met hers she couldn't stop the trembling that vibrated through her body. She hung on tightly as I nibbled at her mouth, barely registering my fingers at the waistband of her shorts. Then my hand was inside her panties, my fingertips circling her sensitive butt as I pushed her shorts off her hips. I dipped one long finger into her wetness and then another, catching her cry in my mouth.

We enjoyed each others bodies that night and over the next

two days I spent my nights in her motel rather than staying at my hotel room at Harrah's Club. As I boarded a bus to return to Camp Pendleton, she stood there with me. We kissed saying we'd see each other soon. As the bus pulled away from the hotel I saw her sports car drive by and pass our bus. We saw each other over the next few months in California but slowly drifted apart.

Ernie and I formed a small group of musicians from the Marine Corp Band and began playing dance jobs off base on the side. We made some extra money playing in a number of officer's clubs and other functions. Our group consisted of Ernie playing piano or trumpet, I played sax, clarinet and bass, while sometimes doubling on drums, and we also added a regular drummer and trombone player. While I was keeping busy playing in the Marine Corp Band and with my music on the side, I began to study karate with a few Marines that had mastered the skill before they enlisted. I continued with that study until my enlistment was up. While studying martial arts, one of my martial arts Marine instructors gave me two books to read, which peaked my interest in alternative medicine and natural healing, *Many Mansions* and *There is a River* by Edgar Cayce. Something else that grabbed my attention was hypnosis and self-hypnosis. With my music and hobbies, I had a lot on my plate while completing my military service.

The Marine Corp Band was one of the best in the world. Its reputation preceded itself everywhere we went. The band was asked to play all over the country. We were constantly playing a concert or parade somewhere in the United States. It was a great job and I was extremely proud to be a band member in the Marine Corp Band. It was the best of both worlds. I was doing my patriotic duty and serving my military obligation, while at the same time I was allowed to operate my own band on the side to make extra money. How great is that?

I Kicked Mona Out of the House

My sister and her boyfriend were living in the same house with mom while I was still in the Marine Corp and on my days off base I quickly saw how Mona and Ronnie were sponging off mom while poor mom was working her tail off to survive. They weren't working and were asking mom for money for things like movies and eating out. Mona refused to help mom clean the house or share in the household duties and never once offered to chip in for food and such. Mom wasn't complaining about the situation and she never told me anything about supporting these two on her dime. When I saw what was happening and how they were taking advantage of her, I became angry and took both Mona and Ronnie into the kitchen, sat them down and told them they'd have to get out of mom's house.

I said, "I'm tired of seeing you both lay around the house and not lift a finger to help mom out. You're eating her food, leaving dirty dishes for her to clean up and you're letting her do all the housework. I want you gone from the house by the next time I come up on leave." I made no bones about the fact that I thought they were both a couple of bums. I said, "Neither of you are working and I don't want your lazy butts living off mom or me, its time for you to support yourselves." They began arguing with me, but I reminded Mona that I was the one that signed over my money to her each month so she could get on her feet. She brushed it off saying it wasn't that much money, and besides I made extra money playing music so I could afford it. They called mom into the kitchen and told her that I was throwing them out of the house and wanted her to intervene. Instead she said, "I agree with Brad, I think it's about time you two go out on your own." When I returned during my next leave they were out of the house, but before leaving they dinged ma for more money. Mona borrowed $900 from mom and she and boyfriend, Ronnie moved into an apartment complex known as Victory Park in Compton.

Mom told me Mona promised to pay back the money if their apartment ever sold in the future. But the payback never happened. Mona never went out to get a job, but boyfriend Ronnie got a job as a minimum wage security guard. Ronnie was a nice person but he was a little slow. He joined the Air Force about the same time I joined the Marine Corp, but due to his mental abilities they released him from the Air Force after only a couple weeks when he was still in boot camp because he couldn't adapt.

Seven months after I finished my military service and left the Marine Corp, Mona and Ronnie had a child, a girl they named Robyn.

Music Side Jobs In the Corp

On our days off, Ernie and I would go to nightclubs off base and sit in and play with civilian musicians. One of our favorite places was the 400 Jazz Club in Los Angeles. The house band was Teddy Buckner's Dixieland Jazz Band and Ernie and I gained somewhat of a reputation and had a small following when we would show up and sit in with Teddy's band. We often played Laguna Beach with local musicians and during one of our jam sessions we made a friend who was a major in the Marine Corp. He wasn't a musician himself, but was an avid fan of Dixieland music. He lined up a number of parties in and around Laguna Beach for us to play at. He and his wife also threw fantastic parties at their house, high on a hill overlooking Laguna Beach. The major was a Marine jet pilot who was based at El Toro Air Station and sometimes following his parties, Ernie and I would run late in getting back to Camp Pendleton, so he gave us his personal car which had an officer's sticker on the window that would help allow us to drive on and off the base without being stopped by the M.P.'s at the gate.

He also arranged for me and Ernie to eat at the Officer's Club, where the meals were prepared to order for the officers and they had a menu to choose food dishes from. The officer's ate at tables that seated only four people and each table had a white tablecloth, a glass of water and china plates at each place setting and the food was ordered and served by a waiter. Compare that to the mess hall where we would eat food from a chow line on a metal tray, sitting on benches at a long table filled with 20-30 other Marines. There was no contest between the two when we had our meals, it was two different worlds. Being friends with a high ranking officer had its benefits and we certainly received quite a number of extra privileges because we were friends with a major.

There were times when Ernie couldn't get off to work extra music jobs so I formed another group and named it after my old band The Encores. My group was playing auditoriums and USO Shows in and around Oceanside, San Clemente, Vista and San Diego and other cities near Camp Pendleton. The band became more popular by the day and I was getting calls from officer's clubs up and down the coast. My group was also asked to play the Governor's Ball at Oceanside, California in 1957. It was at that engagement I met Nicole, who was at the ball with a friend. Her husband was a sergeant on maneuvers and would be gone for nine months. Nicole would come up to the bandstand, put money in the tip jar requesting different songs and asked me to join her and her friends at intermission. We sort of clicked one night. She knew my band was playing at the NCO (non-commissioned officers) Club in Oceanside most every weekend so she began showing up on a regular basis with a girlfriend of hers.

Nicole's house was only a few blocks away from the NCO Club and one night she walked to the bandstand and motioned for me to bend over as if she were going to ask me something. When I did she dropped a note in my suit breast pocket and walked away. A few minutes later I saw her leave the club. At intermission I opened the note and a key fell out into my hand and the note was her address written down with the words, 'I'll wait up.' When we closed out for the night I drove the short distance to her house and used the key she provided to go inside. The living room was dark except for a small glowing nightlight on the wall that allowed me to see my way through the room. As I closed the door behind me I said softly, hello. From the rear of the house I heard a reply, in here. I walked down the hall and saw the glimmer of a light shining through the door which was slightly ajar.

I slowly pushed the door open and saw Nicole lying in bed wearing nothing but panties and a bra. Nicole said "Well?"

I said "Well what?"

Nicole said, "Aren't you going to ask me to make you a drink, maybe coffee?" I looked right in her eyes and smiled. She then said, "But if you have something else in mind," and with that I laid down beside her and brushed my lips across hers. She kissed me back hard and I stood up and began removing my clothes, letting them fall to the floor as she watched. I laid down and my lips moved from Nicole's lips to her breasts. I removed her bra and my lips moved to her belly button to the dampened crotch of her panties which soon found themselves on the floor.

Her sexuality slammed through her leaving her trembling, quivering and sobbing. I gently kissed her tears from her cheeks. As I lay there I moved her legs further apart and with this I pressed closer, my weight on top of her. Soon she'll feel me inside of her, after all, it was her idea. She's the one that dropped the key into my pocket. She could notice a lot of things while the large red digital numbers on her radio alarm glow and move from 3:05 to 3:10. She can also notice my clothes lying there on the floor. She was lying next to me and moved her hand onto my bare chest. I wasn't a muscle man but had a medium build that was lean and my chest was sprinkled with blonde/brownish hair. I moved to roll onto my side to face her. Nicole let her hand slide down over my chest her fingers gently gliding over my muscles all the way down to the middle of my legs. She nipped at my neckline as she reached out and wrapped her hand around my junk. I was big and hard against her palm as she stroked from base to tip. She moaned and groaned as I slid my fingers out and lifted her up so she could wrap her legs around my waist. "Open your eyes, honey," I breathed and she did, slowly afraid of what she would see. I slid and pushed inside her as she met my gaze, shocked at the intensity staring back at her.

That encounter was the beginning of a passionate relationship that lasted for the entire nine months her husband was away on maneuvers. A week before he was to return home, Nicole and I decided to end our affair so there would be no hint that she had been cheating on him.

We took a lot of jobs at parties on Balboa Island near Newport Beach. A number of officers and movers and shakers from the surrounding cities partied it up on Balboa Island. While I was playing on Balboa Island I set in and jammed with Stan Kenton's orchestra. His band was very popular on Balboa Island. After I got out of the Marine Corp, Stan hired me to play as fourth sax with his band on the island for a few months. It was a pleasure working with that super great band, even for a little while.

During our jam sessions off base, Ernie and I would go to Redondo Beach. There was a place there called Redondo Lighthouse. The Lighthouse was an in spot for a lot of the jazz greats who would congregate there for jam sessions on Sunday afternoons. We jammed with fellow musicians like trumpet player Maynard (Fergie) Ferguson, trombonist Trummy Young, saxophonist Stan Getz and jazz great Dizzy Gillespie, along with other good musicians. Those were fun times. The crowds ate it up and the place was always packed wall to wall.

Discharged From the United States Marine Corp (USMC)

On April 16, 1958 my enlistment in the Marine Corp came to an end. Since friend Ernie and I joined the military on the same day we were both discharged on the same day. The Corp offered me the rank of corporal and a small bonus if I would re-enlist. I wasn't interested and neither was Ernie. We decided to go back into the music business where we left off before joining the Corp. For the first couple months after our discharge, Ernie stayed with me and mom at the Lynwood house. We both renewed our musician's union cards and played a few small jobs around southern California for a few months.

Ernie got an offer to play with the famed Kid Ory Jazz Band in San Francisco, so he took the job and went on tour with the band. He later worked with Al Hirt, Pete Fountain and a number of other well known Dixieland bands around the country. Ernie was one of the best trumpet players I've ever heard in my life. He moved up the entertainment ladder fast and all those greats were clamoring to have him work with their bands.

As Ernie went his way I placed an ad in the local paper, seeking musicians that were interested in working in a band that was going on tour around the country. For the next few months I auditioned musicians, gearing up to get a band ready for road and stage work.

Brad, in the United States Marine Corp-1957.

Brad's band he formed while in the Marine Corp.-He used his old band name, the "Encores."-1957.

06

Showtime!

Looking For Musicians

When I was auditioning men for my new band, I hired a trumpet player to play in my music group that was in the Marine Corp Band with me. He was being discharged from the Corp and said he wanted to be a professional. I hired him but he turned out to be more trouble than he was worth. While I was forming my new band I allowed Bill to stay at my house in Compton until he got on his feet. He didn't want to go back to Minot, North Dakota and thought playing music with my group would allow him to stay in California. I used Bill on a few jobs but found when we were between gigs he refused to go out and find himself an apartment or any type of work to keep him going. He imposed on my friendship and took advantage of my ma's hospitality. He would lay around the house and eat mom's food, watch TV and sleep in the spare room, never cleaned up and never once offered to pay for any of the groceries, or room and board. He knew mom was working hard every day but that didn't seem to phase him. He continued to lay around the house and spend his days at the beach until it was time for meals. I got fed up with his attitude and one day I took him aside and told him it was time for him to leave, I'm not going to use you in the band anymore, maybe you'll be better off back in Minot, North Dakota.

Prior to enlisting in the Marine Corp he was working in a mortuary and I suggested that he might be better off returning to that profession, and told him he wasn't cut out to be a professional musician. He asked me to keep him on but I refused. I said, "You had your chance and blew it, Bill. I want you out of mine and moms' house by the end of the day."

"Bill," I said, "somebody has to tell you that you have no consideration for anyone but yourself. You've been mooching off my mother and I for months and its going to end right here right now." He didn't like the reality of the situation, but knew he had to leave so he packed his meager possessions, jumped into his little used red Triumph sports car and drove off. That was the last I ever saw of Bill.

The band I wanted to put together for the road had to be a show band and it turned out to be a tight knit group. The guys had to play more than one instrument so we could switch around while on stage. I had run them through some simple choreography and vocals. I expected each of them to dance and carry a vocal line when we sang and do the dance steps while we were playing and singing. The band costumes were dinner jackets and tux pants. The jacket colors were powder blue, white and plaid. During our performances we would change our outfits three times during the shows. I had them groomed down, we worked hard on stage. I used a lot of the same stuff that I used with my early 50s band. I knew if we wanted to play the Nevada circuit the music group had to do more than just stand there and play a song. To fill out the music sound I would sometimes hire a female vocalist to perform with us. The Encores was a moving, lively group. Sometimes when we were playing rock tunes I'd drop to my knees blowing my sax and it wasn't uncommon for the audience to yell yeah, go-go-go, as I slid across the floor playing.

My band turned out to be a typical 50s show group. As the band seasoned itself, we had the ability to take a song and some choreography, along with a sprinkle of comedy to create an entertainment experience. My goal was to make a group into a classic Las Vegas style entertainment presentation. I wanted to take long time fans and attract young fans. I never thought just singing or playing an instrument was enough. As my group grew and evolved over the years, the member's fine tuned their abilities to combine music, comedy skits and choreography into a neat Las Vegas act. One of our secrets that kept my group going for close to 20 years was to enjoy what you're doing and who you're doing it with.

Traveling Bands

Traveling on the road with my band has always been a great experience. It's sad to say but many of the entertainers of today miss that road experience. The norm for today's entertainers is when a promoter finds a person or a group and then asks them to sing, even if they aren't that good. The promoter puts them in the studio with the music mixer and soundboard to make a recording. In today's music the singer isn't in the studio with the band at all, instead the studio uses computer-generated music and then uses that music to build around the vocalist. The day of the singer rehearsing and singing with a live band in a recording studio is becoming obsolete. Some entertainers today never had to pay their dues by working from the bottom up and touring around the country playing all the little whistle stops along the way. The result is that the artist doesn't appreciate the business.

Prior to the 1950s, we artists traveled in cars, vans and buses, working small clubs and lounges while we honed our skills. Many of us lived out of a shabby motel room. We would press our own shirts, dinner jackets and stage uniforms in the motel room before we walked on stage for the night. There were nights we would also hang our pants and jackets in the bathroom with hot water running in the shower so the wrinkles would steam out of our outfits. All this was done because we didn't have the money to afford professional dry cleaning as we moved from small town to small town night after night.

The music business has changed greatly over the years. There are entertainers today that have the audacity to charge people to shake their hands. I've seen headliners in Las Vegas pull this stupid stunt. First the entertainer charges the audience members to see the show, I'm okay with that. But when they start charging audience member's $50 to $300 dollars or more for a meet and greet to shake their hand or sell a fan a photo, that's a little much. Christ, when I traveled with my group there was never a charge for a photo or a handshake. Most groups and entertainers from the 40s, 50s, 60s and 70s would carry photos with them to hand out to their audience and we were honored to have a fan approach us, shake our hand and tell us how much they like the show.

A lot of musicians and entertains of today get involved with drugs and booze and ignore their fans. I've always maintained that the entertainer shouldn't forget their fans and show a little humility for the fan appreciation. I for one have always looked at the music business strictly as a business and that's why I refused to get caught up in the drug/alcohol scene. It's disgusting to me to see someone with a God-given talent, who might be making outrageous salaries throw it all away by snorting it up their nose or using a needle in their arm and act like the world owes them. If the entertainers of today would have to go through the process of earning their bones like entertainers of old, I would suspect they would have an entirely different outlook on life.

Band on the Road

To get around the country with my band I asked mom to co-sign for me on a new 1959 VW Van, so I could haul all the equipment and instruments along with my band members. She agreed. The cost of the van was $2,400 and the payments were $83 a month. Mom was great, she didn't have a lot of money but she tried to make things easy for me. I used the van for the next two years, traveling around the country touring California, Nevada and the northwest and went as far East as Rapid City, South Dakota.

When I was back in town between engagements I let the band go do their thing and I continued with studio musician work. While working with the music at the studios, mom and I got the idea to open a music store in Lynwood, where we lived. We decided to name the store after my band and called it the Encore Music Shop. We stocked it with a limited number of musical instruments and had a record section and rooms where people could take music lessons. We rented out the rooms to the musicians that wanted to teach. The business never got off the ground, plus the fact that we had a major competitor from the Compton music store located a couple miles down the road. They were in the same location for years and were well established, as well as having a large inventory of musical instruments vs. our small inventory. I worked the store when I wasn't working as a studio musician in Hollywood or working at the clubs in the evenings.

I had hoped my sister Mona and her common law would have offered to help out at the store, but they refused. Mom, on the other hand, was at the store as often as she could be. She and I kept the store for about nine months and then sold it. We recovered some of our initial investment we laid out but not all of it. I went back on the road with my band. While I was on tour in Nevada mom got herself a new job. She began working as a packer at Frito-Lay Potato Chip Company in Inglewood, California. Mom always looked 20 years younger than her real age and she lied about her age to get the job. She told me she

Brad, (with Saxophone) rehearsing his band at home.-1959

Brad-1958-Photo taken at 20th Century Fox Studios. At 22, Brad had chance for movie work. The small gold oscar in Brad's lapel was a gift from Buddy Adler who was head of 20th. Century Fox at the time.

was afraid if they knew how old she really was she wouldn't have gotten the job. Her drive to work was about 25 minutes from our house. She liked the job much better than the donut shop, because she now had vacation, sick leave and partial medical. She worked swing shift from 3 to 11 p.m. She liked the shift and retained it until the day she retired from the company.

While I was on the road in the late 1950s and through the 60s, The Encores were playing both small towns and large cities throughout Washington, Oregon and Nevada and even South Dakota. There were engagements in Jackpot, Ely and Elko, Nevada and large cities like Las Vegas, where we appeared at the Hacienda, Aladdin, Dunes, Tropicana, Stardust and the Fremont Hotels. Any and all places my agent decided to book my music group, I took.

The Chance at a Movie Contract

Early 1959, Jack Kurtze, my booking agent called me and told me to meet him at the 20th Century Fox Studios commissary for lunch. He told me he had a surprise for me. When I asked him what the surprise was, he said he had lunch the week prior with his friend Buddy Adler, the head of 20th Century Fox Studios and said there was a possibility for me to break into acting. He told me that since I was 23 years old and fairly good looking, he'd pitched me to Adler. As a joke I asked him, "Jack, would you do anything to get your 10% of a client?"

"Yes, I would," he chuckled.

We were at a table having coffee when Adler came in. As he approached, Jack stood up, shook his hand and introduced me to Buddy. "This is the young man I was telling you about," he said. During lunch Jack filled Buddy in on my music background and the various places he had booked my band on tour.

Adler looked at me smiling and asked "Do you want to be in a movie?"

Flustered, I didn't know what to say. "Mr. Adler; Jack's my agent and I usually follow his lead when it comes to contracts and such."

Adler said, "I've known Jack for years and trust his judgment. You look the type that's currently popular with movie audiences. Brad, you're just out of the military, you're young, tall and good looking and that could work for you in this business. If I make the decision to start you in the acting business, I'll have you sign the standard seven-year contract with 20th Century Studios. Seven years may seem like a long contract, but actors and actresses that are signed with 20th Century Fox have to attend acting school on the studio lot where a lot of time and effort is expended on their training and grooming."

Adler had my portfolio that Jack had previously given him with a number of photos that were used in promoting my band. As we talked he was flipping through the photos and bio information and he told me if I became a studio property there wouldn't be a lot of money in it, especially during the time the studio trained their contract talent. As lunch was coming to an end, Mr. Adler asked me if I was interested in becoming a studio contract person of 20th Century Fox.

"It sure sounds good, but I have to follow Jack's direction and guidance because he's my agent."

Adler said, "Jack, I'll set up a reading for Brad with one of my talent people and if it works out, then the next step will be a screen test." With that, Adler reached into his suit pocket and pulled out a few pages of a script and pushed it across the table towards me saying, "Brad, take this home and read it. Get familiar with it. This is what you're going to read for one of my associates." Nodding to Jack he said, "Check back with Jack in a few weeks, I'll give him a time for your reading."

I looked at the script as I read the title, The House of Chatsworth. Jack said, "Mr. Adler said get yourself a girl to read the female part." As Jack and I were walking to our cars, he turned to me smiling and said, "Hey, we might get something going in the movie biz too."

At home I read over the part. The script took place in England during World War II. A military officer was leaving for the front and saying goodbye to his girl. There was even kissing in the scene. I mulled over who I was going to get to read the female part. I didn't know any actresses and I didn't want to use one of the girls at my drive-in hangout, so I came up with the idea to contact Compton Junior College and made an appointment with the instructor who taught drama and theater arts. When we met I explained that I could possibly give one of her female students a chance at a shot to get a real movie part and emphasized that she had to be able to read her lines in front of a 20th Century Fox Studio executive from memory and without flaws.

The instructor told me she thought she had the right young lady for the job, a student named Cynthia, who was in one of her advanced classes. She told me that Cynthia was only 18 years old and she would like to get her parents permission to go ahead with the project. The instructor set up a meeting in her office for Cynthia, her parents and me. I explained the situation and told the family this was only a one-shot reading and one chance to read a part for 20th Century Fox Studios. There would be no do-overs and no second chances, but if Cynthia did well then she would have the opportunity to obtain a SAG card (Screen Actors Guild). The SAG card is one of the most difficult for anyone to get. Usually somebody has to know somebody to get into the actors union. Cynthia was over the moon and chomping at the bit to have a chance to read for a real movie part. I showed her and her parents a copy of the script. The parents had no objections and thought the opportunity would be good for Cynthia and they clearly didn't want anyone else in her drama class to take the chance away from her.

I set up a rehearsal date at my house for the two of us, but when the day came around Cynthia's mother tagged along. She seemed very possessive and protective of Cynthia. I explained to the mother that Cynthia and I should be allowed to rehearse by ourselves so there would be no distractions. I told her if she was sitting in on our rehearsals, it might inhibit Cynthia from doing her best in portraying the characters in this script. The mother was concerned because there was kissing in the script. I tried to satisfy her concerns saying that if Cynthia became an actress, there might be many parts where she would have to kiss another person.

Her mother finally consented and said, "I'll leave."

As she was leaving I said, "I'll drive Cynthia home when we finish up here."

Cynthia and I had been rehearsing the part for three days and during that time she would sometimes breakdown and cry, telling me she couldn't do it and her mother would be disappointed with her. She was nervous and afraid she wouldn't be good enough. She was having trouble memorizing her lines too and she blamed it all on her mother and the pressure her mother put on her. On the fourth day after rehearsal she called that evening from a nearby coffee shop and asked to come over to talk with me. She told her mother she was going to see a friend. I told her it was okay with me and 10 minutes later she showed up at my door.

"I want to apologize for my mother's possessive attitude. She's one of those stage mothers you often hear about." As we sat on the couch drinking coffee, Cynthia said if her mother knew she was inside my house without her permission there would be hell to pay. As we talked about the script she said she enjoyed the kissing parts we had to practice and we should practice them more often. "I want you to know I appreciate the opportunity you're giving me here and I'm glad you chose me instead of another student," she said. She slid over and hugged and kissed me very hard. After her kiss I thought for a moment, Cynthia's 18-years old, I'm 23, why not go for it. No harm, no foul.

Cynthia was a cute little package sitting there dressed in her neat skirt and sweater and it didn't take me long to see where this visit was going. I began to return her kisses and quickly had her out of her clothes. We slid slowly from the couch to the floor. I chuckled, a very soft throaty sound that vibrated through her neck as I kissed the spot just under her ear. I wanted to take my time to explore this tight, smooth tempting body. I reached over her with one hand to the oak end table next to the couch and fished around in the draw until I found a condom. I looked at her, while wondering if she was one of those women who liked to slip it on the guy herself. Her nails began to sink into the flesh of my back, her tongue sliding into my mouth. I decided to do it myself and rolled away from her for a moment and then I was inside her. The following day Cynthia's mother dropped her off for rehearsal and afterward we had sex again before calling her mother to come pick her up. Cynthia and I rehearsed the script for about two weeks, at which time she thought she could perform the scene from memory in front of other people.

I called my agent, Jack, who set up a specific time for the two of us to show up for the audition at 20th Century Fox. Cynthia's mother insisted on going along to the audition with us. I agreed to have her go with us because I didn't want to upset Cynthia. I wanted her at her best during the reading. We all piled into my car and drove to 20th Century Fox Studios. A gate pass was waiting for us on arrival and we were directed to Mr. Bernstein's office. It was Mr. Adler's talent person who was going to conduct the reading. I asked Cynthia's mother to wait in a nearby conference room, telling her the reading would only take 20-25 minutes tops. Bernstein's secretary walked Cynthia and I into his office. He looked to be a man in his 30s. He was sitting behind a large walnut desk. The office looked very expensive, yet comfortable. He motioned to a couch saying have a seat. As I sat down I saw a few photos on the wall with him and some celebrities together. He got right down to business. He asked if we were ready to proceed and when I nodded and said yes, he reached into a desk drawer and pulled out a copy of the script and said, "Let's proceed."

I began my lines but when it was Cynthia's turn to respond with her lines she just looked at me and said nothing. Mr. Bernstein sat for a moment waiting and looked down at the script and read Cynthia's line to her. He said that's all right start again. I again read my lines and waited for Cynthia to respond with hers but she didn't. Instead she began to shake, tremble and cry. She looked up and said "I forgot my lines, I can't remember a single line. "

I looked at her and asked her to calm down, take a deep breath and try again. Bernstein also offered a few comforting words, but to no avail.

Cynthia was sobbing and crying, "I'm sorry, I'm sorry, I thought I could do this. Mom is going to be mad at me." She then turned to Bernstein and asked him if she could try again in two or three weeks.

Mr. Bernstein politely said, "I'll think about it," but I knew by looking at Bernstein there wasn't going to be another chance. I thought back to what my agent and Buddy Adler said during our lunch, this was a one-time only reading there would be no second chances.

Bernstein told me that he'd get back to Mr. Adler and my agent, Jack, in the event we were to return, but as I was shaking his hand and we left his office I knew the movie thing was in the crapper. In the outer office Cynthia's mother saw the tears and swollen eyes. Cynthia told her mom that she froze up and forgot her lines and cried all the way to the car. As I was dropping the two of them off at their house, Cynthia's mother turned to me and asked if I could set up another appointment. I reminded her of what I told her the first day. This chance was a one-time shot for Cynthia. However, in order to pacify her and Cynthia I told a small lie and said I would talk to my agent and if things changed then I would call her. A few weeks went by and I received a call from Cynthia's mother, inquiring if I had scheduled another appointment for a reading. I tried to be nice and let her down gently so I told her that I couldn't do that because I was taking my band back on the road. I suggested that she should have Cynthia return to Compton College to finish her theater and drama classes. I also suggested she enroll Cynthia in an acting school or get her an acting coach to help her learn the trade. I wished her and Cynthia the best and never saw them again.

Ernie and I Team Up Again

The 1960s started with a bang, Ernie my old teenage high school chum and best friend called me from Los Angeles and said he had a break from the band he was working with and wanted to get together. I told him he could stay at the house with mom and I for as long as he's in town. He wanted to team up as a duo act and tour some cities in Oregon like we used to. I had a few weeks so it was a no-brainer. We teamed up again and booked a number of supper clubs and dinner houses in and around Portland. Neither of us had been back to Portland since we joined the Marine Corp four years earlier. On the way to Oregon we hit Rick's Rancho, a popular supper club in Santa Maria, California. It was a favorite watering hole for a lot of people in that town. We signed a two-week contract there. The club gave us a two bedroom suite as part of the contract deal. Like always the first thing we did was tie up with a couple of the women that were regulars in the dinner house. They kept us satisfied for the two weeks we were in town.

We left Santa Maria and drove on into Portland and stayed at Ernie's parent's house. His parents were like my second parents. We stayed there three to four days getting caught up with his mother and father. About the second day we left the house to go downtown. When we walked to the van in front of the house, the front door was open and the side window was broken. All of our band instruments and equipment was gone. Some assholes broke into the van while we were asleep in the house and took everything. We reported the theft to the police but couldn't hang around Portland because we still had to appear at our next engagement. Ernie and I wound up going to the local Sherman Clay Music Store to buy new instruments and equipment. The cost of the new equipment would take a big chunk from the money we were to make off our tour, but it had to be done. We had to honor our commitments. We finished our Oregon tour and headed back to California, but we stopped in Portland to say goodbye to his parents and to check with the police department to see if they had made any progress on the theft of our equipment. As we suspected the cops had nothing. They told us the probability of getting the stuff back was zero and they were right, we never heard from them again.

Once back in California, Ernie stayed at my place again for a few days until he received a call to go back to work for Jazz great Al Hirt. He kissed mom goodbye and told me to stay in touch and flew off to Louisiana.

My Time with Redd Foxx and Sonny Bono

It was about this time, my agent Jack thought it would be a great idea for my band to cut a demo record. He said he could promote the record through our bookings from state to state. Dooto Records was a small independent record company and only a few miles from where I was living in Compton. I went to Dooto with photos of my band and met with the owners. Little did I know then that the two men that owned and operated the recording studio, would become household names in the entertainment business. One of the owners, named Redd Foxx, was a comedian who at the time was recording very risqué comedy records, which some people called filthy for the times. His partner, Sonny Bono, was an up and coming songwriter and singer who was trying to learn the record business and get a start as an entertainer. Over the next few weeks the three of us had a few lunches and talked about my band, the types of music we played and the places we appeared.

As months passed we became good friends. Sonny was only a year older than me so we had a lot in common when we talked music. Redd and Sonny agreed to make a demo record of my band on their label. I was excited about the prospect of releasing a recording. The following couple of months I would take my band into the studio where we would jam and kick around different songs. More often then not, Sonny would sing a song as we rehearsed. He had an interesting voice, a little high pitched with a nasal quality but he made it work for him. Redd was a nice guy who was constantly clowning around with the band and Sonny when we were jamming. He was a funny guy when he wanted to be. Every chance he had to rip off a joke he would. Redd never apologized to anyone for his risqué routines that he recorded, saying there was an audience for his stuff and as long as they bought the records he would keep recording them. He would even do some scat songs with

Redd Foxx- Comedian, record producer and
television star. Brad worked with Redd starting
in 1959.

my band as we rehearsed. His gravel voice worked well for him when he sang.

Both Redd and Sonny liked my band's music and they thought the band's name The Encores was a unique name. After a few months of my band going in and out of the studio Redd and Sonny got down to work and finally cut the demo record. They liked the final result, telling me they would release the platter, but as luck would have it they got into a business argument and fought on a regular basis. It wasn't long before the two of them started to put a lot of music projects on the back burner and they began to neglect their recording artists and everyday business activities. One of the projects that languished was my band's demo record. The grudge and hard feelings between Redd and Sonny increased more and more each day, which resulted in them splitting up and going their separate ways. My first music recording contract endeavor fell by the wayside.

After their split Redd and Sonny went on by themselves to become major stars. Redd began working the lounge circuit in Las Vegas and eventually got his own television show Sanford & Son, which became a big hit for him. Sonny got his big break when he wrote some songs for Johnny Otis on the Digs Record label in the 60s. It was Sonny that introduced me to Johnny, telling him he should let me play sax in his band. It was like old home week when Sonny and I got together again. He was his same old self. He would clown around with me like he did when we were at Dooto Records. When I was taking the solo he would say look Johnny watch this, I'll make Brad crack up and he would stand in front of me making funny faces, blow and puff out his cheeks and cross his eyes until I'd break up. The Johnny Otis Band was a smoking hot commodity that traveled all over southern California in the 60s. I recall playing at Stan's, a hot spot club in Norwalk, California and at the El Monte

Legion Stadium with Johnny's band. When we would do the song Hand Jive, the audience would go wild. It was one of Johnny's signature songs and was a winner with the audience. After the few jobs I had with the Otis Band I lost track of Sonny but I couldn't help but follow his career as he climbed to the top.

It was about 1964 when he recorded his first song with his then girlfriend, Cherilyn Sarkisian, better known as Cher. I've never personally met Cher, but he sure got a winner with her. Her stage presence, voice and dry humor that she exhibited in comedy skits really brought Sonny along. He hit his stride when he teamed up with her. The two of them toured the nightclub circuit, performing their singing and comedy act, which eventually brought them to their highly rated Sonny & Cher TV Show. The show went all out and drew a wide audience, but somewhere around 1974 the show ended. It seemed that after that Sonny's entertainment career came to a grinding halt. It lagged for about 14 years, when all of a sudden he roared back into the public's eye when he decided to enter politics and became Mayor of Palm Springs, California in 1988.

When I knew Sonny from my recording studio days it was obvious that he was a good businessman. He always had a lot on the ball and knew how to mix with people, and when he put his mind to it he usually got what he wanted. Sonny was a persistent person, so when I heard he became Mayor of Palm Springs it was no surprise to me. According to some residents of the city, Sonny did some outrageous things as Mayor, making a lot of them angry but knowing him like I did I suspect he had a method to his madness and had a calculated plan to keep his name front and center. His plan must have worked because he built momentum and ran for Congress. Six years after being elected Mayor of Palm Springs, my old friend with the nasal high-pitched voice was elected to Congress in 1994. What can

I say, who would have guessed? From a record producer and songwriter in the 50s to entertainer and television personality and then on to become Congressman, America is great!

I was watching a news program when the word came down that Sonny was dead. The news reporter stated that Congressman Sonny Bono was killed in a freak skiing accident. I was shocked. Sonny made it and made it big. He clearly made his mark on the country and music, that's for sure. The sad thing is the way he went out, I mean, a freak accident like that, what a waste. Some people knew him as an entertainer, others as a politician, but I had the pleasure to know him before he made it as either an entertainer or politician and had that rare glimpse to see him grow during both careers. Sonny was a good man and a good friend.

Redd and Sonny never did make up, the breakup was bitter. Something happened at Dooto Records that could never get them back together again. I saw Redd occasionally in Las Vegas and southern California where we would reminisce about the good ole days. Redd was the type of guy that was a gracious person and if you were his friend he would go out of his way to do for you, but if he thought you crossed him he wouldn't give you the right time of day. He and I stayed in touch through the years and remained good friends. My mom got a kick out of Redd and enjoyed watching his television show, but if I ever played one of his shady records she would shake her head in amazement. Mom told Redd one day, "I don't understand how you started out making off-color dirty records and then came to be one of the best comics on television."

He just smiled and replied, "I don't know either, if you ever find out let me know okay?"

Wayne Newton

My band was traveling in and out of Las Vegas the latter part of 1958. When 1959 rolled around we were appearing off and on in the lounges of the Fremont Hotel, working shifts other groups didn't want to work. The hotel would sometimes alter our hours and reschedule at a moment's notice. Our turn on stage was usually in the wee hours of the morning. We were lucky to have an audience other than the gamblers that lost all their money and were looking for a place to crash with a drink.

During our stint we shared the stage with a newcomer in town, a 17 year old named Wayne Newton. He and his brother Jerry had a good show worked up. It was a fast-paced routine with Wayne singing and jumping from one musical instrument to another. The show was electrifying, especially for the 1950s. He, like me, started performing in the lounges and clubs while still in his early teens. He reminded me of myself when I was his age, except when he was 17 years old he had an exceptional show package put together, which was something I never had at that age, I was just the run of the mill musician. As the years went by my music group got better and I hired musicians that could work together and do some choreography, sing and play more than one musical instrument, which allowed us to perform in Las Vegas lounges and around the country. In that time and era I would have to rate Wayne's performance as excellent. He was a good talent and the crowds loved him.

We talked occasionally in passing and he mentioned he was born in Norfolk, Virginia. He wanted to make it big in show business. From what I saw of his stage presence there was no doubt in my mind that this guy would make it as a top talent one day and he did. As the years went by we crossed paths off and on. I would be working one place and he another. His show routines were getting better and better every year. In the early days Wayne was a friendly congenial person where he would sit and talk with other musicians and he too would bounce around from lounge to lounge like the rest of us entertainers. As the years flew by he became aloof and distanced himself from the everyday musicians. Then one day he got a super big break, when singer Bobby Darin heard him sing the song 'Danke Schoen' and agreed to produce it. Wayne was around 21 when this break came his way and after that he was on his way to becoming an international star. That single was a worldwide hit. If Bobby had never produced that song, life might have been entirely different for Wayne, who knows.

Wayne made his shows bigger and better as the years tumbled by. He began to use dramatic and fantastic entrances onto the stage. There were stages filled with fog and space ships, making his shows true production numbers and the people loved it. I was proud to say I knew him when he was just starting out in the business. He grew and became a staple on the Las Vegas entertainment scene when he earned the tags Mr. Entertainment and Mr. Las Vegas. He worked up and down the Las Vegas strip for years and had the highest grossing act in Las Vegas history. At one time he owned The Frontier Hotel/Casino on the strip and did quite a number of great shows from there. Wayne also bought the Aladdin Hotel/Casino. After the purchase the media outlet, NBC, accused him of buying the place with mafia money. Wayne sued NBC, but when he was in litigation with them he filed for bankruptcy and apparently was $20 million in debt. The court sided with Wayne and he won his suit. I was glad to see him win the lawsuit.

When Wayne's career began to falter in Las Vegas he went to Branson, Missouri and performed a number of engagements there. While appearing in Branson it was alleged that he had problems with his partner, singer Tony Orlando and apparently he sued Orlando for damages. About the late 1990s, Wayne came back to Las Vegas and found work in different showrooms in town, but the crowds weren't as enthusiastic as they once were. However, in the millennium Wayne caught another break. He found a performance venue on the Las Vegas strip, the Stardust Hotel, which became a new home for his shows. Supposedly he signed a $25 million contract and had his own showroom in the hotel, but as to the crowds flocking to see him at the Stardust, I didn't think it happened. I always wondered if the $25 million contract was a publicity stunt or if in fact, he was four-walling his show. Meaning, the entertainer makes a side deal with the hotel casino, promising to fill the showroom each night and in turn gives the hotel a cut of the revenues taken in. Some four-wall artists sometimes make a simple rental agreement with a hotel and pay them a flat fee for the room.

In any event Wayne came a long way from that 17 year old performing at the Fremont Hotel. He carved out a unique place in the entertainment world for himself. I'm proud of him. He earned his acclaim and made his bones in the business. The only drawback I see with Newton is that he seemed to forget a lot of his friends and those that crossed paths with him as he was coming up on the fast track. I always thought he went out of his way to forget and ignore those little known musicians that worked the lounges alongside of him years ago. A glaring example is when I bought a house in 1993. By chance it was directly across the street from Wayne's Rancho Shenandoah residence. Most of the neighbors knew that I was an old 1950s Las Vegas lounge entertainer, but when Wayne would throw any of his parties I was never on his guest list, even though I lived directly across the street from him. I guess that's how each entertainer looks at life, some have style and class and some don't, but to each his own.

In contrast, some of my friends like famed singer Billy Eckstine or Mr. B, as I and many of his friends called him, had class. Maybe it was because Billy was born in Pittsburgh,

Pennsylvania and me a few miles away, but whatever the reason, we remained friends up until his death in 1993. Here's a guy that started in the music business in 1939, even before I was born and he never once thought of himself as a great. He once told me, Brad I just caught a couple of good lucky breaks in life and wound up singing for a living. He said the music business was good to him. He was a humble and gracious person and exuded class. We met frequently to have some soul food at Katie's Soul Food Restaurant, a little off beaten track place in Las Vegas. We both enjoyed the catfish, homemade smothered pork chops and short ribs while talking music. Mr. B never ever put up a front and never forgot his friends. If Billy saw an entertainer he worked with in the past it was like an old home week reunion.

Some of my other entertainer friends that I would have to say had class were Frank Sinatra, Dean Martin, Sammy Davis Jr,, Nat King Cole, Elvis and Frankie Laine. So yes, there are some entertainers that just oozed with class without any pretense and people know it when they see it.

Crossed Paths with Ann-Margret

The 60s rolled in and my band, The Encores, was working the Nevada circuit as usual. The Nevada circuit included Las Vegas, Reno and Lake Tahoe. We also hit the small towns of Elko, Ely, Searchlight, Jackpot and more. On one trip we were playing a gig at the Hacienda Hotel on the Las Vegas strip. Generally, after we finished for the afternoon or evening, we would go around to the other lounges and catch the other entertainer's shows. We walked into the Dunes Hotel and went to the lounge where a new group called "The Suttle Tones", were on stage which had a couple guys and a girl singer. The singer was a real doll. She was a knockout redhead and was singing her pipes out with

Ann-Margret-1965

Ann-Margret-On stage, Las Vegas-1967

the group. This good looking lady was wearing a tight gold sparkling pedal pusher outfit and when she wasn't singing she would grab a tambourine and slap it against her hip, which was par for the course in Las Vegas in the 50s.

That was the first time I ever saw Ann-Margret. She sure made an impression. There were a few 18-21 female vocalists working the Nevada circuit, but most of them working with the bands were there only for eye candy. Most of the girls dressed in skintight clothes and looked cute on stage, but as far as talent goes, they sucked. But this outstanding long legged, 19-year old redhead had talent. She could sing and dance and had a stage presence that would make any guy walking past the casino lounge stop and stare. During one of their breaks they came and sat with our group and we exchanged tour stories. Ann- Margret and the Suttle Tones were working the same tour as my group. They were appearing in the same small towns as we were. This young thing came across as a nice pleasant person. She was friendly and interested in the different music groups playing Las Vegas.

Ann-Margret was 19 and I was 24 when we met. During my engagement in town when I was on break I would wander over to the Dunes and check out her group. We would talk mostly about music but I was hoping I could get to know her a little better so that I could ask her out while she was in town. I couldn't build up enough nerve to ask her out, she was just too good looking and I was afraid of being shot down by hearing her tell me no. The result was that I didn't ask her out and both of our groups moved on when we finished our gigs. Ann-Margret was worried about her engagement at the Dunes. Apparently the group was having some kind of audition troubles and her gig fell through sooner than expected. In one of our conversations I told her that I believed she had what it takes to make it in the music business and it wouldn't be long before she could quit touring the small towns like we were doing at the time. In the back of my mind I knew it wouldn't be long before someone who had connections in the entertainment business would see her, exuberance, and her vibrant musical abilities that were just waiting to be discovered.

And, just as I thought it didn't take long for someone to see what I saw in this Swedish-American, long, tall, drink of water. Ann-Margret was working her heart out at the Dunes Hotel lounge when by chance, a representative of comedian George Burns, came into the Dunes and saw her. He told George about her and when George dropped by and caught her routine on stage he immediately gave her a 10-night gig at the Sahara Hotel on the strip. That did it. After top notch rave reviews she was literally on her way. I would think things were moving fast for her because shortly after her discovery she was signed to an RCA recording contract and shortly after that she was signed to the standard seven-year movie contract at 20th Century Fox Studios. After that the sky was the limit for her and it couldn't have happened to a nicer person. If I had to put money on it I would guess that Buddy Adler, head of 20th Century Fox in 1959 and the man who gave me a shot at a movie contract that year, was the same man who okayed Ann-Margret's contract.

After our brief encounters at the Dunes while we were playing the lounges on the strip I never met Ann-Margret again. The only other time I ever personally heard about her was when Elvis told me he would give her my best. It was around 1964 when he was filming Viva Las Vegas with her. She was his co-star in that movie and he told me he would remind her of the time she and I met in Las Vegas at the Dunes years before. Elvis only had good things to say about Ann-Margret. When I asked him how she was to work with now that she was a big star, he laughed and said, "If you only knew, Brad." He told me she was down to earth, easy going and he enjoyed working with her. Now I know what he meant when he gave me that laugh of his. Everything he told me about Ann-Margret, led me to believe they were very close at the time and I guess the point was brought home when the pair had a highly publicized off-screen romance.

Now, decades later I sometimes see Ann-Margret in a television episode and it appears to me she's still that easy going, casual person that I knew way back when. A great lady.

Some of My Favorite Spots in Las Vegas

When I took time off from touring with my band and wanted to relax, I would usually head for Las Vegas. I guess it's because I worked there so much over the years that it was a town I was comfortable in. I spent a lot of private time at the Tropicana, Hacienda, The Desert Inn, Flamingo Hotel and Caesars Palace. I liked certain things about each of the places. In the late 50s, early 60s I frequented the Desert Inn because of its class and happening entertainment groups, especially in the evenings. The Flamingo wasn't as classy as the Desert Inn, but there was a good feeling for the place after I worked there with the Mills Brothers in the early 50s. It had one of the best pools around and I did a lot of sun and pool time there. Caesar's Palace, now there's a quadruple class-A hotel/casino. I remember when it opened in the summer of 1966.

Soon after it opened I was hanging out there and it became my favorite of all the casinos on the strip. I would take all my ladies to Caesar's when I brought them into Las Vegas for a weekend or getaway vacation. Caesar's became my absolute favorite place in the 70s when they built the Cleopatra Barge. It was an attraction I loved to hang out at. The barge set in its own miniature Mediterranean Sea inside the casino and the barge swayed back and forth as if you were actually out at sea. The patrons could sit at the tables and enjoy their favorite drinks and dance. Cleo's barge always had a great musical group appearing on it. There were many nights I had the pleasure of sitting in and jamming with musicians that were playing there. Even today, decades later I'd have to say Caesar's is still my favorite place to wine and dine my ladies. When I worked there off and on with different groups I came to know many of the employees and when I stayed there I could count on some of my favorite foods.

Personally, I'm a coffee shop guy and have always taken many of my meals in coffee shops and as coffee shops go, Caesar's has one of the best. In the early days the coffee shop served chicken livers, one of my favorite dishes. On my stays there with my ladies, we would leave the room to have breakfast. I would order the chicken liver and eggs and the server would bring a tray with my eggs, potatoes and toast and beside the plate they would set out a large silver gravy boat filled with super tender chicken livers in a gravy sauce that would make anyone's taste buds scream hallelujah! After a few years the coffee shop quit serving the livers, but on occasion when I would walk in to eat and there was an old employee that I knew, I could be assured the dish would be made for me.

Another favorite of mine was the Hacienda Hotel/Casino. It was one of those places anyone could go just to relax and meet the average, run of the mill tourist that might be visiting from anywhere USA. To me the place felt homey. It wasn't for those looking for glitz or glamour. As a Las Vegas strip hotel it was one that priced their food and rooms so most anyone could afford to stay there. When I appeared at Hacienda over the years with the band, I found their audience most appreciative of the entertainers. Most were just regular everyday people, who just wanted to have a good time on a small budget. In the afternoons and early evenings I would hang out at the

Tropicana, quite often, lying around the pool for hours.

In those days, the 50s and 60s, some women were allowed to sell sex at the hotel/casinos and one of those girls was Sheila. She was a regular fixture and hooker at the Tropicana. She would sit around the pool in her skimpy bikini and concentrate on the men that had big bucks and wanted her company. Other times the bartenders working the pool area or bell hops would get the word from inside the casino that a high roller wanted someone sent to their room and they often sent Sheila. She was a very attractive brunette with a great looking body and bubbling personality. I came to know her quite well from previous visits and gigs at the casino. When she wasn't working we would have something going between us. I got to know her so well over the time I spent performing in Vegas, we hooked up whenever we could and there was never a mention of money. Our sexual relationship was based on two people wanting to be together.

I remember the first time with her. We went to her apartment following dinner. We sat and talked for a while and I told her I had to call my agent and discuss some business. She poured me another cup of coffee and told me she was going to bed. After she went to the bedroom I stayed up talking on the phone with my agent. After the conversation on the phone, I poured two more cups of coffee and walked into the bedroom. I closed the door with my foot balancing the two cups of coffee. I brought you something I whispered to sleeping Sheila. Opening her eyes she pushed down the green satin sheets enough to lift her hand. She took the cup of coffee with a devilish smile on her face and then pushed the sheet past her naked breast and down to her tummy. Slowly she poured the warm coffee between her breasts, want to toast? As our bodies became entwined her head dropped back, her body quivering with the intensity of unexpected emotion. She felt my lips on her breasts, moving up and over her neck to the top of her chin. She lifted her head, her eyes closed as she waited to feel my mouth against hers once more. After that night she and I formed some sort of bond that lasted between us for a few years.

My Band and the Mob

When anyone dares to talk or whisper the word 'mob', they should be smart enough not to mention real names. For obvious reasons and in the best interest of my own well-being and theirs I've taken the liberty to change some names in this section of the book. The 50s, 60s and even into the 70s, was an era when it was a known fact that the casinos had mob connections and the Tropicana was no different than any other casino in town. The mob attitude was, if a customer had the money they could get most anything they wanted and the casino would make it happen.

There were those people that would never admit they were a mobster, and if asked, they would deny ever being mobbed-up, but the threads of the mob weaved its way throughout Nevada like a patchwork quilt that ran from the tiniest town and casino to the largest casinos into the largest cities in the state. The tentacles of the mob wrapped around lawmakers, bankers, business executives and attorneys who gladly did the bidding of the Costa Nostra. Those tentacles ran deep and the greed for money and power handed down by these people ruled Las Vegas for years.

At one point in time two brothers owned the Tropicana Hotel and casino. It was rumored they were tied to the mob, but who really knows, right? When I had occasion to work the place with my band, I found they were good guys. Most musicians and entertainers in those days learned to keep their mouths shut, do a job, turn a blind eye to what they saw or heard and

Brad's band- He reorganized the "Encores"-1958 and took the group on the road .Brad- (playing sax, second from left).

Photo on stage in Las Vegas, Nevada-1959

what was happening around them. The mob owners generally treated the entertainers well. If we towed the line we would receive some of the freebie gratis benefits such as good food, drink, hookers and sometimes a handful of gambling chips, all courtesy of the mob guys. The mob also knew how to work the entertainers. Many entertainers had a credit line with casinos where they appeared so they could gamble and have their losses deducted from their weekly salary. Sometimes those entertainers would go overboard and exceed their gambling limits and when that happened they became in debt to the casino and if the music group or entertainer was a great draw for bringing in the crowds that's just what the casino wanted.

The mob guys would then tell the entertainers they would have to renew their contract and continue playing at the casino so the debt could be paid off. Worse yet, the entertainer would have to work free for a few weeks to pay off the gambling debt. The result was the mob got free entertainment from the musical group that would draw customers to the casino. I've seen that ploy happen to some big name entertainers over the years, they owed their souls to the casinos, sometimes for weeks and months.

One casino I worked in, the 50's and 60's was the Stardust Hotel. My band appeared in the lounge quite frequently and we worked the stage with notables like the beautiful Kim Sisters, a Korean singing group and comedian George Wallace. The Stardust Casino/Lounge was an in spot at the time but it was not immune to the mob influence that extended from the East Coast. There were those times the mafia bagmen from the East would come to the Stardust and walk out with suitcases stuffed with cash. The Stardust was a personal piggy bank for the syndicate boys back East and even with all that skim action going on there was still time for the mob to hold onto entertainers in their joints. I saw some fellow entertainers

Sonny Bono-Brad
first worked with
him in 1959 at Dooto
Records.

Top: Sonny in his
early career. Bottom:
Sonny, about 1985.

Brad and his "Encores" did a gig at the El Rey Resort, Searchlight, NV-1959. At the time the casino catered to both Movie Stars & everyday tourists.

Brad, on tour with his "Encores"- 1959.

I worked with in the casinos on the hook for week's worth of paychecks and they were nothing more than indentured servants performing on a tab, in order to pay their gambling debt and serving the will of the syndicate. What a racket!

In those early days of Las Vegas, before all the corporations owned and operated the hotels, they were owned by individuals, partners, groups and syndicates. Many were also owned by the mob and persons that had ties to the mafia. Knowing what Las Vegas was like in the 50s and 60s and seeing what it is today is a big disappointment to me. I think the city and casinos were run much better when the mob had its foothold in Las Vegas. Customers were happy and treated well. There were times I saw the average John or Jane Doe from Hicksville, USA lose all their money in the casino and it wasn't unusual for one of the casino bosses to give the loser money for a one-way bus ticket home with a warning not to come back and expect the same treatment. I've seen a cocktail waitress tell a floor boss that it was a gamblers birthday and he would write up a comp for them and their entire party to have dinner in one of the best restaurants in the casino. The same would occur if one of the bosses walked by and saw a person playing a machine for a long time. He would stop and say you've been playing that machine for quite a while so dinner is on the house and he would write a comp to the gambler.

One thing you have to say about the Vegas mob in the 50s and 60s is that they knew how to treat customers. They also kept the town in line. No one would dare even think about stealing or robbing a casino. If any employee was caught stealing from the casino they had to pay the piper and payback was a bitch. I've seen broken fingers, legs and some physical pain handed out to the thief that no one could ever imagine. Some of the idiots that were stupid enough to think they could get away with stealing from mobbed up people in Vegas were punished, shown the highway and told never to return. For anyone walking into a casino with a gun in an attempt to rob it was unheard of in those days, because the person knew they would have to pay severe consequences if they got caught. In today's corporate Las Vegas it's nothing to hear of someone using a gun and walking out of the casino with a wad of money or chips.

One bad experience I had with some shady types, some say they were mobbed up, some say who knows, I don't know if they would ever publicly admit they were connected but it was a group of people in Searchlight, Nevada. My band was scheduled to appear at the El Rey Lodge in Searchlight. When we were booked into the casino I had no idea there may be a mob connection involved; however, I soon got a fast education on who's in charge. The entire small town was run by connected individuals, or at least I thought so. These guys had a squeeze on most of the motels and had their fingers in the other small casinos around town. My band arrived in town and pulled into a small motel. I was going to check the band in before showing up at the casino, when the motel owner asked me why we were in town. I told him the band was appearing at the El Rey Lodge. "I can't give you a room here," he said.

"Why I asked?"

"If you're the band at the El Rey you'll have to stay at the El Rey Motel."

I laughed it off and left. We drove to another motel and tried to check in.

The manager of that motel gave me the same story adding, "No motel in town will rent you a room, go stay at the El Rey Motel."

We drove to the El Rey Casino and I told the band members I was going to check in with the owner to let him know we had arrived. I instructed my men to get their instruments and set them up on the bandstand while I talked to the owner of the casino. I asked a card dealer at a black jack table where I could find Angelo Contino and he pointed to a booth in the corner. Angelo was sitting there smoking a cigarette and had a drink in front of him. Sitting with him in the booth were two men that looked like Neanderthals. I introduced myself and he invited me to sit down. When I told him the trouble I had trying to check into a motel down the street, he said I was to stay at his El Rey Motel. He explained that if he was going to pay a band good money to perform in his casino then they were going to get some of that money back in rent and, "By the way," he said, "the rent you pay for your rooms will be double what other motels in town charge." He told me flat out that all entertainers that work for him have to stay at his property so that he could recoup some of the money he pays them. I saw that he was serious and didn't want to get into an argument with him before we even started our gig.

I motioned to my drummer and told him to take the band next door and check into the motel. While Angelo and I were talking, I told him not to give any gambling credit to any of my band, explaining that a couple of the men got in a little over their heads at one of the casinos we worked at.

"I won't extend any credit to the band," he told me.

We were to be at the casino for a two week gig and through the first week things were humming right along. The customers liked what they heard and when I asked Angelo how he liked my group he told me that if he didn't like my band he would have tossed us out of the casino the first night. He was strict but all the employees in the joint liked him. He was generous to his help. One of the dealers told me that he would give them big bonuses on holidays and gifts on their birthdays. I saw his generosity one evening when Angelo came up to the bandstand and told me to shut down the music and asked the band to go with him. When I asked where we were going, he said "It's a slow night so I'm taking a few employees and your band to Las Vegas for a few hours." He had two cars outside that we all piled into.

On the way out the door I asked one of the dealers why Angelo was doing this.

He said, "Enjoy it, it's something Angelo does frequently for us when things are slow at the casino."

I rode in Angelo's car. He had the two bruisers that were always around him drive us. Angelo and I sat in the backseat. On the road he was smoking and taking nips from a metal flask that he pulled from his suit jacket. Some of my band members rode in the second car. When we arrived in Las Vegas he had his drivers pull into valet at the Hacienda Hotel/Casino. As he stepped out of the car it was obvious that everyone knew him. When the valet opened the car door for him he greeted him by name saying, "Good evening, Mr. Contino." Angelo nodded and handed him a $50 bill. The cars were taken to a private section near the front entrance while Angelo and the rest of us went into the casino. Inside he gave each employee and each member of my band $50 and told them to go do some gambling, while also telling them we would meet for dinner in the restaurant in 90 minutes. They thanked him for the money and walked off.

He grabbed me by the arm saying, "Come with me," and we walked to the nearest roulette wheel. "Brad, do you like to play roulette," he said?

"Sometimes," I said, "but my favorite game is black jack."

"I like black jack too and we'll play some together later." he said. As we stood at the roulette table he reached into his pocket, pulled out five $100 bills and told the dealer, Money plays," as he threw the $500 down on #11.

Acknowledging the bet the pit boss said, "Money plays."

Angelo looked at me and said, "If the number hits, it will pay for the night out for my help and if it don't, why ask?" Laughing he said, "Brad it's only money."

The roulette wheel was spinning and slowly came to a stop and the dealer yelled, "Number 3," as he scooped up Angelo's $500.

I was standing there shaking my head and all Angelo said was, "Maybe next time."

We found a black jack table and sat down when he shoved a $50 bill in front of me and said, "Here's your $50, let's play." I was betting $1 a hand and Angelo bought $25 chips and was playing one and two chips a hand. We played for about an hour. I came out $20 ahead and Angelo walked away from the table a $200 winner. It was getting close to time for dinner but Angelo and I stopped by the lounge where we had a drink. I had my regular orange juice while we listened to the trio playing there. Angelo said, "They have nothing on your sound, Brad. They do a good job but your group is better. "

We left the lounge and met the rest of our party for dinner. There was good conversation at dinner, which included hearing about different situations that happened at his casino over the years, Angelo paid the tab and we left the casino. Valet brought the cars around and Angelo again tipped the guys $50 apiece. When we got back to the casino my band and I thanked him for the trip and turned in for the night. The rest of the week went on without a hitch.

Angelo really had a good thing in this little town of Searchlight. He promoted the El Rey Lodge all over the country and hired air conditioned Greyhound buses to bus customers from major cities, especially from California and/or Arizona. He advertised the El Rey Lodge as a place for luxurious seclusion and privacy. Everything was geared to cater to the crowds and he had the pool, comfortable rooms, gambling and the privacy. There was even a chef out of Chicago that put out some of the best food I've ever tasted. This guy was ahead of his time in promoting his casino by busing and flying people into the place. He also scheduled flights into Las Vegas and would bus the customers the 40 miles to his casino. The transportation was free to the customers, all they had to do was come to the casino and gamble for a few days. It worked. The crowds Angelo bused and flew in, resulted in many nights where it was standing room only and the dance floor was belly to butt. We even had movie stars frequent this small out of the way casino.

In our second week there, actor Rory Calhoun showed up and hung out for the rest of the week. The band my group followed in was the famed Wingy Manone Dixieland jazz band and some of his fans stayed around for another week to dance to my music. When we finished our second and final week, it was time for me to collect our wages so I could pay the band. Surprise, Angelo didn't keep his word. When he told me he wouldn't let any of my men run a gambling tab, he lied. My piano player Paul went behind my back and asked for an advance and Angelo gladly gave it to him. As I was sitting there in Angelo's booth with my coffee asking for my wages, he shook his head and said, "Brad, you have no money coming, I don't owe you a penny. On the other hand, you owe me $1,800."

Thinking he was joking I smiled and said, "Sure, do you want it all in hundreds?"

Angelo lit another cigarette and said, "It's no joke, I want my money."

With that I quickly became concerned. Angelo told me that Paul was gambling at the tables all week and lost not only his salary, but the salary for the entire band and was still in debt for another $1,800 on top of that. I was shaking and felt sick to my stomach. Hell, my band's price for an appearance was $1,800 for the week and in the 50s that was more than good money. It was money I couldn't afford to lose. It was hard for me to understand why Angelo could let this moron piano player of mine gamble away the band's paycheck and more. I reminded Angelo about our talk when I told him not to give any credit to my band members, but he just threw his hands in the air and told me they're grown men they don't need your permission to gamble.

"Angelo, we played and honored our contract to you and I want my money. My band doesn't play for free for anyone."

He started to become angry saying, "Your band has to pay the piano player's gambling debts and if you don't have the money, your band can work for an additional two weeks for free and I'll cancel the debt."

My mind began racing. I knew I needed to get out of this mess and buy some time for a plan. I told Angelo I'd talk to my piano man and get back to him the next day before we were scheduled to leave.

I met with the band in my motel room and broke the news as to the happenings and the trouble that Paul had gotten us into. A big argument broke out. The guys said they wanted their pay and Paul was responsible for his own debt. They were ready to beat on him for his stupid gambling stunt but I told them we had to figure out something and there was no time for brawling now. I knew Paul didn't have $1,800 and all of us together didn't have that amount. I told the band to pack up all the instruments in the van and we would sneak out of town at about 2:00 or 3:00 in the morning. It was a plan and the only one we had. We started to leave town under the cover of darkness and drove onto the two lane road out of town. A few hundred yards down the road we saw two big black limousines blocking the road, one in front of our van and the other behind us. When our van tried to get by one of the limos two men stepped out and told us to return to our motel. One of the men said we were not going anywhere until the piano man's debt was paid and they told me I should see Angelo when we got back to the casino.

There was no doubt these muscle-bound goons had guns and were probably ready to use them so I told Vince, my drummer, to turn around and return to the motel. The men went back to their rooms and I walked over to the casino to meet with Angelo. In the privacy of his booth, Angelo told me I shouldn't try to leave town before the debt is paid or me and my men would be hurt very badly. "A debt is a debt," he said.

I asked Angelo if there was a way to work it out somehow because the band was booked for other engagements that we had to make. He again suggested that the band work free for a few weeks for him.

"It's not going to happen," I said. I also have to honor my contracts elsewhere. He said I should borrow the money from friends or relatives to repay the debt and I rejected that idea, but told him if he would allow the band to leave town with food and gas money and wipe out the debt, that I would leave all my musical equipment with him so he could sell it to recover his money. We both knew the musical equipment and instruments was worth much more than the $1,800 he demanded. It didn't take long for Angelo to accept my offer. We shook hands to seal the deal and I gave him a note showing that I would leave all the band instruments and equipment. He then motioned one of his henchmen over to the booth and instructed him to let us leave town without any interference. He gave me a $50 bill for gas and food home.

I returned to the motel and told the men what it would cost us to leave town. They were upset and irate at Paul, but I told them to forget about any fights or arguments and try to concentrate on getting the hell out of town. We took all the musical equipment back into the casino and set it on the bandstand while Angelo was eyeing our every move. We then jumped into my van and headed out.

From Nevada to Rapid City

Once back home I had to replace all the band instruments and equipment so we could meet all our other engagements. I called my agent in Beverly Hills and told him what had happened in Searchlight, Nevada. He reminded me that I had to get to Rapid City, South Dakota for the next gig. We had to honor the two-week contract in Rapid City. I told him I had already replaced all the gear and we were set to go. We were booked into the well-known Esquire Supper Club and only had a few days to get there. Jack, my agent, was also concerned that if we didn't make the engagement on time he would have contract trouble with the Esquire Club. We then drove to Rapid City, South Dakota and arrived a day ahead of schedule.

During the first night there, Beverly, the coat and hatcheck girl took a liking to me. She said that some of the bands that appeared at the club had a bunch of old men in them and she was glad to see a band with young guys in it for a change. Vince, my drummer, hit on the cocktail waitress. He and I now had our women lined up to help us get through the two-week gig. Beverly was half Cherokee and was a long tall sweetie with long jet-black hair. One early morning we left the club after our second breakfast date and I took her home to her apartment. Inside the apartment we stopped in the living room. Only a small table lamp lit the room. We sat on the couch and began kissing. I caressed her until she melted in my arms. She wet her palm with her tongue and reached for me. On the completion we moved towards her bedroom as she dropped her clothes along the way. I continued to caress her naked smooth tight body, making her hungry for the completion that my blue eyes promised.

With both of us naked and lying there, I let my lips linger over hers for a long time. I memorized the feel and the taste of her and was secretly hoping she was doing the same. My common sense told me not to hope because we have only known each other for a few days. My tongue rimmed the outline of her mouth and sought out its moist interior. She moaned. I held the nape of her neck in my hand and with my left hand on the small of her back, I eased onto her until I was on top of her and she was cradled beneath me. My kiss grew more intense. Over and over again I devoured her mouth as if I had no love for a long time. That morning was followed by many others over the course of my two week stay in town. I quickly found out that Beverly was a very jealous woman. When I had occasion to talk with some of the women that came into the club, Beverly would shake her head no at me as she stood at her hatcheck station.

After the club closed one night, she let me know in no uncertain terms that she didn't like me talking to other women. I told her that both of us knew that our hookup was only a sexual thing and she knew I would only be in Rapid City for two weeks. That didn't make a difference to her. "I don't care if its two days or two weeks, you're my man as long as you're in town."

"You're enough woman for me babe," I said.

"I better be enough for you, because if I see you screwing around on me, I'll do what a lot of Indian women do."

"What's that?"

She reached down, touched my crotch and told me she would take a knife to it. With that announcement I was sure glad we only had a couple days left for the gig and I could get out of town and away from this crazy. Once I was away from

Rapid City and on my way back home to good old California I was thinking about the next guy that tangles up with this Cherokee looker. I was never so glad to get out of town and away from a lady.

Once the band finished up its tour and returned home to California I fired Paul's ass as soon as we got back home. I also told him I would put the word out to all the musicians in the area about how he treated his fellow band members.

Howard Hughes – the Downfall of Las Vegas

I believe Vegas really began to deteriorate and fall apart when billionaire Howard Hughes came to town in 1966. He snuck into town on Thanksgiving Day by railroad car and immediately moved into the Desert Inn Hotel and Casino. He didn't want to leave the hotel but the hotel owners wanted him out. A fight between Hughes and the owners began and the confrontation resulted in Hughes buying the place in 1967 and taking up residence in the penthouse. The hotel's 8th floor became ground zero and command center of Hughes' future dealings in Vegas.

It was no secret that Hughes' would often covertly leave his hotel in disguise and take private jaunts here, there and everywhere, on his own. As one story goes, according to a small restaurant owner, shortly after Hughes' settled in Las Vegas he was hitchhiking by himself at night in the desert around Joshua Tree, California. His hitchhiking persona was to look like a scruffy bum. He wore a scraggly beard and his clothes and appearance was unkempt. It's up for grabs whether or not he purposely dressed like that to go incognito or if in fact, it was some sort of mental condition affecting his decision making.

Near the highway was a small, popular steakhouse that Hughes' wandered into. He told the female manager that he

Brad's "Encores" appearing at the exclusive
Esquire Dinner Club:Rapid City. South Dakota-1959

Brad and his "ENCORES" appearing at the noted Esquire Club in Rapid City, South Dakota-1959.

was on his way to Las Vegas and wanted a hamburger asking, "Do you take credit cards?"

"Yes, she replied." With that, he ordered a hamburger and a drink. After this grimy looking bum finished up his meal he presented the lady with his credit card. She looked at the name on the card, which read, 'Howard Hughes'

"Are you Howard Hughes?" she asked.

"Yes, I am," he replied.

She ran the card and it went through without any problems. He left the steakhouse and continued hitchhiking toward Las Vegas. The manager kept the credit card receipt and later had the signature checked for authenticity and reported it was said to be an authentic Howard Hughes' signature. You have to admit Hughes was a real fruit cake in his later years.

Between a short time span of only two years 1966 to 1968, Hughes bought up several other hotels/casinos in Las Vegas. He also bought up a number of television stations including KLAS TV. All of Hughes' business holdings in Las Vegas were handled by a specific group of close contacts, which became known as the Mormon Mafia, because the business committee had so many Mormons affiliated with it. Howard Hughes wielded enormous clout because of the businesses he owned and operated in Las Vegas. He had substantial economic and political influence that stretched throughout the entire state. Hughes wanted to change the face of Las Vegas and make it more glitzy and en vogue than it was. It's reported that he sent a memo to one of his confidantes that said, 'I like to think of Las Vegas in terms of the well-dressed man in a dinner jacket and a beautiful jeweled and furred female getting out of an expensive car.'

My Las Vegas was from 1953 and up, until the time this looney-tunes billionaire bought up the city's businesses, gaming properties and politicians. In my opinion, once Hughes converted Las Vegas into the corporation structure the place went to hell in a hand basket. It's ironic, Hughes said he wanted to see men in dinner jackets and women in furs and jewels, had he looked around when he came to town in 1966 he would have seen just that. In the 1950s and through the 60s that's how people did dress when they came to Las Vegas. The women decked themselves out in their finest and the men wore dinner jackets and expensive suits on their visits to Vegas to see a show or catch a lounge act. It was common practice to wear evening clothes, suits with ties and a lot of expensive jewelry to the shows, but alas, after Hughes did his number in Las Vegas, look what we have today.

People show up to shows in the major hotels and casinos wearing cargo shorts and flip flops. I recently took one of my ladies, visiting from back east to a show at a major hotel on the strip. To my surprise, in an audience of about 200 people, I was the only man in the audience wearing a suit and tie, with a date wearing evening clothes and nice jewelry, no joke! The rest of the men in the audience were wearing attire such as shorts, t-shirts, baseball caps, jeans and open work shirts. I know this because prior to the main act performing, the opening act was a magician and he needed a person out of the audience who was wearing a suit and tie to use in his act on stage. Prior to performing the magician walked the aisles of the casino theater looking for a man who was wearing a suit so he could use the person in the act. He finally came to my booth and explained the situation, and literally begged me to come on stage so he could perform his magic trick.

The old Las Vegas had well-known entertainers appearing as headliners in the showrooms and there were tons of lounge acts appearing in the hotels. Now the modern day corporation titans build billion dollar hotel/casinos and fill their showrooms with circus acts and magicians, but to me that's not Las Vegas, it's an amusement park.

Lou Rawls- Brad played sax and bass for Lou's shows in Southern California and at Caesar's Palace in Las Vegas, NV. Brad's "Encores" also backed Lou on numerous engagements over the years.

07

The 60's Were Good Years

I was discharged from the Marine Corps in 1958. My home base for my band was southern California and I was living in the City of Lynwood. Mom and I sold the Lynwood house and bought another one in Compton. It had an extra screened-in room attached so that I could rehearse with my band. From the late 1950's and into the early 60's in addition to doing my studio music, my band would often open for name acts at the El Monte Legion Stadium. On the bill at the Legion Stadium were major acts like Ike and Tina Turner. Wow! That was a high energy group. Tina would dance and sing until she looked like she was going to drop. She was really something to see and listen to with her long luscious, legs and short miniskirts glistening under the stage lights. She was magical on stage. Tina made the group.

I also played sax and clarinet with the rocking Johnny Otis Group at the Stadium. His band appeared there quite often. The El Monte Legion Stadium was a place for fans to go to enjoy top flight rock and roll groups. Headliners like Ike and Tina Turner drew standing room only crowds. Yes, these late 50s and 60s had me playing local spots like the El Monte Legion Stadium and doing studio work and appearing at local dinner houses and clubs. To keep my band in tip-top shape, I held rehearsals at my house and the neighbors and their kids would sit on the brick wall fence around my house and listen to my band. I didn't mind. I thought it was good morale for the band.

When I was off the road and not traveling with the band, I found a little place to hang out. It was Richie's Drive-In on

Soul legend, Tina Turner: Brad worked with the Ike & Tina Tuner show at the El Monte Legion Stadium, El Monte, California during the 1960's.

Ike & Tina Turner..
Brad worked the
same stage with
the Ike-Tina Turner
Revue at El Monte
Legion Stadium in
the 60's. Tina is an
outstanding talent.

Rosecrans Avenue in Compton. The place drew a large local crowd who liked to show off their vintage autos and the carhops were exceptional in their looks department. Their uniforms were little red miniskirts, white blouses and little white sneakers. Me, I could usually be found inside at the counter or sitting in a booth by the jukebox. The place was like a second office away from home for me. The employees and regular customers knew that I was a professional musician and some of the carhops would come to some of the places I worked, even some of those under 21 would sneak in. A few of the carhops were married but they still showed up without their husbands just to get a night out away from their home life routine.

Over the years, the help at the place got to know me as a regular. I'd have breakfast there most every day and many of my friends in and out of the music business could find me there. My mother and sister could always call the place and find me there if they couldn't locate me anywhere else. Anyone could leave a message for me at Richie's and know that it would get to me because there usually wasn't a day that went by that I wasn't hanging out there having a cup of coffee and a smoke. It was my hangout. Sometimes I would leave my car at the Drive-In and pile into a friend's car and a bunch of us would hang out at the beach all day. After the beach trip, we'd return to Richie's and I'd pick up my car and go home and get ready for my gig that night. I was a beach hound. I loved California beaches.

The carhops at the Drive-In liked to hang out with some of us regulars. When we got together we would bowl at Compton Bowl, go to the drive-in movie and then drag the Boulevard. Cathy was a carhop I took out quite a bit. For me, the hook-up was just a sex thing but for Cathy I found out it was a little more than that. She began to be very possessive. One evening a group of us from the Drive-In was at a party being held at one of the girl's apartments. We were all dancing and having a fun time

Brad and his group the "Encores" listed in Talent
Directory for World-wide engagements, Part 2.,

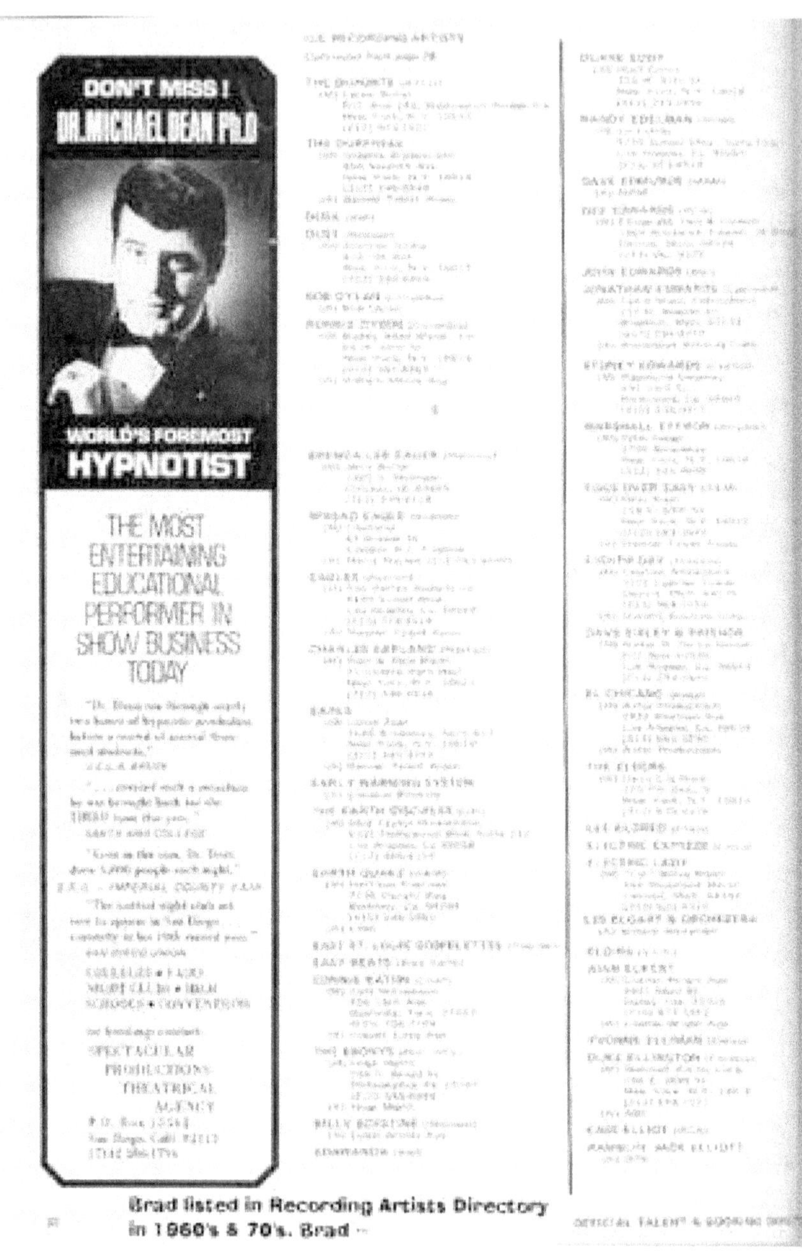

Brad's and his group the "Encores" listed in the Talent Directory.

when she accused me of showing more attention to another girl at the party. She became very loud and shouted, "You're dating other women. You have no feeling for me anymore." She became hysterical and began crying. She locked herself in the bathroom and said she was going to kill herself.

Some of us tried to talk her out of the bathroom but it was useless. Cathy screamed through the door that she had slit her wrist with a razor blade and wanted to die. Some of us guys broke down the door to get to her. All the guests became upset and some began to panic. During the commotion, one of the girls called the police and asked for an ambulance. The police arrived, had Cathy transported to the hospital and they interviewed all of us in the apartment. I had to give a statement to the cops about what was said between Cathy and me and what caused her to try to commit suicide.

The cops left the apartment and told us what hospital Cathy was taken to. It was big news around Richie's and I was razzed about having a woman trying to kill herself over me. It wasn't funny to me and I told the loud mouths to let up and stop the gossip. Three days later Cathy was released from the hospital. She returned to work and when I showed up for breakfast she took me aside and apologized. She told me she was just jealous and it wouldn't happen again and asked for my forgiveness. The whole situation was embarrassing to me and I felt bad that she did something so dumb like attempting suicide. I told her that our hanging out together was over and there was no relationship. I let Cathy know I couldn't be involved with any woman that flew into a rage and considered killing herself. She said if we couldn't get back together, she couldn't take coming to the restaurant where we would see each other every day.

"Cathy," I said, "I don't know what to tell you." A couple of weeks later she quit the restaurant and moved on. I never saw her again.

Glen Campbell-Singer, stage performer and television personality. Brad and he both worked as studio musicians in Los Angeles and appeared on stage together in Southern California. They jammed together in the 1960's quite often.

Karate Defense

Some of my friends that would hang out around with me at Richie's Drive-In asked me to teach them some karate. I told three or four of them that I would only teach them a few moves because I really didn't have the time to train them every day as a school would. They agreed to that arrangement, so I tried to set aside Saturday and Sundays at noon. That time would allow me to get home from the nightclub and catch some sleep before I started my day. I usually slept until 10:30 or 11:00 o'clock a.m. I agreed to tutor my common law brother-in-law, my friend Bill and Red. They would show up at my house and we'd go into the back yard where I would work them out. The first couple of weekends went well. They showed up but they soon gave up the workouts because they found out it was more difficult than they expected. They didn't want to put the work in to learn the skill. That was sad, because I wasn't hard on them at all. I treated them with kid gloves. These guys couldn't take half of some of the things I went through learning karate. A person has to work at it and it was evident that these Pillsbury dough boy softies didn't want to put in the time. Hell, when I was learning martial arts in the Marine Corp I carried it over into my civilian life and when I was between gigs back from a music tour I would schedule practice time at any studio close by. I was lucky enough to secure a private personal instructor in my home base, Compton. I met the guy by chance. In the 60s it was popular to go to after hour joints. In Compton a popular spot was the Royal Room. During the early evenings it was a local watering hole but come closing time at 2:00 a.m., the place would close, all the booze was put away and then the place would reopen at 2:30 a.m., as an after- hours hang out. The club sold soft drinks, coffee and sandwiches. Musicians from around the Southern Cal towns like Long Beach, Lakewood, and Downey would jam and play for the customers until 7:00 a.m.

When I would finish one of my gigs I would show up at the Royal Room and jam with the other musicians. The place was always packed and because of the crowds the club had an in-house bouncer and bodyguard. The guys name was Sammy, he was a small stature mixed Asian person that stood only about 5′ 2″. He was thin and gaunt, always wearing shorts and a Hawaiian shirt and flip flops. His dark, jet black hair ran loose all the way down his back to his butt and his eyes had a piercing, determined gaze.

To look at Sammy one would think he could be blown over with a big gust of wind. He looked like a derelict, a bum. But believe me, looks are deceiving. Anytime there was trouble in the place the owner would call on Sammy to resolve the matter.

He just had to walk over to the person that was causing the disturbance and ask them to leave. Most did leave, but for those that didn't, he would lay them out cold with one swift blow. He looked crazy when he went into action. The man didn't care if there was one person or ten he had to deal with, he would take them all on and come out on top every time.

The regulars at the club knew about Sammy and would give him a wide berth. They didn't mess with him. Whenever this guy got into a scrape it was as though he couldn't feel pain. Wham, bam and it was over. On the surface he was an easy going friendly, person. It was when he went into his fighting mode that he seemed to lose all perspective. Over the years of jamming at this night spot I came to find out that Sammy was a friend of the club owner who allowed him to teach a few people karate in a private conference room at the rear of the club. I came to know him quite well. He was a music fan and we became good friends. As we became closer friends, Sammy knew that I had studied karate for years and it was no surprise to him when I asked him to teach me his style. Even though he held closed classes with only a few students at a time, he agreed

Brad, at home, off the road, teaching friends karate.-1963

to take me under his wing in private and group sessions.

I studied with this easy going wild man all through the 1960s and into the early 70s. Sammy was a tough task master. In group sessions he would have four or five of us attack him and he made short work of us. Outside of martial arts expert Chuck Norris, he was one of the fastest martial artists I had ever encountered. He looked as though he was a Tasmanian devil. Whenever he left the mat jumping into the air, he would twirl and twist and his long hair would trail in the breeze as he landed his foot or fist on his opponent. His Asian features, his long hair and his loud kee-i, a loud scream, made him a fearsome sight for anyone. Sammy could take a large man down with one hand, even with one well-placed finger. He really knew his karate.

In our private sessions he pushed me to the limit. To build up my karate fist and knuckles he would have me stand in front of a bucket filled with rice kernels, other times it would be sand, and he would have me thrust my open hand and closed fist into those buckets every day for at least one-half hour. Other times he would take me out in back of the club and do push-ups on the cement driveway using my knuckles and a closed fist. Sammy demanded obedience and discipline. Eventually my first and second knuckles on my fists had a large callous built on each knuckle. His determined training reminded me a lot of the Marine Corp. After a few weeks it was nothing for me to do push-ups on the cement or the street using my knuckles. I guess there was a method to his madness. But it did the job. Sammy taught me a lot.

I asked my friends why they wanted me to teach them karate if they didn't want to put in the time to learn it. They told me they wanted to learn karate because they saw me use it a few weeks earlier in a local bar. I recall the incident they referred to. It was one afternoon, Bill and Red and their dates came to a country and western club I was working at. They asked me to join them at a local bar nearby when I got off later in the evening. I left the country and western club with my date and we joined the party. When we were there, three bullies sitting at the bar began to harass us and tried to pick up on our dates. These idiots were causing problems in the bar for all of the customers. They were foul-mouthed and vulgar and every other word was the "F" word. They were making rude remarks to our dates and to the other women in the bar. It was apparent these obnoxious mutts were three sheets to the wind and well on their way to being stupid drunk. They were itching for a fight. I could see it.

Each time my date would get up from the booth and walk to the jukebox, these clowns would try to grab her ass. About the third time this happened, I got up from the booth, walked over to them and asked them to either stop their stupid antics or leave the joint. I guess that's what they were waiting for. My remarks brought a bunch of boo's and hisses from all three and one of them puckered up his lips and made kissing sounds toward my date. His friend started swinging as he rose from his bar stool. Before he made it to his feet, I hit him with a karate punch to the throat and he went down, dropping to his knees and he fell to the floor like a limp sack of potatoes. One of the other guys started to move and I laid into him before he could make it all the way up off of his stool. The third guy I hit so hard, I found out later that I busted his arm and shoulder. All three guys wound up lying on the floor hurting. I turned to my girl and said, "Let's go." Bill and Red grabbed their dates and we left the bar. On the way out I apologized to the bartender. All he said was, "They deserved what they got."

The next morning I drove to Richie's to have my breakfast. Red and Bill were sitting at the counter. When I sat down in my booth, they slid in beside me with Red asking me if I saw the morning paper. When I said no, he pushed the paper in front of me pointing to an article that basically read the bartender of the tavern reported to police at the scene that a man in a party defended himself and took down three unruly men that were harassing his date and other customers. The paper indicated that one of the man's arms and shoulder were broken and all three men were taken to the hospital before being arrested. When asked, the bartender said he didn't have any idea who the man was that took these guys out. I have to say that was the one and only time in my entire life that I had to defend myself and my friends to such an extent, but I was sure glad I had the training and ability to do so or we would have been in deep, deep doo-doo.

The Rustic Room

A local place I worked was called the Rustic Room in North Long Beach. I could always count on that place to use my music. I played there off and on for seven years when I wasn't on the road. The supper club was a local spot for Long Beach and its neighboring cities. It was a cute place. It had red leather booths, a large dining area and a large bar. It also had a pitted fireplace in front of the bar and the dining area. It was an attractive spot to be seen at. It served good food and large drinks. It was well known for its steaks and prime rib. Our music usually had the dance floor packed and there was always a waiting line for a seat at the bar.

One night I asked Helen, one of the carhops who was a luscious blonde from Richie's Drive-In, to come into the club. She was married but I knew she saw other guys on the side. We were to go to breakfast when I got off. She came into the place early and while she was sitting at the bar waiting for the night to end, she danced with customers when they asked her. While she danced, she would wave and flirt with me from the dance floor. Between the dancing and the drinks, she got sloshed. When the club called last call and the bartender locked the doors, she put some money in the jukebox and started to dance by herself on the dance floor. I was packing up some music equipment when I heard the bartender and a couple of his friends that were still in the place start yelling and clapping. I heard them say, "Take it off, take it all off."

When I looked up, there was Helen in the middle of the dance floor dancing to the music all by herself. She was stripped down to her panties and she was unhooking her bra and motioning to me to come dance with her. I took off my dinner jacket and ran onto the dance floor and covered her up and sat her down in a booth. I told the bartender to pull the plug on the jukebox. All she said to me was, "I want to make you happy." I knew she was feeling good, she was high but not fall-down drunk. I grabbed her clothes up in one hand and her in the other hand and left the club. Holding onto her to keep her steady, I took her to my car and told her to leave her car in the parking lot and we would get it tomorrow. As soon as she got into my car, she started to kiss me. Since she was dressed in only her panties and my jacket, we began to make out.

I brushed the jacket from her shoulders, my hand slid to her waist, to the belly, to the top of her thigh. With her panties and bra off and my hand still on her thigh, my kisses followed my hand and worked their way down until my head was between her legs and then I looked at her as if asking for permission with my eyes. It seemed to excite her, just the thought of kissing her there. My head was in shadow. My arms scooped under her legs. My breath blew a lightly warm feeling on her thighs. I very slowly began. I felt that if she could have screamed at the top of her lungs, she would have. After that night, Helen and I would meet when her husband was working nights and

I could get her home before he got in from work. We continued our relationship for close to a year until the two of us decided it was time to call it quits.

On one of my return engagements to the Rustic Room, I got involved with the bartender's girlfriend. Sheri would come in each night and sit at the bar, have some drinks and wait until Andy the bartender would close up the place. There were some nights she would get pissed off at Andy because he would flirt with other women sitting at the bar. When I was on intermission, she would corner me and cry on my shoulder about the situation. After a few weeks she began telling me she should give him some of his own medicine and see other men. Hey, I was for that. Sheri was cute. She had a spectacular figure and was a nice trim thing. This lady always kept herself looking sharp. She worked at the Estee Lauder cosmetic counter at May Company in the Lakewood store, which was only a few blocks from the club. Better yet her apartment was only a couple blocks from May Company. On my way to the club one evening, I stopped at May Company and went in to see Sheri. I told her to take a coffee break and we sat down for a conversation. I talked her into going out with me and she did.

That night after the club closed, Sheri told Andy she had things to do and didn't want to see him because she was still angry over an earlier argument they had. She left the club alone and after I packed my instruments up, I headed for her apartment. It was the Christmas holidays and I love Christmas. That's my favorite holiday. As I was driving to Sheri's apartment, I was hoping I could score and have her as one of my early Christmas presents. We were lying on the floor, me with coffee and her sipping wine. Beside us was a small Christmas tree she had up. The lights were shimmering and we were listening to Johnny Mathis Christmas albums. I got her stripped down to her panties and I arranged myself up on one arm and kissed her breast for a long time as she ran her hand up my back and slowly rubbed my buttocks while the Christmas lights cast a faint shimmering shadow across the room. After that night together we began a three- or four-month relationship behind Andy's back. He had no idea what he was missing. He shouldn't have let Sheri sit on the sidelines while he tried to pick up other women.

Once Sheri and I split, I began an affair with a cocktail waitress at the club. Dee was a tall blonde. She wore tight black slacks and a white silk blouse as a club uniform that she sure looked good in. We got together and she started bringing presents into the club for me. First it was a nice sweater, then a watch here and a ring or bracelet there. I wasn't about to say no. They were super expensive gifts. It was obvious she wanted to get together and we did. Dee was someone I could take home to her place most any night and have a great time with and she didn't screw around on me. As long as we were together, it was just the two of us.

A lot of celebrities and musicians and sports figures are always bragging about exactly how many women they bedded down. I recall one sports figure saying he'd slept with hundreds of women. Me, I'll never put a figure on how many women I've been with. Let's just say there were many, many women over the years. Most of them were for the sex only. They knew it and I knew it. Out of all the women I have had, there were only two or three that I was actually serious about and considered marrying. With those ladies, I had a rule. The rule was, don't screw around on your lady. I had the idea that if you don't screw around on her, she won't screw around on you and I always held to my rule with those ladies that I had a serious relationship with.

Mr. Tequila

As one of my engagements was coming to a close at the Rustic Room, I told the owner I couldn't renew a new contract because I was scheduled to take my band into a club in Anaheim, California, for a few weeks. I told him I would find a good replacement music group so a few days before I was to finish up I called my friend, Chuck Rio, who I knew was between engagements. We both worked Long Beach and Southern California for years and we would recommend each other for jobs. Chuck had the music group, The Champs, who recorded the famous song 'Tequila'. I asked him if he would be interested in bringing a trio into the Rustic Room for a few weeks. He said he would like that so I told him to meet me at the dinner house on my closing night. When he showed up with his men, my group took an intermission and I asked Chuck to take over on the bandstand. The Champs rocked the house. While he was on stage playing I walked over to the owner and asked him, "What do you think of this band? Will Chuck and the Champs do it for you?"

The owner saw the reaction of the diners, who were applauding, and said, "He'll do."

Chuck and I also held membership in the Long Beach musician union local #353, and we had worked a lot of jobs together. Chuck, whose real name was, Danny Flores, grew up in the Long Beach area and we would go the same jam sessions. Chuck was seven years older than me. He taught me a lot about the music business over the years. I would sometimes call him, 'Mr. T' or 'Mr. Tequila', he got a kick out of it. He played sax, guitar and a few other instruments. It was his "dirty growl" sax part that made the song, 'Tequila', the big hit it was. His song 'Tequila' went number one on the Billboard charts and won a Grammy in 1959. Danny began using the stage name, Chuck Rio about the same time he recorded 'Tequila' because at the time he was under contract to another record label.

Danny started playing professionally three years before I did. He was only fourteen years old when he started work with a trio who played Mexican music. Once he recorded 'Tequila', he became known as "The Godfather of Latin Rock." That song became a classic and was used in a number of commercials and TV shows. It even became popular with an entire new generation after it was used in the 1985 movie "Pee Wee's Big Adventure." Danny died on August 24, 2006. The doctors said the death was caused due to complications from pneumonia.

Cheryl Tiegs

While appearing at the Rustic Room and doing music work at Desilu Studios, I put a trio together and played for different modeling agencies doing their fashion shows in and around Hollywood and Los Angeles. They were fun jobs and paid well, and my trio was working with some great looking ladies. One of my favorite models was Cheryl Tiegs. My group frequently had occasion to work shows where she appeared. Cheryl is a gorgeous, gorgeous lady. She knew how to work the shows and in the 60's was one of the top models in the world. Our meeting during a break consisted of every day chit-chat. Cheryl came across as a super nice person and when she spoke to you, it was as if she knew you for years. Everyone that had a chance to work with her really liked her.

Phyllis Diller

The 60s were a super busy time for my band. I was doing a lot of movie/TV studio music, playing hotels, clubs and private parties. During this time in my life I was meeting interesting stars and entertainers. On one of my engagements I met comedienne, Phyllis Diller, for the first time. It was when we

Brad played a number of fashion shows with Cheryl in Southern California area during the 1960's

Phyllis Diller-Fantastic comedianne , Brad's band
played a few engagements in the 1960's with Phyllis
on the show. A gracious lady. Easy to work with.

both were working a Bob Hope military benefit in Hollywood, where we were entertaining the troops. I saw Phyllis on stage in 1955 at the famous "Purple Onion" in San Francisco. I was on my way to perform in Hawaii and I dropped into the club while in Frisco. I told her I caught her performance in San Francisco years before doing her "fang" comedy routine, which was based on her life as a house wife and stories about her very dumb husband, who she called "Fang." Phyllis told me that was one of her first club dates after being asked to go into show business. One thing many people don't know about Diller is that she is a very accomplished concert pianist and played with more than one hundred symphony orchestras. She's a classy lady. That Bob Hope benefit was the one and only time I had occasion to work the same stage with this funny lady. Years later, in 2002, I went to see Phyllis last stand up performance at the Suncoast Hotel and Casino in Las Vegas. We talked back stage for a short while and Phyllis told me it was time for her to stop the touring and quit while she was ahead.

During this swan song performance, at 84-years old, she came on stage and told the audience she was calling it quits as a stand-up comic because she didn't want to totter onto the stage, forgetting her lines, or be embarrassed on stage, or embarrass her audience, or worse yet, have the audience feel sorry for her. Talk about class, this raucous, delightful lady has tons of it. The last contact I had with Phyllis she was living a comfortable life in her mid-90's at her Brentwood home, in the Los Angeles area, writing her memoirs - a funny lady.

Frank Gorshin, Impressionist

Many of my private gigs during this era took me to the Hollywood Hills where many movie stars and celebrities frequently threw big bashes. At one of these private parties I

Brad's friend, Frank Gorshin,-comedian, impressionist and actor. Bottom photo is Frank in his Bat Man movie costume.

became friends with impressionist Frank Gorshin. He liked the music my band put out and asked me if he could hire my group for some of his parties in the future. During our initial meeting he told me he was from Pittsburg, Pennsylvania, which gave us common ground from the get-go, since I was born in a little coal town outside Pittsburg. On top of that, he was only three years older than me and we could relate to the same things as we grew up. During a number of parties that I had occasion to work where Frank was present, he always provided laughs. Frank was an excellent impressionist. He would always perform at the parties and his impression of Kirk Douglas was outstanding. He could contort and twist his face and lips like they were made of rubber.

Frank and I remained friends for years and did the occasional Christmas card thing. Frank's love was his wife, Christina. He would always have something nice to say about her. He was one of those entertainers that never got into trouble, or ran with an in-crowd. He was a nice man and a family orientated person. During some of our conversations he told me that he was embarrassed about his early "B" movie films like, "Hot Rod Girls", but I think he overcame those doubts when he became famous for playing the Batman character, "The Riddler."

Edgewater Inn

The Richie carhops were good action for me. It was 1962 and I was 26-years old. I was appearing at the Edgewater Inn Hotel in Belmont Shores at the Port of Long Beach. It was a plush upscale hotel geared for all the affluent people that frequented the marina. Out of all the bands and musicians the hotel could have hired to inaugurate the place, they hired my band. I signed on for a month's engagement. When the carhops at Richie's found out I was working at the Edgewater Inn Hotel,

Brad- (in rear) Appearing at the Edgewater Inn, on opening day, Long Beach, California marina-1962.

Brad and group appear at the famed Edgewater Inn, LongBeach. California 1962-Busboy pulls plug on dancers.

they wanted me to get them in. One of the carhops, Patti, was a knock out redhead. She was also a year into a recent marriage that wasn't going too well according to her. She was only 18 but I told her even though I couldn't get her into the hotel ballroom while customers were there, I would meet her at the coffee shop after the band finished up for the night and I would buy her breakfast.

I guess she planned ahead and put her nightclub clothes in her car before she went to work. When she finished her shift, she changed out of her carhop uniform into the let's get down outfit and drove to the hotel. I really didn't expect her to show up but as the band members and I were sitting in the coffee shop having coffee and a cigarette, in walks this breathtaking lady all dolled up. Her hair was done up just right and she was wearing a dress that showed off every curve in her tight body. I don't think there was a guy in the place that didn't stop eating and look at her as she slowly walked toward our booth, all of them wanting a piece of her. The guys in my band just looked at me and one said, "You know how to pick them." Another just let out a "Whew."

When she got over to our booth, I introduced her to the rest of the band and they immediately excused themselves, telling her they had to get home. We sat in the coffee shop for a couple of hours talking about her new marriage, what she wanted to do with her life, her plans and a lot of other everyday chit chat. Before we left the Edgewater Inn, I took her on a tour of the hotel. I showed her the ballroom where my band played and we strolled the marina. We left the hotel in the wee hours of the morning. During our stroll along the marina and after a few small kisses, Patti told me her husband was out of town for a few days visiting relatives. I suggested I follow her home. She nodded yes and we walked to our cars. Patti invited me in for coffee. Inside we sat there and I began to kiss her and thank her for showing up. She reciprocated returning the kisses. I brushed her hair back and my tongue brushed her soft smooth ear. I blew a very soft small light breath over the moist spot and she shivered gently and let out a small moan. She couldn't gather enough strength to resist when my closeness alone encompassed her entire being. We moved into her bedroom and enjoyed an hour or two of bliss.

As I was leaving her apartment, she promised she would see me again. That again came quite soon, because a few weeks later a bunch of us from Richie's Drive-In decided to drive to Ensenada, Mexico for a couple of days. Patti's husband didn't want to go and everyone called him a party pooper until he finally gave in, so off we went. We drove down to Ensenada and on the way we stopped in Tijuana for some shopping. Patti's husband was a wet blanket all the way and constantly complained that we should turn around and go back home. Patti was frustrated and angry. Even after we arrived at Ensenada and had dinner on the beach near the motel, Patti's husband Chuck was angry. It was clear he was very possessive and jealous. That was one reason Patti thought her marriage sucked.

After dinner we all went to the adjoining bar and had a few drinks. Chuck kept telling Patti that they should go to their room. He didn't want to stay up and party with the crowd. Patti was enjoying herself. She was dancing to the music from the jukebox and was flirting with the men in the bar. Her actions made Chuck even more angry and he finally grabbed her by the arm and bid the rest of us goodnight and marched out of the bar. Later that evening, I was sitting outside on the beach by a fire pit drinking a cup of coffee watching the fire dance and crackle. From behind someone covered my eyes and said, "Guess who?" It was Patti. She said her husband fell asleep and she wanted to be with me. I grabbed her hand and walked her down the beach away from the motel. We found a spot on the beach behind a sand dune and it was like we picked up where we left off in her apartment about a week earlier. Sex, the beach and the ocean made me a happy camper.

She quietly tiptoed back into her motel room as the sun was coming up. We all stayed at Ensenada for another two days riding horses, parasailing and swimming on the beach. Chuck was a drag all the way. I asked Patti if Chuck had any hint that she was cheating on him. He may have suspicions, she said. He was so jealous but he didn't want to confront me because all the people at the Drive-In knew that I practiced karate and was teaching some friends from the Drive-In how to use it. After that trip to Ensenada with Patti, that was my last encounter with her. I moved on and I told her to go back to her husband.

My Disc Jockey Days

While I was appearing at the Rustic Room in the early 60s, an owner of a local radio station brought his wife in for dinner. They sat and listened to the band and danced. On one of our breaks, he asked the cocktail waitress to have me over to his table. He introduced himself and his wife and asked me if I would be interested in doing some radio disc jockey work at his radio station. He told me I had a good voice for radio. The station was located only a few miles from the club. It sat atop the City of Signal Hill, California. I told him there may be a problem with the Musician's Union and mentioned my work schedule and how sporadic it was with me being in and out of town with my band. He asked me to give it a shot and he would work around my schedule on my days off, so I accepted.

So that I wouldn't get any static from the Musician's Union, I used another name on the air. I used the alias of William Carson. My show broadcast late at night and into the very early hours of the morning on Station KLFM-FM 105.5 FM. My late night show was called The Dream Maker. I would open by saying, "This is William Carson broadcasting from high atop Signal Hill, the view of seven cities." The station was located in a commercial trailer at the top of Signal Hill behind the Hilltop Restaurant, which was another popular dining spot in the Long Beach area. People used to drive to the top of Signal Hill, which was loaded with oil derricks and park and look out over the cities below. It was a known make out spot for lovers.

Vikki Carr

While I was working as a radio disc jockey at KLFM-FM, I met up and coming singer Vikki Carr. It was the early 1960's and she was just starting her career in the music business. I was one of the first radio DJs to begin playing her newly released records in Southern California. Vikki was cute, a nice pleasant happy person. She was always polite to us DJs that spun her records. She came to the station often and I would give her a lot of airtime. I'd play her records and interview her. She and I often went to lunch at nearby Belmont Shore and would talk about her music desires. Vikki had a great hook that would grab the audience. She would sing a song and actually cry while she was singing. It was not uncommon to see tears rolling down her face when she was performing. She had good musical chops and a good vocal range, that's for sure.

One of her engagements close to the radio station was at Mr. C's. The nightspot was located at the Long Beach traffic circle. The décor of the club was a Tahitian motif with tiki torches and the whole nine yards. It was a major spot in its day. I would take a remote set to the club and record her live on stage and then play the show on the air. I also recorded her live when she was appearing at the Holiday Inn in West Covina, California. I wanted to give her career a boost when I could because I thought she had a lot of talent and radio airtime could only

Vikki Carr-Outstanding vocalist. Brad played her new record (s) on air when he was working as radio disc jockey, "William "Bill" Carson" on radio station KLFM-105.5, Long Beach, California-1960-1962.

help her chances. I would like to think that my efforts giving her a lot of radio playtime helped her career. She did quite a number of albums after my association with her, and through the years she became a star in her own rite.

A few years following our association, I was in Las Vegas. I saw her name on the marquee and I contacted her at her hotel. Her sister answered the phone and I asked if it was possible for Vikki to get me a couple of tickets for old time sake to catch the show. I told her sister who I was and explained my association with Vikki but she wouldn't let me talk to Vikki and said she couldn't get me the seats at the show. That was disappointing but a few weeks later in the mail I received one of her recent albums and a photo. Both were signed, With Love, Vikki. I assumed Vikki's sister told her about my phone call. An apology from Vikki? Possibly. During the 60s I was working about 48 weeks out of the year. When we were between bookings and my five-piece band was inactive, I continued to work the trios and duos that I would put together. Other times I'd just hire out as a sax and clarinet player and a drummer with other bands.

Southern California Local Clubs

In 1964, Don Perry, the organist who worked with me at the Edgewater Inn, and I opened up a duo act at the Lion Dior. It was a new plush supper club in Downey, California. It was a popular hangout for the Los Angeles Rams. It was a party place. Don and I drew a following at the place and we would let visiting musicians and singers come in to perform with us. Don began dating Mary, the manager of the club, and she had an 18-year old daughter Susan, who was a little over barely legal. She worked as the bookkeeper. It wasn't long until I jumped her bones. We worked this club off and on for two years and by now Don's relationship with Mary had cooled down. My hook-up with

Ohio Players still ready to play its funky stuff

the daughter also began to fall apart because I was seeing other women and she began seeing someone else. As Don's relationship began winding down with Mary, he had a heart attack and had to have heart bypass surgery. After getting out of the hospital, he gave up the job and moved back East. I hired a new organist, Gene Jay. He did a good job and also had a good singing voice, so we continued to perform at the place for another two years when I wasn't working Vegas or on the road.

Another favorite spot I enjoyed working was at Disneyland Hotel. I was hired to play sax by the bandleader who was working his group in the club atop the Disneyland Hotel. The nightspot was another hot spot for those that liked to get out and be seen. The band was encircled by the entire bar. Our stage was set right in the center of it. The club was super busy every night. I played the Disneyland Hotel off and on for about two months. Like a lot of hot spots that rocked during the 60s, there was no shortage of women. We band members could take our pick and we did.

On our off nights at the Disneyland Hotel, some of the band would visit a club a few miles away. The group there was drawing crowds from all over Southern California. The men were two local talents appearing at the nightclub called Bourbon Street. These two artists packed the house every night. The group was The Righteous Brothers, Bill Medley and Bobby Hatfield. They made the club. They made the club's reputation. The guys were gaining a reputation during the 60s. Bill and Bobby were stand-up guys. They didn't rub their talent in the faces of other entertainers, nor did they have an attitude. They would talk music to any of us at any time. Many of us musicians who worked the area knew that these two men were destined for fame. Talent is talent and when another musician sees it, they know it and they like it.

The Righteous Brothers, like many of us musicians, came up by hard work and hard knocks. They played small clubs over and over again, going from place to place and working their butts off. They earned their bones and deserved their fame. The next time I saw Bill and Bobby was years later when I took one of my ladies to see their shows in Las Vegas. They worked the stage just as hard as they did years before. It was a high energy performance. Again years went by and I didn't see Bill or Bobby again until the time I was appearing at a small dinner house in Las Vegas. Lo and behold, they were at a club a few miles down the street from where I was appearing. They were at the Orleans Hotel, and to top that off at the same time Wayne Newton, another entertainer that I crossed paths with in the late 50s, was appearing at the Stardust Hotel. In fact, the Review Journal Newspaper had each of our pictures in the same section of the entertainment page during our separate engagements. Show business is a funny animal. People you may have crossed paths with years before all of a sudden find themselves appearing across the street from each other. Go figure.

Eilene

It was the early 1960s and I was being kept very busy both on the road, appearing in Las Vegas and working all the local jobs near home in Southern California. By this time I gave up my radio disc jockey side job and was concentrating on some local work. I also closed out my entertainment at the Edgewater Inn at the marina in Long Beach, California. One day I was hanging out at Richie's Drive-In having breakfast when one of my friends, Al Dauray, came in and sat down next to me. He was a graphic artist who worked out of his home. Al married one of the carhops at Richie's. Her name was Marilyn, a cute redhead. Al wanted me to come over to his house for a cookout

EILENE — 1964 Ports Call
Eilene-Ports of Call,
Long Beach, CA.
Great looking lady. We
were together 3 Yrs.
PORTS OF CALL - 1963

that evening. He said he wanted me to meet Marilyn's sister. He didn't say much about the sister but I told him I would be over that evening.

When I arrived and walked into the kitchen to say hello to everyone, I was bowled over. Standing there was this long tall gorgeous thing that was wearing white short, shorts and a pastel blouse. Eilene was helping Marilyn fix dinner. Her eyes were the deepest green I've ever seen on a woman. She was beautiful. We ate dinner in the back yard at a picnic table. The dishes were cleared and she and I sat and talked for hours. In our conversation, she told me she left California and moved to Alabama, had two kids, Johnny six and Eddie three, but when her marriage went south, she decided to return to California where her sister and her parents were living. Her parents only lived a few blocks from Marilyn and Al's house.

Finally, Al and Marilyn told us they were going to turn in. They went to bed leaving Eilene and I in the back yard at the picnic table. We sat there having coffee and cold drinks. Over the hours, we got to know each other quite well. We kissed and made out a little and at 6:00 a.m. we decided to call it a night, promising each other that we would see each other again. Over the next few weeks, we found her a nice comfortable apartment and Eilene and I began a relationship. She was only three years younger than me. The apartment was located near her sister and parent's house. While she was getting settled in California, I drove her to different companies while she filled out job applications. She landed a job as a secretary at Aerospace in Downey, California, which was a few miles from her apartment, but she soon left that job for one with the Murietta Company, which was even closer to her apartment.

Eilene's folks were dead set against her dating a musician. They told her over and over again that musicians were bums that couldn't be counted on for security and a steady family life, but Eilene and I continued our relationship. I spent most every night at her apartment. When I started to see Eilene, I immediately stopped seeing other women. Eilene was my only squeeze. She would come to see me on stage every so often but her hours at work and the kids kept her close to home. On her days off, we would take the kids to the beach and spend the whole day in the sun and sand and ocean. When the sun went down, we would go to a nearby beach café and have dinner. It was a regular family outing for us. We loved the beach and spent a lot of time there. Other times Eilene would leave the kids with her parents while we would go on trips with Al and Marilyn to places like Yosemite National Park for a day or two, or just the two of us would take a mini vacation and drive down to Mission Bay in San Diego and stay at one of the hotels there for a weekend.

She and I were also regulars in Vegas. We would go off for the weekend to gamble, eat and have a ball in Las Vegas. Since a lot of people at the Flamingo knew me, we would generally stay there. I was given quite a few comps by the employees. In Vegas we would hit most of the clubs on the Strip but we spent a lot of our time at the downtown casinos because the machines were always looser and we could win more money there than on the Strip. Our relationship went on for three years. At one point she became pregnant but quickly aborted the child without any discussion with me. I didn't say much regarding the abortion because I loved the lady and I didn't want to cause problems with her family. I also believed that she had the right to make her own decision and do with her body as she wants. In the back of my mind I always wondered how much pressure was on Eilene from her parents to abort the child.

As relationships go, we got along fine. We very seldom argued while living together and we had a nice home life. In our sex life, we were very compatible. It was great. Wow, was it good. I remember one occasion when I was to play a New Year's Eve gig at a club in a nearby town. Eilene made arrangements with her parents to take care of Johnny and Eddie and she came with me to the gig. She sat there at a table with all the other women that were with band members and patiently waited until we finished up for the night. I felt sorry for her and the other women just sitting there, not dancing, but she told me afterward that she would rather sit and listen to the band.

After the band played Auld Lang Syne for all people in the joint, I jumped off the stage and went to Eilene and kissed her and wished her a Happy New Year and then ran back on stage. Once the band wrapped up the music for the night, she and I went out for breakfast and back to her apartment. I took her keys, unlocked the door and we both went inside. I led the way to the kitchen and started to fill the coffee pot with water, but Eilene told me to forget it. She then leaned against my body and kissed me. While she forced my lips wide with her tongue, she grabbed hold of the front of my shirt with both hands and pulled sideways and took two or three buttons off from the shirt. She didn't stop there. She took me by the hand and we went into the bedroom. "I'm yours," she whispered, pressed against my lips.

I then returned a passionate kiss and began to remove her clothes while she removed mine. Both naked, we fell to the bed and I began to move within her, sending cycles of pleasure through her body. I watched her eyes close again while giving herself over completely to the feel of my lips and tongue moving down the nape of her neck, my body locking tightly to hers. She felt whole as some part of her she hadn't even known was missing and being fulfilled. Moving with me, she matched my movements and she gave herself over to spirals of passion. The passion became stronger, exploding from her entire being. Then she was floating, all the tension draining away as she collapsed into my arms. I hugged her against my chest, kissed her neck and then we lay there sprawled out, breathing heavy and staring up at the ceiling. We both lay in silence for a long time and then fell into a restful sleep. That was a New Year's Eve I'll never forget. I will always remember it.

The pressure from her parents to move on was overwhelming. They kept telling her that getting involved with a musician was a life of instability and it wasn't long before we began to drift apart. She began to see someone else and I couldn't take it knowing that she was going out dancing and running around with other men, so we sat down and talked it out and decided to go our own ways. Eilene wound up marrying the man she was seeing. She had two more children. Over the years I would see her parents and her sister and brother-in-law, and we would talk about how much different our lives may have been if I had continued on with our relationship and married Eilene. Somewhere in the late 90s Al, her brother-in-law, called me and said Eilene had died of cancer. To this day I still receive an annual Christmas card from Al and Marilyn, even though we haven't seen each other in over 40 years.

After Eilene

In 1965 and my relationship with Eilene was over. After Eilene, I went back to dating and hooked up with every lady that showed any interest in me at all. It was about this time that mom and I bought an old wood framed house on an R-3 lot in Compton. We tore down the old house that was there and had a brand new three-bedroom house built from the ground up. We also had two separate bedroom apartments built in the rear of the lot. Our idea was the apartments could be rented out and would help pay for the new house. Mom was still working at Frito-Lay Company in Inglewood, California and I was in and out of town on the road with my band.

Eilene- 1963 Brad's main squeeze for three
years. She and Brad considered marriage.

When I was back at home, mom and I very seldom ran into each other because when she was either going or coming from work, I was on my way out the door to a gig. When back in town, I began taking a lot of local work. I returned to the Rustic Room and also signed on to play at a country music nightclub a few blocks from the Rustic Room. I liked the situation because at the Rustic Room I was playing dance and dinner music, but then I would wear another hat and play some good old country music at the other gig. The country spot drew a lot of well-known country singers and musicians. It wasn't unusual to see my old friend and fellow studio musician, Glen Campbell, mosey in, unpack his guitar and jam with us musicians. Glen and I were the same age. He was three months younger than me. Both of us were studio musicians brought up in the same era so we related very well.

Another friend that used to come in and sit in and jam with Glen and I was Danny Flores. His professional name was Chuck Rio, or as I liked to call him 'Mr. Tequila' because he penned the song 'Tequila' in the 50s and made it an international hit. I don't think there is anyone in the world that hasn't heard the song Tequila who doesn't sing the one word Tequila when they hear the song. Glen, Chuck and I often played the same clubs around Southern California for years. During these stays in town, my friends that hung out at Richie's Drive-In were always asking me to do something with them. It was let's go to the beach, let's go to some new nightspots around town or teach me some karate.

One time it was, be my best man at my wedding. My friend Bill met Pat, a bartender at a local watering hole. She and her sister were from Dallas, Texas and these ladies were very easy on the eyes. They both had great figures and were a lot of fun to be around. I've got to say Texas grows some nice women down there. Shortly after Bill met Pat, he proposed to her. They decided to get married in Mexico. Bill asked me to be his best man, so Pat, Bill and a few of us that hung out at Richie's Drive-In drove into Tijuana, Mexico. I stood as best man while Pat and Billy were married. We drove back to Compton that same evening so that they could celebrate their honeymoon at home.

Pat had two children of her own, Robin, about 12-years old, and Gale, a few years younger, and it wasn't long before they had a child together. I had a hunch maybe that's why they decided to get married when they did. These two people were like night and day. Pat loved to go out and party and Bill was a stay at home, sit in a chair and watch TV type guy and wanted Pat to wait on him hand and foot. Pat told me she was disillusioned about their marriage and said that before they married, Bill liked to go out and have fun but as soon as they tied the knot, he became a homebody. Their marriage began to crack and Pat took a job as a bartender and began to drink and run around. The two separated for a while and during that separation, I would take Pat and their kids to the beach for the day. We would beach bum all day and then have dinner at a restaurant on the beach.

Pat would also show up at the clubs I was appearing at and sit and wait for me to get off. I used to sing the Sinatra song Summer Wind, and that became a favorite of hers. Every night she came in, she would ask that I sing that song for her. I began seeing her more and more. One night she showed up at the club and told me when I finished up I was to come over to her apartment. She said she would leave the door unlocked and wait up for me. Well, being the hound dog I was, since I'd left Eilene, I went over to her apartment. Once inside, I locked the door behind me. There was a small soft light shining through a half open bedroom door. She was lying in bed dosing off. I leaned in very close and I tugged and pulled the little string on her teddy and pulled it back off her shoulders. She made a feigned grab for the teddy but I caught her hand and held it down to her side. With one finger, I brushed the teddy lower and then put out the light and in the dark kissed her forehead, eyes, cheeks, her lips and chin. I continued very slowly with a soft lip touch to the arches of her feet. In a matter of moments, we were entwined and enjoyed the rest of the night.

Pat and I began an off and on relationship for a year or so. I moved on with my life and she left the area. I didn't see her for years. It was one of those out of sight, out of mind situations. Then out of the blue 13 years later, she found my current phone number and called me. At the time I was living in Upland, California and she was living in Palm Desert. She then drove into Upland to see me. We met at a coffee shop and talked for a couple of hours, filling each other in on our lives. She was again single and tending bar in Palm Springs. After that meeting I saw her one more time a few years later. She again found my phone number and wanted me to come up to her place in Palm Desert. Pat was living in a mobile home and was still tending bar. She called into work to take the night off and we went into Palm Springs for dinner and dancing at a few hot spots. I stayed over but there was no sex. The next morning we went out and had breakfast. Following breakfast, I kissed her goodbye in the restaurant parking lot and never saw her again.

While I was sleeping with Pat, I was also sleeping with a few other groupies that followed my music from club to club. There was always a groupie that I could grab onto for the night. That's one of the perks of being a musician. Many of the women I was seeing knew that I appeared in Las Vegas quite often and they wanted me to take them for a day or two of fun. I never had a problem with that. I would usually take them to some of my favorite places. One of the favorites to show the ladies a good time at was at Caesar's Palace. Caesar's restaurant offered up great food and had one of the nicest pools on the

Las Vegas Strip. A person could lie around the pool and soak up the sun all day and order up anything their heart desired. In the evening, I would take my ladies for drinks and dancing on Cleopatra's Barge. It was an all around great place to spend time with a loving partner.

Brad, during an intermission at one of his shows-1961

Brad, played drums, sax and sang when he formed a duo for the Lion Dior nightclub in Downey, California in the mid 1960's. Brad hired Gene Jay, organist and piano player to work with him. 'The duo known as the Jay-Evans duo earned the title: "One of the nations most versatile duo's."

WAYNE
NEWTON
NOW
Saturday through Thursday
Showtime 8 p.m.
For Ticket Information
Call 947-5577
STARDUST

08

Elvis

It was April, the spring of 1961. I was at Desilu Studios on Gower Street working as a studio musician. Desilu Studios was then owned by actress Lucille Ball and husband, Desi Arnaz. Paramount Studios covered a massive track of land around Gower Street and it was a mega center for studio musicians. Jack Kurtze, my agent, had offices in Beverly Hills and Palm Springs, but spent a lot of time at Paramount and Twentieth Century Fox Studios. He was a well-respected talent agent and I was lucky to have him handle my band.

This particular afternoon Jack called me at Desilu from Paramount Studios. He said he was on the set of 'Blue Hawaii' and asked me to meet him there. He said "Since you're only a stone throw away from Paramount, meet me here. I have business at Paramount and I also want to discuss some engagements I've set up for your band. I can kill two birds with one stone." When I got there he told me this was Elvis' eighth movie. The plot had Elvis playing Chad Gates, just out of the Army and who was in Hawaii. Elvis' mother was being played by a very good actress named Angela Lansbury who in later years would have her own television show called "Murder, She Wrote."

During a break in shooting some of the cast decided to go out to eat at a popular eating spot. Jack, Elvis and his manager Colonel Tom Parker, his security people, myself and a few studio security men went to Martoni's. It was owned by celebrity chef Ciro Marino. It was known for its superb food menu. It was actually a celebrity hangout. Actors, musicians and agents hoping to be discovered or hoping to sign deals frequently met at Martoni's. You could find agents, actors and musicians working as busboys and waiters so they could have a chance to pick up on local gossip or to promote their own talent. It was a mover and shaker deal-making spot and some celebrities had so much juice that even when the place was closed they could have it opened just because of who they were.

Chef Ciro's clientele included Frank Sinatra, Nat King Cole, Phil Spector, The Beatles, Jackson Five and it was a favorite of Elvis when he was on the west coast. A popular spot? You bet it was. In the evenings it would be two or three feet deep at the bar. Martoni's was a spot where major contracts were signed on nothing but a napkin. It was here that my old friend Sonny Bono wrote the song 'Look at Me' after he was refused service because of the flashy, glitzy clothes he was wearing. I guess the sight of Sonny glitzed out was too much for the bar so he was asked to leave. Sonny's song that he scribbled out that night became famous because of the flipside which went down in history. That song was 'I Got You Babe'.

Martoni's was suggested by someone in Elvis' group because they knew he liked the place. I left my car at Paramount and rode with Jack. Elvis and Colonel Parker had their own ride with security people. While we were dining in a private area Elvis' security man Red West and Red's cousin Sonny West stood close by our table and kept an eye on Elvis and the Colonel. Elvis appeared to be relaxed and comfortable during the meal. He talked about his trips back and forth to Hawaii while shooting the picture. He also spoke about his producer Hal Wallis saying how well Wallis treated him and gave him most anything he wanted. He seemed interested in my studio work and asked me, "Do you like studio musician work?"

"Yes, I like it, but to break up the boredom of reading music charts, I'm on the road quite a bit with my group."

He laughed. "I can understand that. Boy, do I know what road work is, but it gets old after a while," referring to the times he was traveling getting his start in the music business. "Do you have any tapes of your group?"

"Yes, but not with me," I said.

"Hey, the next time we see each other, how about a copy? I enjoy collecting tapes of different groups and musicians. I listen to them in my spare time."

I was surprised he asked for a tape of my band, but said, "Yes, I'll get one to you next time."

The rest of that year I had occasion to meet Elvis at the studios and during one of those brief meetings I kept my promise and gave him a tape recording of my group. Each time we met he became more at ease and comfortable. He began to come across as though we knew each other for a long time. He became more and more relaxed. Whenever we met over lunch or dinner in a public place outside the studios or in a hotel suite, he would have Red or Sonny book the reservations under the alias John Barrows. That's the name he used when he came to see ma at home when she was recovering from one of her surgeries. I hate to say it, but he also used Barrows when he had his people get prescription drugs for him. It was a favorite moniker of his.

We discovered we had some things in common. Both of our birthdays were in January, his was on the 8th and mine on the 30th of the month. Age-wise we were one year apart, Elvis was born in 1935 and I was born in 1936. I worked in Hawaii with my band and he also worked in Hawaii. I played in Hawaii in 1955 and in 1957 he appeared in Hawaii for the first time. He loved the islands. More common ground between us was we both had an interest in karate and both of us studied under private instructors and continued our study of karate after being discharged from the military. He was Army and I was a Marine. My karate style was Kempo Kung Fu and Elvis used

Elvis, on train leaving Florida to see agent-1960's

Brad's friend, Elvis., King of Rock & Roll, movie star and stage performer. Both remained friends from 1961 until his death.

Elvis with his mother Glady's. Elvis gave this photo
to Brad's mom Mary, in 1960's.

Elvis, at the Pacific War Memorial in
Hawaii-March 25,1961.
One month before Brad and he became
friends..

a mixture of different styles. He received his first-degree black belt in March 1960.

When he found out what year I got out of the military, he told me that was the year his mother died. When he talked about his mom I could tell they were very close. When I mentioned I was taking care of my mom the best I could he said "Brad, make sure you take care of mom because you only have them once."

"I will, thanks," I said. That was a nice gesture on his part. It would be later when he got to know mom that he gave her a picture of him and his mother together.

When we talked about music he asked, "How do you like playing Las Vegas backing different entertainers? I like Las Vegas and would like to appear there on a regular basis some day," he said. He thought Las Vegas was electrifying and full of action. Little did either of us know at the time he would later dominate the Las Vegas scene.

We talked about everything under the sun from music to politics over the years that we knew each other, even though we weren't close buddies like the relationships he had with his childhood friends. Instead, we were more like the kind of friends that whenever you saw each other you could be comfortable talking about a lot of things knowing it was among friends. Elvis had his own circle of close, close friends, but explained our friendship by saying, "I try to have friends with people that I choose myself because it helps me stay grounded and it's a change from all the other people that are always around me."

After our first few get-togethers, I didn't hear from Elvis until my birthday the following year in 1962. He sent me a birthday card telling me he would be back on the west coast in Hollywood to shoot 'It Happened at the World's Fair'. The note in the card said that his producer Ted Richmond would have him shooting both in Hollywood and Seattle and if his schedule permitted we could at least meet for coffee or a cold drink. I saw him very briefly one time during that shoot.

Elvis was doing a string of movies during the '60s and when he was on the west coast, if nothing else, I could count on a phone call just to say hi and most calls would end with him asking, "How's mom?" or "Is she there?" If she was he would say hi before hanging up. Mom liked that. I usually sent him a birthday card over the years because our birthdays were in January. One day I asked him, did you ever receive any of the birthday cards? "Brad," he said, "some of my people watch me so close they isolate me from some of my friends and there are many times I don't get half of the mail that's sent to me. That's one part of the business I don't like."

Another two years went by. It was 1964 when mom answered the phone and Vernon, Elvis' dad, was on the other end. Elvis came on the line briefly to say hello to mom. After mom's hello, he told me his new film "Viva Las Vegas" was his latest project. How do you like working with Ann-Margret, I said? "She's a real doll and her long legs run all the way to you know where. I'll tell her hello for ya." He knew I ran into Ann-Margret a few years prior while she and I were both working the Las Vegas circuit. It was nice of Elvis to pass on the greeting. I wonder if she did remember.

A few years into our friendship he offered me a small bit part in a movie project that was on the drawing board. The proposed title was "Hillbillies Go Hollywood". The gist of the story was Elvis was a country singer from down south who had a small hillbilly band traveling around small towns and the movie would depict the hardships of the band as they struggle to get to Hollywood to snag a recording contract. My very small bit part was to be one of the sidemen in his band. The movie was to be produced by some executives that worked at Twentieth Century Fox. "When the movie goes into production I'll see that you get a Screen Actor's Guild Card (SAG)," he told me. But as luck would have it, the financing fell through and the entire project was cancelled. I've always wondered how my life might have been different or changed if the movie went forward. Elvis did these favors for a lot of his friends. In fact, with Elvis' help, Red West, long-time friend and security guy, got into the movie business doing stunts and acting.

It was 1966 and I was appearing at a popular supper club, The Lion Dior, in Downey, California. Mom and some of my friends decided to throw me a birthday party at the club on my 30th birthday. Between the party-goers and the regular customers it was packed wall to wall. Just before I left for work at the club that evening Vernon Presley called. "Happy birthday, Brad, did you get the two shirts from Elvis?" I did and said thank you. There were times over the years when I received an occasional birthday card from the Presley's, but the shirts I had just received were a real surprise. They were both the same style and had high collars and were great colors. Surprised was not the word for it, because it's been a couple of years since I'd heard from Elvis and out of the blue these two shirts. Vernon said "Elvis bought the same two shirts for himself and thought you would like the style." That's typical for Elvis though. If he liked certain clothes or a particular item, he would buy two or three of the same thing for himself and friends without any rhyme or reason. He sent presents all over the country. He told me he had bought cars, clothes, diamonds and jewelry for his friends over the years and I've seen him lavish some of those homes, cars, jewelry and money on his security people. He was a generous giving person. I accepted the shirts gracefully with thanks. I wore those shirts on and off stage over the next few years until they became shaggy and too shabby. When they gave up their last gasp of wearing life I gave them to the Salvation Army.

Elvis' generosity even extended to mom. There was an

occasion when he invited a group of friends, which included me and mom, to the Brown Derby Restaurant on Vine Street in Hollywood. His people bought out the place; it was closed to the public. The Brown Derby was famous for its food and the many celebrities in the movie industry that were regulars. Some celebrities would have the owner prepare their favorite dishes and at times even ship it by air across the country to the spot they were appearing at. This evening Elvis could have probably had his choice of any gourmet meal prepared for him, but he had the chef make him a plate of pork chops with all the fixings. I've always thought of pork chops as a working man's meal and I didn't expect him to order a simple dish like that, but he did. However, through the years and as I came to know him a little better, I have to say that was Elvis. Burgers, hotdogs, pork chops; he'd eat them right along with the rest of us.

It was at this gathering that he told mom "You work too hard, mom. How can I make life a little bit easier on you, how about a new house?" She politely refused saying "I have a job and I'm doing okay. I'm used to making my own way and earning my own money." He smiled and hugged mom. "Okay, let me know if you ever change your mind," he said. Elvis and mom got along pretty good. He was always courteous to her, but she wasn't afraid to bawl him out when she thought he deserved it. When she thought he was pushing the envelope she sometimes told him point blank about easing up on the drug dependence. When she got on his case his usual response was, "I hear ya, ma. I'll try."

That night at the Brown Derby made an impression on me because Lucille Ball, who owned Desilu Studios where I did studio music work, filmed her first of the Hollywood episodes 'I Love Lucy' there. The episode had Ethel (Vivian Vance) and Fred (William Frawley) and Lucy having lunch in a booth with actress Eve Arden and actor William Holden. The episode led to the unexpected scene where Lucy accidentally causes a waiter to hit Holden in the face with a pie. That scene wasn't scripted, but it added to the dramatics of the scene. It's a classic scene now.

The Ambassador Hotel on Wilshire Boulevard was another outing with Elvis. Like the Brown Derby it was frequented by celebrities which included a few that I had the privilege to work with. Inside the hotel the Coconut Grove Nightclub hosted Sinatra, Lena Horne, Judy Garland, Vikki Carr, Perry Como, Sammy Davis, Jr. and band leader Benny Goodman. It was amazing to me how Elvis would get an idea in his head and want to go some place or do something on the spur of the moment and his people would put the wheels in motion and make it happen. Following my 30th birthday party another year flew by when I received a card from Elvis telling me he was going to marry Priscilla and it happened. He married her on May 1, 1967.

1968 was a busy year for me. I received a call from an aide to the Speaker of the California Assembly, Jesse M. Unruh. The aide advised me that the California State Assembly was going to adopt the resolution as of October 22, 1968 honoring me and my band, The Encores. The aide asked me to stay on the line for Speaker Unruh because he wanted to congratulate me for my music contribution. Wow! That was an honor for me. It was during the same year when Vern Presley told me that they saw a blip in the newspaper about my receiving the music award from the State of California and wanted to congratulate me and also tell me that Lisa Marie was born and Elvis was a daddy. There were congratulations enough to go around for everybody that year.

Still another year passed. It was a steamy, warm, humid California summer before I heard anything from Elvis. He said he was going to open an engagement at the International Hotel

Brad Evans-36 years old. Wearing one of two shirts that Elvis Presley gave Brad as a birthday gift.

in Las Vegas and would be there for a four-week stint. "Do you want to catch the show?" he said. "Yes, love to." "Great bring your date and check in with Red or Sonny. They'll have tickets for you." I jumped at the opportunity because other than seeing him on screen I've never seen him at a live performance. This was going to be a first for me. I flew into Las Vegas that July 31st, I was finally going to see Elvis in a live stage performance. Before the show bodyguard Red, who was also a musician in his own right, had my tickets for me. He also extended an invitation to say hi to Elvis in his suite after the show. Since Red and his cousins were going to be the gatekeepers at the suite, I knew there would be no problem with hotel security. In his suite Elvis was surrounded by his inner circle of old friends, many of them known as the Memphis Mafia. Colonel Parker was also glad-handing around the room.

I'd say Elvis was really charged up after his super spectacular performance. I had the brief opportunity to say hi to him and the Colonel for a few minutes. I introduced my date to both of them, congratulated him and told him I had to leave. As we started to leave Elvis and the Colonel walked us to the door telling me he would be going to the Sahara Hotel at Lake Tahoe that summer. I didn't want to over stay my welcome and a few minutes of conversation was okay with me. During the brief time we had to talk, Elvis reflected back to the first time he ever played an engagement in Las Vegas. He looked at the Colonel and said "This is far different than what happened in 1956, isn't it?" Nodding in the affirmative, the Colonel said "Yes, it is." I looked perplexed as to what they were referring to when Elvis said "Brad, back in 1956 I was booked into the New Frontier Hotel, it was my first time to appear in Las Vegas. When I went on stage and started my routine the audience began to boo me. They booed me off stage. People were waiting to see comedian Shecky Greene and they didn't want any part of me. The crowd continued their booing and hissing until I gave up and walked off stage. I was upset and embarrassed and swore to myself I'd never play Vegas again." He and the Colonel laughed and Elvis said, "But here I am now with a new contract to appear in one of the largest hotels in the city."

As the years came and went our talks together touched on most everything. For example, when I asked him what song he liked the most out of the many that he recorded over the years without hesitation he said, "In the Ghetto". Another time when we were goofing around talking about songs, I said what's the worst song ever recorded by anyone? "That's easy," he said, "Monster Mash." He hated that song with a passion. That's one song no one ever brought up around Elvis, especially on Halloween. I mean come on. Who else could talk about such loony things as the 'Monster Mash' and still stay friends? It's conversations like that which impressed me about Elvis. He was the kind of guy that once he considered you a friend he continued that friendship for years and our friendship was one that lasted for 17 years.

Some of our other conversations touched on Vernon, Priscilla and some of his security people around him. His dad, Vernon, he didn't have much love for. He resented how Vernon treated his mother before her death. Elvis thought his mother could have been treated much better and at times he blamed Vernon for contributing to his mother's death. He tried to steer clear of Vern when he could. According to Elvis, the relationship between them was strained. He made no qualms about how he felt about Vern saying he knew the relationship was very poor, but he said, "That's how he likes it." In his early years, apparently, Vernon was a motivating guy and he bounced around from project to project. It was clear his mother, Gladys, wore the pants in the family because Vernon would always do what Gladys told him to do. His mother was three years older

Brad's award from the State of California honoring his band, the "ENCORES"-October 22, 1968

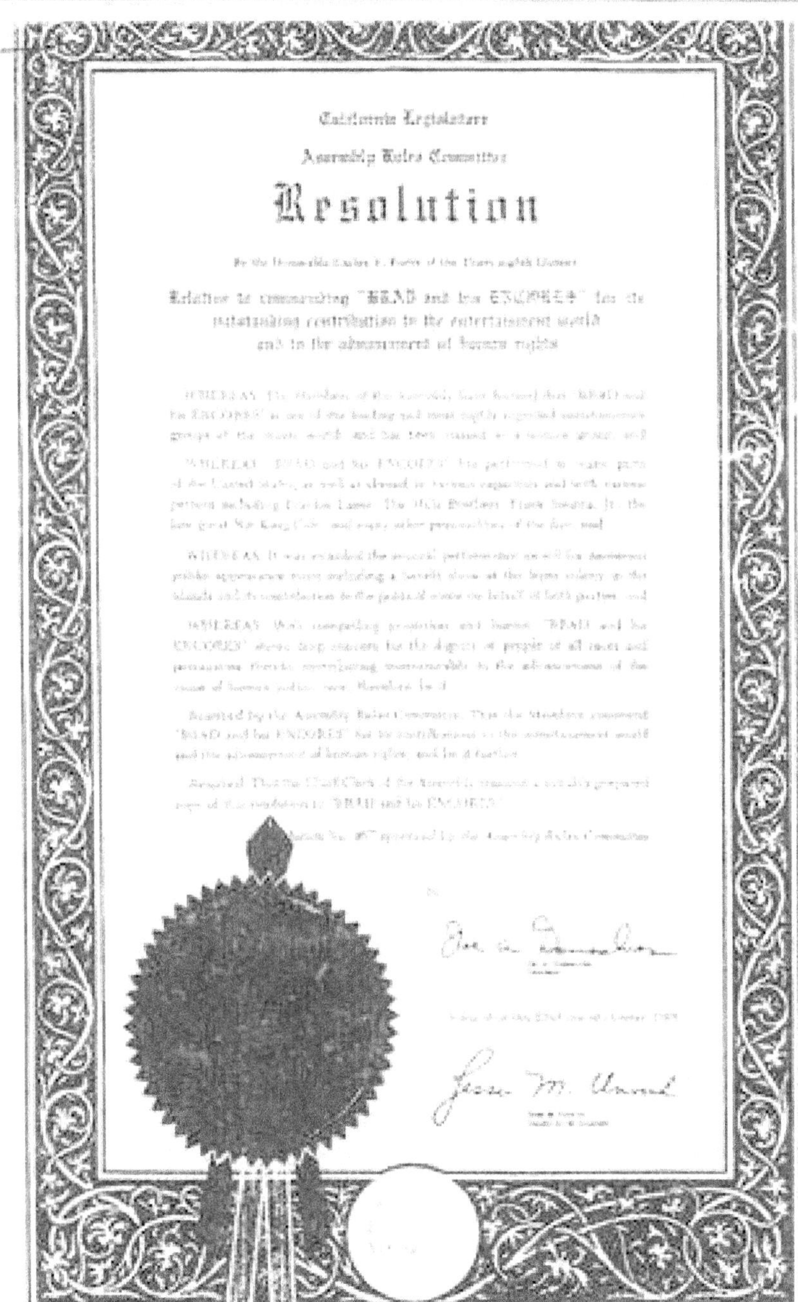

than Vern, according to Elvis. He also had the feeling Vernon loved him, but he had a hard time expressing his love. Vernon worked as a laborer on many different jobs when they moved to Memphis in 1948, but he hurt his back, suffering a lot of back pain and wound up disabled and on disability. With Vern not working the only thing that kept Elvis and his family treading water was federal housing assistance.

Following Elvis' mother's death Vern met Dee Stanley. They met while Elvis was still in the military. Vernon married Dee in 1960, a year before I met Elvis. Elvis was so angry at Vern that he didn't even attend the wedding. Another frustration of Elvis was Dee's attempt to redecorate and remove some of his mother's things from Graceland. The anger became so fierce that he asked his father to live somewhere else other than the Graceland mansion. Elvis said he loved his dad and resented his ways, but couldn't bring himself to throw the man out into the street so he arranged to have him live in a house near the mansion. Hell, the grounds covered about 500 acres so it wasn't a real inconvenience.

There was a time he said he was having problems with Priscilla. As he sat across from me he just shook his head, cupping his face in his hands and saying he was at his wit's end. "I'm one of the luckiest people on earth. I have a lot of money, more than I could ever use, but even with all of that wealth and fame I can't get a handle on my family life." He took a lot of the blame for some of the problems in his marriage and was ambivalent about getting a divorce. One minute he thought divorce was the answer and the next minute he wondered what affect divorce would have on his life. Elvis loved Priscilla and wanted to hold on to her and be a family man. He was torn between maintaining a picture of a happy family and enjoying the freedom of doing things he wanted to do. He also considered the impact of a divorce on Lisa Marie.

To that I said, "Christ, Elvis, you named your plane after her. If you didn't love her you wouldn't have did that, would you?" Smiling, he said, "I guess not. I love her with all of my being and I hope she knows that." But like a shining light on the facets of a diamond and ever changing life changes, they separated in 1972 and divorced in 1973.

Elvis' Drug Use

When the subject of drugs ever came up he knew that I didn't even drink alcohol and never did drugs. At times I thought Elvis remained friends with me because I was one of those friends that didn't use drugs. He once told me that some friends he chose to be with helped him keep grounded. Maybe that was the case of our friendship, whatever it was I was glad to be able to say we were friends. Sometimes he would comment, "I don't know how you did it all these years, working in the entertainment business and steering clear of all this garbage." At one time he said, "Brad, you know and I know I can get my stuff from almost any doctor at any time and under any made up name. It's always available. I think a lot of my so-called friends that hang with me would rather see me use." He said, "I know I should quit and I know it's wrong to do. There are times I feel I'm being torn apart from both ends."

Colonel Parker

When any conversation mentioned the Colonel it would be an understatement to say there was a love-hate relationship there. According to Elvis the Colonel had a strong hold on him, one that he couldn't break. He thought the Colonel was cheating him and only using him to squeeze every dime out of the fans for his own personal gain. In the beginning of his career Elvis thought he had a good thing by associating himself with the

Colonel, but as the years passed he came to the conclusion that the Colonel's only interest was his own, that being money. The relationship slowly became very fragmented between the two of them. Elvis believed the contract between them was one-sided and the Colonel refused to budge whenever any mention of renegotiation of the contract was brought up. According to Elvis, "He's screwing me and there's not much I can do about it, but Parker will get his one day."

Elvis' Security

Elvis always treated his party guests well. Personally, I thought many of the people around him took advantage of his generosity. Most of the parties were always supervised and all of the guests were screened. At this one invite I got off the elevator, approached the suite and said hello to security man Sam Thompson and Dick Grob, who was monitoring the guest list. They cleared me on the list, but as I was about to go inside a group of four or five people behind had a person yelling and cursing in the group. Apparently, there was only one person in the group that was on the guest list and the loudmouth became more agitated when he was told he couldn't get into the party. The guy became more belligerent by the second. I just stood there and watched the entire show unfold right before my eyes.

Sam and Dick asked to see each person's ID in the group and that set this idiot off in a frenzy. He was yelling, "Do you know who I am?" while every other word was a cuss word directed at Sam and Dick. He refused to show his ID and I could see the others in the group were embarrassed, but they tried to stick up for their friend. I guess Sam and Dick had enough and very gently took the guy by the arm, one on each side of him, walked him a few feet away from the group and backed him up against the wall. They talked very softly to him for a few minutes out of earshot of us and of the people who were standing there. The bodyguards came back to the rest of the group and told them to leave saying no one in their party was welcome. A couple of people in the group with this jerk off continued to ask Dick to let them into the party to no avail. They pointed to the elevator and just said leave. I could hear some mumbling and grumbling as the people walked toward the elevator pushing the drunk along as they went. I thought the security guys handled the situation very well. I would have liked to have been a fly on the wall to hear what the security guys told this obnoxious drunk before sending him packing.

These two guys were just part of Elvis' security detail, though it changed quite often. A number of the men hired for the security detail were Elvis' friends from childhood. Many people in the media used to refer to the bodyguards as babysitters, drug and women providers and much more.

Some of his security had specific duties. Joe Esposito was usually the road manager and personal aide. He held that position for about 17 years. Sonny generally handled security at Elvis' concerts along with his cousin Red. The security crew wasn't really paid that much. In the early days of protecting Elvis they were paid $250 a week. They mostly depended on the generosity of Elvis, with him giving gifts, money, clothes, cars and any women that Elvis had left behind for them to enjoy. Elvis got a kick out of giving these gifts to his security. He knew he could shout and scream at them and they'd take the abuse just for the largesse. He knew that they knew they were there to do his bidding and to address any whim he may have had at any given moment. It wasn't until about the 1970s that the security wages were raised to $425 a week. None of his security people ever made more than $500 a week and they were often belittled and insulted by Elvis when he felt like getting into their face.

A few of these ever-changing security people had been arrested with false prescriptions when they tried to collect drugs for Elvis. Elvis' childhood friend, bodyguard Red West, was my age. He was kind of a hell raiser. Red also became a stuntman and actually appeared in about 16 films that Elvis made in the 1960s. In 1976 Red got involved in an incident where he became irate and hostile towards some Elvis fans and the media jumped all over it and criticized his behavior. When Vernon Presley got wind of Red's action he fired Red and two other bodyguards. Vern thought the dustup with the fans tarnished Elvis' image.

Sometimes a few years would go by before I heard from Elvis or his dad. I can understand why, this guy was always busy in one way or the other because of who and what he was. He was a bigger-than-life icon. Me, I kept humming along and doing my thing playing my music when and where I could. As the '70s popped up I got a call from Harry, one of the Mills Brothers. He asked me if I wanted to be a guest with him and his singing group at the International Hotel in Las Vegas. When I asked what the occasion was, he said that Perry Como was going to revive his singing career by performing a three-day engagement at the hotel. Harry, I said, it would be an honor. He told me to call Redd Foxx for all the information, details and arrangements. My name as a guest came up when Colonel Tom Parker was talking to him. The Colonel apparently told Harry since I worked with the Mills Brothers frequently he thought I might enjoy the show.

I called Redd Foxx who was in Las Vegas at the time. After we got caught up Redd said, "I'm arranging some of the guest list for Perry's show. Flip Wilson will be on the guest list too." Laughing he said, "Don't worry, the Flipper won't be attending in drag." That's what we used to call Flip Wilson. Anyhow, Perry's opening night was like old home week for a lot of us entertainers. Besides the Mills Brothers, Flip, Redd Foxx and me, the rest of the audience looked like something out of a who's who. In the audience sitting in the VIP seats were Johnny Carson and his bandleader Doc Severinsen, comedian Bob Hope, movie star Sal Mineo, singer Andy Williams, the Osmond Brothers and friend Colonel Tom Parker.

Prior to going into the show, the Mills Brothers, Redd Foxx, Flip Wilson and myself sat around and reminisced about the good old days. Redd and Flip had us all in stitches. Those guys can't do anything or go anywhere without cutting up and being funny. As we were walking to the showroom, Colonel Parker took me by the arm and he said, "Say hello to your mom, give her my best." I thought that was a nice gesture on his part. This was Perry's first non-televised stage performance in over 25 years and the entire opening night was being recorded. The performance would later turn into an album on RCA Victor. They titled it 'Perry Como in Person at the International Hotel, Las Vegas'. This was Perry's first live album ever.

I think the album is out of print now, but it did become one of Perry's most popular live recordings. It featured Cole Porter's 'I've Got You under My Skin'. He also performed 'You'll Never Walk Alone'. It was an outstanding performance. After the three-day engagement it sure gave Perry's career a big boost. He was signed to a three-year contract to appear at the Hilton Hotel. It looked like Perry was on a roll in the '70s because his songs 'It's Impossible' and 'I Love You So' were going strong, not to mention his Christmas albums. After his show I never ran into Perry again until the late 1980s. He returned to Las Vegas for a few weekend performances at the Riviera Hotel. I caught a couple of his shows and sent a congratulations card.

As powerful engagements go one stands out in my mind. The reason I remember it so vividly is because it happened on my mother's and Frank Sinatra's birthday, December 12th. It was on this date in 1976 when I attended the last and final performance of Elvis at the International Hotel in Las Vegas. Elvis left tickets for me with the security people. Can you imagine tickets for Elvis' show back then were only $22.50? Elvis' dad Vernon told me Elvis would be in Vegas for an 11-day gig, so I asked Vernon to set me up with tickets for the December 12th show because that date had a lot of meaning for me and if I could have the tickets for that night I would have one more reason to celebrate December 12th.

Both Elvis and Colonel Parker had a fondness for the International Hotel in Vegas. He liked to work the place and it was like a second home to him, especially since it was this hotel that gave him the chance to regenerate his career with the concert of July 31, 1969. I hadn't seen Elvis for a long, long time and it was something to see. He was dressed in one of his white jumpsuits with blue turquoise and a lot of gold accents that gleamed and shimmered and shined beneath the lights. The showroom with all of his fans waiting for Elvis was like one large living thing, an anxious thing. The air was scented with anxiety and anticipation and holiday cologne. I could hear small talk, nervous laughter, the sizzle of anticipation and there was muted contemplation, all waiting for Elvis. The audience was black, brown, white and all shades of color in between, all the colors that makeup an international audience from around the world.

Most of the fans assembled in the showroom were in business-attired outfits that were suited for a night out in Las Vegas. Women were wearing furs, diamonds and stiletto heels. Men were wearing three-piece suits; some were in black and white dinner jackets. When it was all over I could only rate his performance as spectacular and electrifying. Incidentally, the young tall blond on my arm was seeing Elvis for the first time and like all women she fell in love with him right then and there. She leaned into me and said she loved his dark hair hanging down in his eyes. I didn't tell her that Elvis dyed his hair, it wasn't public knowledge. He was dying his hair that signature jet black for years. Originally, his hair color was dishwater blond until maybe he finished his first movie 'Love Me Tender' in 1956. Following that movie, Elvis began having his hair dyed that signature color which everybody recognized.

Since I last saw Elvis he had lost a lot of weight. He was trimmed down and looked really sharp and lean up there on the stage. His performance was remarkable that night. As I watched him on stage I remembered that he told me how he preferred a live audience rather than his movie roles. He didn't think his work in films were the greatest. He said, "Brad, do you know what's worse than seeing a bad movie? The only thing worse than seeing a bad movie is working and acting in a bad movie." He thought he was typecast in his roles. Elvis did 32 movies, but one of his favorites was 'Viva Las Vegas' co-starring Ann-Margret. Out of the 32 movies he did he told me he could count on one hand the number of those he himself liked. "I'd rather do the movies where I can sing. I wish my producers would stop trying to make me into another James Dean playing dramatic roles. That's not me. I'm not up for that. I like the music roles," he said.

During the show I waved to Colonel Parker who was in his private booth with his girlfriend, Loanne. I mouthed thank you to acknowledge the tickets. He nodded and waved. Also in the Colonel's booth was Mel Sherman, who I found out after the performance was the Vice President of RCA Records who went on to become Chairman of the Board of Sony Records. Only in America, right? Some people have all the luck. As I looked around the audience I spotted Elvis' new squeeze Ginger Alden. At that time she was 21 years old. Yep, Elvis and I liked them young. We used to joke about dating ladies 12 and 14 years younger than ourselves, sometimes even younger.

Speaking of young things, there was a young good-looking lady that Elvis dated briefly while he was working in Las Vegas. She was the youngest showgirl working the Las Vegas strip at the time, only 17 years old. It was 1968. She came in from Colorado Springs, Colorado. According to her one of her idols was Ann-Margret. She wanted to dance and thought Las Vegas would be a place to show off her talents. Elvis saw her dance and began a brief hook up with her. He also encouraged Cassandra to chase after a singing career. She went on to carve out a special niche in show business for herself. Cassandra Peterson, better known to her fans now as Elvira, Mistress of the Dark, eventually hosted her own horror film television show in Los Angeles and did some movies. It never ceases to amaze me how show business has its twists and turns for those in it. One day I'm talking to someone like this 17-year-old who's dancing her butt off and a few years later I'm back home in California and see her on television with her own show. Nice girl, she worked hard for what she accomplished. I'm proud of her.

Elvis' current lady was a cutie. She was sitting with Elvis' dad Vernon and Wayne Newton. I waved to Vern and mouthed thank you, to let him know I appreciated the tickets. Wayne? Well, that's another story. I personally always believed he was on a constant ego trip and failed to recognize musicians and groups that ran into him on the way up, so I ignored him.

That 1976 show was the last time I ever saw Elvis. I can remember the evening I got the news he had died, it was a hot, lazy August night in 1977. I was visiting relatives in Pennsylvania who I hadn't seen for about 30 years. Lou Rawls, a friend of mine who I had performed with in southern California and Las Vegas, had an engagement in a nearby town and he arranged for me to have tickets to his show. I took my half niece Lana to see Lou. After the performance we were

Cassandra, (aka) (Elvira- Mistress of the Dark).
Elvis dated her in the 60's. She was a great dancer
and was the youngest showgirl (17 years old) in Las
Vegas at the time. She's a great talent.

Cassandra, (Elvira), dancer~singer, movie star and television personality. Brad, knew her in the 1960's when she was performing as a showgirl in Las Vegas, Nevada. She was a neat person.

driving home when an announcer on the radio interrupted the music and declared "Elvis is dead." What a shock, damn it. I'll always remember that August 16th night, it seemed unreal. I could hardly believe what I heard. When I returned to southern California I contacted Vern Presley and offered condolences from me and mom, telling him to pass them on to everyone in the Presley family.

Two more years went by and in 1979 I again heard from Vernon. It was a few days before my 43rd birthday a parcel was delivered. It was a gift from Vernon. It was a large framed drawing of Elvis and it had two brass plates attached. One read 'Presented to Brad Evans, a gift award for his work and friendship through the years, 1979', the other read 'To Brad, a good friend and entertainer. Always, the Presley Family, Friend, Vernon, 1979.' I've always assumed that Vern was disposing of some of Elvis' possessions following his death and out of all the gift items the family gave to friends Vern directed this one to me. I consider that gift one of my favorite pieces of entertainment memorabilia. It's been hanging on my wall since I received it.

As the years go by I can see many of the friends and musicians that I work with and who worked with Elvis leaving us for the big casino in the sky. In August 2004, a musician friend, Al Dvorin, was killed in an auto accident in California. I saw him just three days earlier. Christ, he was here in Vegas at the Aladdin doing a gig. For those that ever saw Elvis perform live they would know of Al, even though they never met him. Whenever an Elvis live performance ended his fans always heard someone say "Elvis has left the building." Well, that was Al. He started spouting that phrase during Elvis' comeback performance at the International Hotel in Las Vegas on July 31, 1969 and Al used that signature concert call at all of Elvis' concerts since.

Gift-To Brad, From Vemon Presley, Elvis'
step-dad,-1979

Brad and Lana-1977
Belle Vernon, Pennsylvania
The day Brad learned Elvis died..

At the time of Al's death, I would estimate he was about 81 or 82 years old. The same year Hank Garland, a super great guitarist, who I and Elvis both worked with, passed away. We used to jam together over the years. He was a legendary country rock guitarist. He'd not only perform with Elvis, but also with the Everly Brothers, Roy Orbison, Patsy Cline, Charlie Parker and many other entertainers, like country greats Brenda Lee, Mel Tillis, Marty Robbins, Hank Williams, Jr. and Boots Randolph. Hank even jammed with jazz great George Shearing. Some of the Elvis hits he worked on were 'Little Sister' and 'Big Hunk of Love'. He wound up working with Elvis from 1956 to 1961. He was a Nashville favorite. Hank died when he was 74 years old. His last years were spent trying to collect music royalties from the record companies and talking to producers about a movie about his life. It's too bad the movie didn't come to pass before he died. I would bet big money that it would have been a smash hit.

09

My Time With the Rat Pack

It was January 29, 1960, one day before my birthday, when Frank Sinatra, Dean Martin, Sammy Davis, Jr. and the rest of the Rat Pack were booked into the Sands Hotel Casino. Frank always carried two or three of his regular musicians with him, they were piano player Bill Miller and Al Viola, guitarist. Bill had been playing piano with Frank for close to 50 years. He was playing in the lounge at the Desert Inn Hotel back in 1951. Apparently, Frank was having trouble finding piano players around this time and a friend recommended Bill to Frank and suggested he should listen to him play. Frank went to the Desert Inn Lounge, he listened, he liked what he heard and he hired him. Bill continued to be Frank's regular pianist and accompanied him around the world on his engagements. However, they had a falling out in 1978, but Bill was invited back in 1985. When Frank died of a heart attack in 1998 at 82 years old, Bill played the song 'One for My Baby and One More for the Road' at his funeral. Following Frank's death, Frank, Jr. hired Bill to play in his band.

Al, the guitarist, was raised in an Italian family out of Brooklyn, New York and like me played in the military band and formed a jazz trio while serving in the military. He played in the Army Band and I played in the Marine Corp Band, forming my trio, quartet and five-piece group. Al gained a reputation for his playing and like a lot of us did a lot of studio work on the west coast. He finally wound up playing for Sinatra and from 1956 through 1980 he was Frank's regular guitar man for 25 years. Al died in 2007 at 88 years old.

Besides these musical greats like Bill and Al who were Frank's regular band members, he would supplement and round out the band with other sidemen like myself who worked the Las Vegas strip. I got my chance to play saxophone and clarinet in Frank's band. He was great to work with. During one of our engagements I met Henry Wayne Hale, better known as Wayne, a bass player who used to work with Frank in his early young days. He always spoke well of Frank and said we current musicians were lucky to work with him. He would tell us a lot of neat stories about Frank's early days. The last I heard of Wayne he was in a nursing home in Ohio. He should be in his 90's today.

The Rat Pack did a lot of good comedy routines and the musicians got to play a lot of good tunes when we backed them up. Frank got along with all of his musicians very well, but he was a perfectionist and if you didn't play the music just right he got pissed off. But, hey, when there's talent; that should be expected. Overall, he was a good guy. There were many times the band really didn't know what he was going to do because he would sometime ad lib from the program and do a joke or comedy bit that wasn't scripted in the act. When he was appearing in Las Vegas he and a few of us musicians would go out to grab something to eat. One of his favorite places for a quiet getaway in the '60s was the Green Shack. It was a family-owned business owned by the McCormick family and was sort of a historical landmark restaurant. The place was off the beaten track and the McCormick family operated it for decades. They served good food and Frank could count on not being bothered by anyone. It was a hangout for many personalities of the day.

Another place you could find Frank and a few of us musicians was at the Thunderbird Casino/Hotel on the Las Vegas strip, it was next door to the Sands where we worked. Most every professional musician and entertainer in town stopped in the

Brad's friends-The one and only Rat Pack at the Sands
Hotel/Casino, Las Vegas, Nevada.- 1960's.
Left to Right: Frank, Dean, Sammy, Peter and Joey.

Thunderbird on a regular basis for after-hour sessions. After-hour entertainers included Elvis, vocalist Sarah Vaughn and Ella Fitzgerald. It was a real hotspot in the '60s for an after-hours hangout. Anybody that was anybody used to stop in and the nice thing about the place was that most of the entertainers of the day that were appearing in Las Vegas knew each other, so this after-hours scene was a nice thing at the time for strip entertainers.

There were some good times and some funny interesting times had by all of us musicians with the Rat Pack while appearing at the Sands. I've seen Frank go to one of the tables and drop anywhere from $5,000 to $30,000 during a regular night of gambling. Gambling and losing that amount of money didn't seem to bother him one bit, he just shrugged his shoulders, lit a cigarette and walked away from the table. It was as if I would have played $10 and lost; no big deal. He may have owned a piece of the Sands Hotel, but you'd never know it to look at him. He never flaunted his piece in the place. Many people just thought he was an entertainer that worked there on a regular basis.

One night after the show I recall a fun time when Sinatra went out on the casino floor, walked up to a black jack table, tapped the dealer on the shoulder and told him to take a break. There were no ifs, ands or buts about it, the dealer nodded yes and left the table. The pit boss then sent the customers who were playing at the table to another table and Frank stood in the dealer's spot and began dealing cards to the rest of the Rat Pack, Dean Martin, Sammy Davis, Jr. and Peter Lawford. Customers were in awe, they loved it. There was Frank dealing black jack hands to the rest of his buddies. The Rat Pack was having a ball, they were joking and clowning around and ribbing Frank. The table and the people watching were in stitches.

The Rat Pack was so popular in the '60s, especially at the

Top: Sammy Davis, Jr. & Kaye Stevens on T.V. show January, 1967. Kaye worked frequently with the Rat Pack crew. Bottom: The Rat Pack on stage.

Sands, they could do most anything they could dream up and get away with it. When they pulled stunts like taking over the gambling tables the patrons loved their antics. Las Vegas had an entirely different atmosphere, a different feel in those days. It was a good time then. The people and the casino owners and managers had a different attitude. It was a fun, freewheeling time for Las Vegas. Yes, we had the mob and there were exceptional entertainers constantly appearing in most of the strip hotels and there was most any type of music anyone could want and see performed in any hotel lounge in the town. Nowadays, I would venture to say that there's no entertainer that could get away with taking over a black jack or crap table for their own use.

The Sands in the '60s was a moving and shaking place for anyone that wanted to be seen and the customers knew they could expect to be entertained. Frank and his crew were so popular that no matter who was appearing there if any of the Rat Pack walked onto the stage at any time they could take over the entire show and they often did just that. They would suddenly appear out of nowhere and ask the artist or the band on stage if they could sit in and they did. It was great, great times.

Kaye Stevens

We also had a female regular that frequently appeared with the Rat Pack. Singer and actress Kaye Stevens was a favorite of Frank's and she performed with the group a number of times through the '60s and '70s. She was a good singer. I mean she had to be or Frank and the Rat Pack would have never let her crash their party to perform with them.

Kaye was only four years older than me and she and I were on the save wave length when it came to music. We had a lot in

Frank at the Sands Casino/Hotel, Las Vegas, NV-1966

The famed Rat Pack-Brad worked with them in the 1960's. From Left to Right: Frank Sinatra,Dean Martin, Peter Lawford, Joey Bishop and in center is Sammy Davis, Jr.

Left to Right: Frank Sinatra, Peter Lawford, Dean Martin
Outside the Sahara Hotel/Casino, Las Vegas, Nevada
1960's.

common. She was brought up in the same area of Pennsylvania that I was. Kaye was born Louise Stevens in Pittsburg then her family moved to Cleveland where she began as a teenager playing drums and singing. She was a frequent guest on the Johnny Carson Show. In fact, Johnny's sidekick discovered Kaye while she was on a gig in New Jersey. She got her really big break when she was playing the lounge at the Riviera Hotel in Las Vegas. Debbie Reynolds was appearing in the main showroom but became ill and couldn't go on stage. Kaye filled in for Debbie and shazam, she became an instant star. Kaye also performed with the Rat Pack at Caesar's Palace. She also performed solo at Caesar's where I played sax behind her. We also worked together on a couple of USO concerts with Bob Hope in the Los Angeles area.

She did a number of shows with the Rat Pack on television in the '60s and went on to act in movies where she won a Golden Globe nomination in 1964 for 'The New Interns'. She also did a lot of game shows that were popular in the '60s and '70s and became a regular on 'Days of Our Lives' in the mid and late '70s.

Sinatra made no bones about letting the band know he was mobbed up. He half jokingly told us, "If anyone messes with me, my friends or my band, they'll wind up with no kneecaps." Following one of the Rat Pack's appearances in 1967, Sinatra told us musicians that he was going to give up working the small rooms in the near future and go for the large showrooms using big bands for his backup. It was about September that year when Frank signed a contract with Caesar's Palace Hotel. It was a good place for him to move because he and his friends knew that Caesar's had mob interest and the Cosa Nostra would treat him well. When Frank signed the contract with Caesar's it was reported to be a $3 million deal and that was a lot of money in the '60s. I thought hey, why not. The mob could afford the money and they were getting Frank. It was a winner for Caesar's.

I have memories of the day Frank signed on with Caesar's Palace. His then wife, Mia Farrow, had lost maybe $20,000 at the tables at the Sands. Frank became angry, but I'd say irate would be more like it. He bought $50,000 in chips and went to the tables and tried to win back the $20,000 his wife lost, big, big, big mistake. In less than an hour he had lost $50,000. Wow! In all the time over the years I had occasion to work with Sinatra, he very seldom mentioned his wife Mia or discussed anything about his marriage to her. All I ever heard him say was, "I was 51 years old when I married her and she was 21." The marriage only lasted a year and he divorced Mia in 1967. Could it be the large gambling loss contributed to the divorce? Who knows, but I bet it was a big issue.

The incident with the big gambling loss didn't stop there. Billionaire mogul Howard Hughes came into Las Vegas, bought up, owned and operated a number of hotels on the Las Vegas strip and the Sands was one of them. When Hughes heard of the losses by Frank and his wife Mia, he immediately shut down Frank's credit line. When Frank got wind of Howard Hughes cutting off his gambling credit he retaliated by trashing his hotel room at the Sands. He even commandeered a golf cart and rode it around the casino floor. When a casino manager tried to intercede and calm him down, Frank threw a large bunch of his gambling chips into the manger's face. Well, suffice to say, that didn't go over too well with the casino manager, so he hauled off and smashed his fist into Sinatra's face knocking out some of Frank's teeth.

A few days later, after all the ruckus cooled down, some casino executives floated the rumor that the entire fiasco was planned so that Frank could break his contract with the Sands Hotel. If anybody bought that line I have a bridge I'd like to sell them. Preplanned? No way. I think Frank just lost his temper and went ballistic when Howard Hughes cut his gambling credit line. After all that and even though Frank signed on with Caesar's Palace, he still continued to appear at the Sands Hotel.

Another incident worth mentioning is when Mr. "S", a moniker that some of us musicians used when addressing Sinatra, approached the casino entrance with famed singer, Billy Eckstine, at 2:30 in the morning, who was scheduled to appear at the Sands. A security guard greeted both with, "Good morning, gentlemen, how are you?" The guard pointed at the entrance telling Sinatra, "You can go through, but your friend will have to use the rear entrance, around back." Frank became unglued. He told the security guard, "I want you to call upstairs and get Jack down here, right now, not later, but right now. I don't care what time it is, or if he's sleeping, in the shower or with a woman, get him down here now. Not later, now. Tell him I want to see him."

The guard called upstairs and a few minutes later the mobbed up official stepped off the elevator. He was standing there with a sleepy-eyed look, wearing his jammies, a bathrobe, and slippers. With a gravelly, gritty, gruff, greeting he asked, "What can I do for you, Mr. Sinatra?" Frank looked him in the eye and said, "Billy's to be allowed to walk in the same entrance as me or any other white person. Do you understand? If Billy's not allowed to walk with me through the same door, you can forget about my shows over the next few days, and you can refund all the tickets for the sold out house." Frank continued, "As of today and anytime in the future, as long as I work here, any black person coming into this casino will be allowed to use the same entrance as a white person."

The honcho apologized to Sinatra and told the security guard to let Eckstine proceed. Frank had a knack of getting his way. The mob guy then shuffled off toward the elevator knowing that if Sinatra cancelled his gig, the casino would take a big hit and lose big bucks. It wasn't too long following that incident at the Sands and many major casinos in Vegas followed suit and allowed colored people to use the same entrance as white people. You can bet Frank had an impact on casino bosses.

While traveling between Las Vegas and California doing my off and on work with Sinatra it was clear he was having trouble with the Nevada authorities, particularly the Nevada Gaming Commission. The Rat Pack, some friends and a few of us musicians knew that it was no secret Frank had an affiliation with the mob and that he knew many of the family members on the east coast as well as the wise guys operating out of Las Vegas during the '50s and '60s. It didn't bother us musicians because many of us had worked for the mob establishments through the years and they treated us great. There came a time when a lot of pressure from the Nevada authorities, politicians and others, who I believe had their own agenda, backed Frank into a corner and forced him to sell his interest in the Sands Hotel. They exposed his mob ties, which up until that time was pure speculation. But the funny thing was, even though Sinatra sold his interest in the Sands, he continued to work the place and, as always, still packed a crowd of standing room only capacity.

I was sorry to see him lose his interest in the Sands. When the topic of the Sands would come up in conversation it was clear he was still bitter over having to give up his interest in the place. He used a string of foul words to describe some of the politicians and those that tried to embarrass him and expose his mob ties. I recall him saying, "Someday those same people that did me in will get theirs." I had no doubts that someday, somewhere those people that did him wrong would get what they deserved. If you were around Frank for any length of time you picked up on the fact that he'd do what he said and most always followed through on his promises.

It was a pleasure working with Sinatra. December 12th was always an important day for me. One reason was that it wasn't only Frank's birthday, but it was also my mother's. When Frank found out that mom's birthday was the same as his, they would often reminisce about the old days in New York City. Mom didn't know him then in 1940, but she told me stories about seeing Frank ice skate at Rockefeller Center while she was skating there. According to Frank and mom, he would sing for drinks and lunch at the Center just so he could be seen. Frank described those early '40s as some of his lean years. He would laugh it up with mom and they would talk about those days when he was getting his start. This guy was a gentleman. An example that comes to mind is whenever I was hired to play with the band at a party or at one of his birthday bashes, he made it a point to always ask me to give mom his regards and make sure I wished her a happy birthday for him. That is class. I had a lot of respect for him because of his birthday greetings to ma. It's little things like that which made him the person he was.

When Frank would talk about his early years he mentioned his turmoil with his MGM film contract in 1950 because of his affair with movie actress Ava Gardner. I guess the studio gave him a lot of grief over Gardner. Frank said his career was so bad from 1949 through 1953 his own agent at MCA Talent Agency dropped him. It was also during this period of time his radio show had been dropped and some of his concerts in New York City went over like a dud. He said he was angry about MGM Films releasing him from his contract, especially when he was only 34 years old and in his prime. He married Ava Gardner in 1951, but they separated a few years later and finally divorced in 1957.

Frank said he lost his voice in the late 1940s and early '50s because of a vocal cord hemorrhage. According to him, he was feeling down at this time in his life and actually attempted suicide by using pills and booze. For one, I'm glad the pills and booze didn't work because he got his voice back and he went on a roll. He climbed back with a number of movies in the '50s and '60s such as the 1953 film 'From Here to Eternity' and the 1955 film 'The Man with the Golden Arm'. I remember seeing that film with my band member, friend Ernie Carson, in Portland, Oregon. Little did I know at that time that one day I would be playing sax and clarinet in a band backing Frank.

There was one incident I remember when Frank was celebrating his birthday at The Compound, which was Sinatra's home located in Rancho Mirage, California. It was one of the very few times I had occasion to be invited to play at The Compound. I was really impressed. I've never seen a place like it. In addition to the main house it had guest bungalows and it even had one bungalow named The Caboose and that's what it was, a converted train caboose. Frank really loved trains, all kinds of trains, especially electric trains. Next to The Caboose bungalow there was an old train and some railroad memorabilia and a house that contained nothing but electric trains. There were shelves lining the walls of probably thousands of antique electric train cars. In the center of the room there were about eight or nine trains that were running all at the same time. They even made train noise and puffed out smoke. It was amazing. He loved electric trains.

While at The Compound a few of us regular band members that often worked with him and the Rat Pack crew of Dean Martin, Joey Bishop, Sammy Davis, Jr. and Peter Lawford, who was a relative of President Kennedy's family who was the political connection for the Rat Pack, were all there. Dean and Sammy began to cut up and they took Frank aside and took some of his birthday cake icing and blobbed a spot on Frank's nose, forehead and cheeks. Then Dean and Sammy standing on either side of Frank kissed him on the cheek and licked off some of the icing. Frank busted up. He took the joke very well and everyone at the party was cracking up. I would bet a million dollars though that no one else in the world could have lobbed cake icing on Frank Sinatra's face and gotten away with it other than his buddies in the Rat Pack.

I recall the time Frank announced he was going to retire, it was 1971. However, he didn't really follow through with retirement and returned to the circuit to perform in a number of concert tours. The concert tours began to take a toll on him. Those of us musicians that had worked with him over the years began to notice that his voice began to break and come apart during his '70s concerts. In 1976 he married Barbara Marx, widow of Zeppo Marx, one of the famed Marx Brothers. Maybe it was because he missed the spotlight that he again teamed up with friends Dean Martin and Sammy Davis, Jr. to perform in multi-city tours. As I watched him perform in these tours, I felt a little sad because I thought his voice was getting worse and it appeared he had some memory lapses and had difficulty remembering the words to the songs. I would have liked to have seen him bow out of show business well before those final tours.

Frank had his share of medical problems moving into the twilight years of his life, but like any show biz trooper he kept them mostly to himself and trudged forward. In the late '80s, somewhere around 1986, he had surgery to remove part of his intestines. Then came the ravages of chronic heart disease, kidney disease, bladder cancer and dementia. Frank's last performance was in 1994, about four years before he died. Frank died on May 14, 1998 at the age of 82, as a result of a heart attack. On his tombstone there couldn't be a more fitting epitaph. It reads...*The best is yet to come!*

Here's a man that began his career when President Herbert

Hoover was in office, a man who hit his peak in the 1950s and finished up his career when President Clinton was in office, which says a lot. His powerful longevity as a major talent spanned the decades. As one of the many musicians that had the pleasure of knowing Sinatra and breathing the same air as him, I know he'll be missed but I also know that Frank left a very rare indelible mark on show business around the world. This beloved icon, my friend, will always be the chairman in my eyes.

Dean Martin

Dean was a real cut-up when he wanted to be. Here is a guy that played an inebriated airhead to the hilt. In real life Dean drank fruit juice and apple juice, instead of those Martini's he sloshed down on his television show or in the Rat Pack skits. Dean was an all-around great guy. The entire Rat Pack was a class act. They had the class, talent and style who took their attitude to the nth degree. It was a pleasure just to be a part of the music in the background while they were performing. I have a lot of good memories working with these guys.

I was watching television years after Frank and Dean died, the movie was about Dean Martin and Jerry Lewis' life. It covered about 10 years of the Martin and Lewis years. I watched the movie and thought it was a bunch of gobblygook. The story line only punched up Jerry's side of the comedy duo. The movie was a shallow dull offering in my opinion. My memory of Dino was that of a much better person than they depicted in the movie. He was someone who had talent equal or better than Lewis. After seeing the movie, a flood of memories came rushing back.

I remember the first time I met Dino, Frank and the Rat Pack in 1960 at the Sands Hotel in Las Vegas, Nevada. I was a

Dean Martin "Dino". Brad worked with him and the Rat Pack in the 1960's in Las Vegas, Nevada.

Top: Dean Martin and Frank Sinatra. Mid 1960's. Bottom: Dean Martin Mid 1960's.

Dean Martin and Lucille Ball, television and movie
star and comedianne . Las Vegas, Nevada, 1960's.
Brad worked for both of these extraordinary talents.

musician, so I'd been hired to play saxophone and clarinet with the band and continued to play with the band off and on for a number of years. I came to know the Rat Pack fairly well— Frank, Dino and Sammy were a musician's friend and treated all of us in the band very well. As I thought about those good times in the 60s, it was like my own movie replaying in my head. I recall the times Dino told me about his life. He certainly had a lot of interesting stories.

His real name was Dino Paul Corsetti and many of us who worked with him called him Dino. He was born in Stubenville, Ohio in 1917 on June 7th. He was an all-around type regular person. Dino, like me, played drums when he was a teen. Me, I started with the clarinet and then the saxophone and then the bass and drums. He dropped out of school in the 10th grade to make money doing odd jobs. At one point in his life he was an amateur welterweight boxer using the name Kid Crochet. Dino also waffled back and forth between legal and illegal work. He told me about a time when he ran liquor across state lines during the prohibition era and a time when he sold illegal lottery tickets and worked as a bookie. He also worked as a car dealer and croupier in the large gambling spots in and around the Ohio area. He really had a colorful and interesting life. He was married three times and had four kids by his first marriage, three kids by the second marriage and he adopted a daughter Shasa, during his third marriage.

His entertainment career started when he was 17 years old, like me. He decided to change his name to Dean in 1940, while he was touring as vocalist with the Sammy Watkins Band. Dean was doing very well on his own even before he met Jerry Lewis. According to Dino, in 1943 he had an exclusive singing contract with MCA Records to sing at the Rio Bamba Room in New York. In 1944, he was given his own 15-minute radio show, "Songs by Dean Martin", which broadcast from New

York City. Dean got his start with Jerry Lewis in 1946 and they began making movies together in 1949. Between 1949 and 1956, these two guys were a popular comedy team. Dino did his last gig with Lewis at the famous Copacabana in New York City on July 24, 1956, which is when I was serving in the Marine Corp. Little did I know that four years later I'd be working with him. It's spooky sometimes how show business works. Entertainer's cross paths through life in mysterious ways.

After leaving Lewis and being back on his own, he renewed his singing career. He signed with Capital Records and did some great songs like, 'That's Amore' and 'Memories Are Made Of This'. By the time I was discharged by the Marine Corp in 1958, he was moving onward and upward. He was acting in the movies by now. That year he received critical acclaim for his portrayal with Montgomery Clift and Marlon Brando, in The Young Lions. Was Dino doing well on his own without Lewis? You bet. It was also about this time in 1958, when Dean began appearing in Las Vegas with his movie and Hollywood friends, the Rat Pack. They were a very close knit group of guys that impressed audiences so much that they expanded their Las Vegas skits and shows to the big screen.

It was 1960 when I first met the Rat Pack crowd. I was hired to play saxophone and clarinet with the band, backing up the zany, crazy magnetic group and it was this same year that they made the film 'Oceans' 11'. The only member of the Rat Pack I didn't really care for was Joey Bishop. From all the scuttlebutt floating around, this guy reminded me a lot of Jerry Lewis. He was arrogant, self centered, a person thinking only of himself and always on a big 24/7 ego trip. I thought his attitude stunk. How Frank and the rest of the Rat Pack put up with this guy is beyond me, but I was told that Frank liked Joey's dry sense of humor so he let him hang around. According to all the back stage gossip and from people that worked with Bishop, they said he was a hard person to work for. Joey told all the people who would listen, that he was better than Frank, Dean and Sammy and he made the Rat Pack what it was. Do you believe that? What an ego.

Dean took a really big hit in 1987, when his son Dino Paul Jr., from his second marriage, was killed in a plane crash during a military exercise. He took the loss hard and to many of us who knew him he never seemed the same after that. I saw him once after that incident. We met in a small restaurant and bar in Hollywood. I said hi to the bartender and as I did, he said Dean came in quite a bit and sat in the same booth but didn't talk to anybody. He said, "Maybe you can cheer him up." That day he looked depressed and down. He was sitting there in dark horn-rimmed glasses and a cashmere sweater. I walked over, said hi and sat with him. Dino returned the greeting and said, "I just feel lost and don't like talking to people I don't know, it's good to see you." I said, "How are you doing? How are you feeling?" "Not too good," he said, "I haven't been well lately, breathing problems, headaches and feeling sick a lot of the time. "

As we sat and talked over the next hour and a half he said he was thinking of doing another gig with Sammy and Frank. Dino said the show would be put together in the latter part of the year and the three of them would then tour around the country. When he talked about the tour his eyes had that old sparkle that was there when he used to perform live on stage in Vegas. We kicked around old times and I told him if he needed anything or if there was anything I could do to let me know. He smiled saying that just talking to a friend helped and today was a big help. Sure enough like Dino said, within the following year he was back with Sammy and Frank doing the tour we had talked about at the restaurant. The three of them toured during 1988 and 1989, but I guess those ailments he told me about less than a year earlier in that restaurant got the best of him.

Dino became ill on tour and was replaced by Liza Minnelli. I hadn't seen Dino since our restaurant meeting in 1987, but I did enjoy following his tour and career on television, it really brought back old times. At the same time I felt sorry for the group. I thought the pressure, the work and the travel on the tour by these three great talents strained them to their limits. They weren't spring chickens anymore and sometimes Frank's voice would crack and other times he would forget the words and lines of the songs, which were on the tip of his tongue years earlier. In my heart of hearts I was hoping the guys would close the tour and retire gracefully.

The Rat Pack days were really at their peak in the early 60s. They soon followed their Oceans 11 movie with Sergeants 3 in 1962 and Robin and the 7 Hoods in 1964. It was about this time that Joey Bishop finally got his when he pissed off Frank. Frank was preparing to film Robin and the 7 Hoods in 1963, a comedy about a bunch of gangsters. Bishop was signed to a contract for $75,000 for his appearance in the film. This was destined to be the Rat Pack's last film together. In fact, I still keep video copies of Oceans 11 and Robin and the 7 Hoods as a nostalgia memory boost. Anyway, Bishop signed the $75,000 contract but as the film was being prepared, Joey was quashed from the film. He was evicted and banished from the film and set because he got on the wrong side of Frank.

Joey was too demanding over too many times. He got on his high horse and demanded a lot of perks from Frank, which didn't sit well. Because of Joey's list of demands he became a big fat zero in the Rat Packs inner circle. The straw that broke the camels back, so to speak, was when Frank asked Bishop to fill in for a weekend gig at Cal-Neva Lodge in Lake Tahoe. Frank was part owner of the lodge, which was a popular spot for the entertainment scene in the 50s and 60s. Joey told Frank that if he was going to fill in for a weekend, he wanted Frank's personal plane to fly him to Tahoe and he wanted everything to be comp'ed for him and his entire entourage, which included his friends and relatives. He also wanted more money than he usually got for an appearance. Because of these outrageous demands, Bishop became a leper as far as the Rat Pack was concerned. Frank didn't want to hear the guy's name spoken. Joey was a nobody for more than a year, but eventually Frank forgave him but still harbored bad feelings towards him. Frank said that no one made him laugh like Joey when he used his off the cuff ad-lib jokes.

The re-introduction of Joey to the Rat Pack happened in 1964 when Frank was in Hawaii shooting the movie 'None, But the Brave'. Frank almost drowned during the shoot. He was caught in the undertow off the island of Kauai. What got Joey back in Frank's good graces, following the near drowning incident, was when he sent Frank a telegram that read, I thought you could walk on water. After that telegram, Bishop was welcome back into the Rat Pack. My dislike for Bishop grew stronger because his demanding attitude never changed. In my opinion, the Rat Pack could have done very well without him, but I guess there's no accounting for judgment. If it wasn't for Sinatra, Bishop would have been nothing.

Did Dino do a job as a solo performer without Lewis over the years? I would think so. Even years after the Lewis-Martin break up it was like pulling teeth to get Dino to talk about those 10 years he put in with Lewis. It was obvious he had a bad taste in his mouth for the man, but there were times when with a few friends he would occasionally discuss the situation. As best as I can recall from the stories and conversations we had about the comedy team, these two guys only appeared one other time in public together, which was 20 years after the 1956 break-up. According to Dino it was just a cordial thing and he said he was polite doing the appearance.

Dino's dislike for Lewis covered a lot of things. He said the reason their relationship came to an end was because of Lewis' big fat ego. The story goes that Lewis always wanted to be in the spotlight and on one occasion Lewis told Dino he could get by without him because he was the main person making up the Lewis-Martin team and he didn't need Dino. Wow! Besides all the Lewis ego trips and him trying to upstage Dino every chance he got and taking control of everything that had to do with the handling of the comedy team, Dino became fed up. Lewis told people that he was a perfectionist, but in reality it was nothing but Lewis' ego, that's what Dino said. He told some of us that Lewis wanted everything his way and if things didn't go his way and if he didn't get or receive the bulk of the attention, he became very angry and an unhappy person.

I could see this happening because the Dino I knew was an easy going laid back type of person who rolled with the punches. I heard Dino say things like hey, if things don't work out don't worry about it things will get better. Over the years I had the privilege to know Dino and he struck me as a person that was never in a big hurry and took most things with a grain of salt. If he liked you and you were lucky enough to be a friend of his he would help out when he could. He really had a neat attitude, but don't get me wrong because the other side of the coin I saw was, don't push this guy. It would be fair to say that he wouldn't be pushed to the wall. Dino had a rough background growing up and he could handle himself when and if he needed to. If people gave him trouble he wouldn't back away.

I liked Dino as a performer and a friend. He was a nice and generous person who like Frank and Sammy Davis Jr., had that special charisma and tons of class about him. This guy did well for himself, rising to the top by using nothing but his own talent and it is my opinion, he had nothing to regret or be sorry for in his life except maybe for the 10 years he spent with Lewis, who I visualize as a big ego tripping boob. I've personally never met Lewis, but after hearing some of the stories about his whims, dumb antics and attitude, I have a feeling I wouldn't like him.

Dino's death occurred on Christmas Day in 1995 from acute respiratory failure. Looking back, these great guys Frank, Dino and Sammy may be gone, but I'll always have the many memories they provided to a musician friend. I predict that it will be years, even decades before another group with the raw exceptional talents of the Rat Pack guys will come rolling down the pike.

Sammy Davis, Jr.

Sammy was an exceptional talent, one of a kind. He was a person that anyone in the entertainment business today couldn't duplicate or do what he did. He was a man who could go on a bare stage with nothing but a chair and give the audience a spectacular performance. He could sing. He could dance. He was a comedian, a movie actor and played an array of musical instruments. You name it and he could do it. He was a quadruple threat to any other entertainer.

Sammy was a heavy hitter with the Rat Pack. As to how he got along with people, I found him to not only be talented but humble and personable. After you met the man it was as if you knew him your entire life. He never used a pretense or tried to be an obnoxious person that flaunted his fame. Sammy was down to earth and I've always believed the reason for that was because of the tough times he had growing up while earning his bones. Being a musician himself, needless to say, he loved talking and working with musicians. He would get right down with the band members and jam with us frequently.

Over meals or during our rehearsal breaks he would talk

about his life and how tough it was. Here's a guy that never went to school while growing up. The Rat Pack knew and some of the musicians knew that Sammy never had one lick of schooling in his life. But just the way he came across and expressed himself to others, I got the feeling that he was proud of that. As a young boy, Sammy said he was dancing in the streets for pennies and nickels. He was brought up very poor but acquired so much talent from those early days of dancing in the dirt streets I would have to say he earned a Ph.D. in street smarts and talent, which he projected onto his audience. For a person that had zero education, he sure came a long way.

He became nostalgic one day and told of his recollections of his first ever television show. He remembered the incident like it was yesterday he said. He was 27 years old then and during those times in the 50s, television was just coming of age. It was 1952 when he was allowed to appear on the Eddie Cantor Television Show. He appeared with his father Sammy Davis Sr. and some other family members. Sammy was 11 years older than me so we could relate to a lot of the same things that were happening in the 50s.

I remember one occasion when the band was rehearsing at the Sands in Las Vegas. Sammy came in smoking a cigarette, wearing his fine jewelry and clothes and sat down to watch some of the dancers run through a dance routine only one time. After they finished he said, "Is that it?" He got up and left and then came back that evening for the show and did the routine to perfection. The guy could just look at a routine and have a total grasp of it without ever running through it himself. Sammy was a super talent and a kick to work with.

Peter Lawford

I thought Peter Lawford was a nice enough guy, but sometimes a little aloof. He also had some problems that were

A great Rat Pack talent-The incomparable, Sammy
Davis Jr., on stage.

Sammy Davis Jr. dancing on a table in his hotel room-May. 1966.

kept under wraps from the public. Lawford loved his booze and drugs. He used them quite extensively. According to some stories from Frank, there was a long standing feud between the two of them because Lawford had been dating movie star, Ava Gardner and Frank resented their relationship. The animosity went on for years. However, in 1954 when Lawford married into the Irish first family of America, the Kennedy Dynasty, his union with Patricia Kennedy, sister of then U.S. Senator John F. Kennedy, changed Frank's mind and Sinatra made the decision that the long running feud should end. This is where Peter Lawford's entrance to the Rat Pack began. Frank knew that Lawford had JFK's ear and Sinatra, being the staunch Democrat he was, began his Democratic campaign for Kennedy.

Peter had four children with Patricia Kennedy and became an integral part of the Kennedy clan and Frank was aware that Peter had influence within the Kennedy family. After Lawford became part of the famous Rat Pack he performed in Las Vegas and films with them, including 'Oceans Eleven' and 'Sergeants Three'. In fact, it was Lawford who brought the project 'Oceans Eleven' to Frank.

The Rat Pack gained super notoriety through their high-rolling comedy antics campaigning for John F. Kennedy's presidential election. My personal view of Lawford was that he was the forgotten member of the Rat Pack. He was there but seemed invisible to most people when the Rat Pack performed before their audience.

As a bit of trivia I should mention that Peter Lawford was the last person to speak to Marilyn Monroe before her death and he was the man who introduced Marilyn Monroe at Kennedy's Democratic Convention when she sang "Happy Birthday Mister President." Monroe and both Kennedy brother's had something going on between them and Lawford often acted as go between for Marilyn and the brothers. Lawford and Monroe were close confidants and Marilyn cried on his shoulder when conflicts arose between her, JFK and Robert Kennedy.

Lawford and his mother had a serious falling out when Lawford was being signed to a movie studio contract at the start of his movie career. Lady Lawford, who was well established in the elite social circles in the United Kingdom, stuck her nose in Peter's acting career and called the head of the studio telling him that her son Peter should be paid more money and that she was his personal manager, which was not true. The head of the movie studio said, no and refused to bend to Lady Lawford's demands. Lady Lawford then went off on a tangent, getting in the movie mogul's face and telling the man that her son was a loser and a no good, hoping the studio would not hire her son, Peter. When word got back to Lawford about his mother's interference in his career, he stopped talking to her and cut off all contact with her.

Lawford became a citizen in April of 1960. He prepared for this in time to vote for his brother-in-law JFK in the upcoming presidential election. When Lady Lawford found out her son, Peter, was pals with the Rat Pack she issued a bulletin in media circles saying, "I don't know why Peter associates himself with that Rat Pack crowd and that dried up piece of spaghetti, but I do like his singing, he is the villain of the piece." I guess Lady Lawford believed her son Peter was too good to be associating with the Rat Pack and that the Rat Pack was beneath her son's station in life. Can you imagine?

Another story about Lawford in the 60s, which came from Frank, was that he became angry with Lawford over a number of bad moves on Lawford's part. One incident happened in 1961 when Sinatra and Lawford had a falling out over brother-in-law Robert Kennedy's objections to Sinatra's alleged Mafia connections. The other major incident was when Lawford failed to use his ability to convince the Kennedy administration to get the president to stay at Frank's compound in Rancho Mirage, California, the "West Coast White House" as Sinatra sometimes referred to it.

While we were doing a gig at Frank's compound he told us about the scheduled presidential meet which fizzled out. Sinatra said the people who had written about it a number of times got it all wrong. The incident happened about a year after I met, and began working with Frank in 1962.

Frank said the media reported that the White House administration informed him, a few days in advance before the scheduled JFK meeting, that the president was cancelling his visit with Sinatra. According to Sinatra, those reports were a bunch of crap, and a lie. Frank told us that the cancellation came the same day he was expecting the Kennedys to arrive at his house.

As Frank tells it, he and a small group of guests who would be welcoming the Kennedy's that evening, were told the Kennedys would be a no show. His long time friend, Jack Entratter, the well-known icon of the Sands Hotel/Casino was with the welcoming committee. Also present was Entratter's ex-wife, Corrine, who was married to Entratter two times. Others on the invite list, who were waiting to greet the president, were actors, Kirk Douglas and Yul Brenner and song writer Sammy Cahn. Also waiting was Frank's wife, actress Mia Farrow.

The Entratter's were regulars at Sinatra's compound at Rancho Mirage. Frank and Jack went back to the days when Entratter hired him to appear at the Copacabana club in New York City. Entratter and Frank were such close friends that when Frank was at his lowest and was struggling to restart his career Jack allowed Frank to stay at the Sands and provided for him, basically carrying Frank on the cuff until he could get back on his feet.

A month or two prior to the president's scheduled visit, it was rumored that Frank planned to build a guest house for him, but Frank told us that was a bogus report. Another erroneous report in books and papers regarding the JFK incident was that Sinatra built a helipad for JFK's arrival, but in reality according to Frank, not true. Frank liked helicopters and would ride them to his home but had to give them up because people using the golf course complained his helicopter rides interfered with their golf game.

There was no advance call to cancel the visit, Frank said. The call came in from the White House the same evening he was expecting the Kennedy's to arrive. He slammed the phone down saying, "That fuckin' Bobby!" referring to Attorney General Bobby Kennedy, and he stormed out of the room. Clearly everyone waiting to greet the president was disappointed and hurt.

Sinatra did a lot of things to see JFK was elected. He even put together Kennedy's inauguration party. As if the cancelled visit by President Kennedy wasn't enough, Sinatra was hit with a second blow. The president stayed with actor/singer, Bing Crosby, who was a good friend of Frank, but a staunch Republican. Sinatra felt as though he was stabbed in the back and snubbed.

After these incidents Lawford might as well have dug his own grave. Sinatra was a nice guy but when anyone got on his bad side, look out! There would be hell to pay.

Lawford was ostracized by Sinatra and the two men never spoke again. Did Sinatra have power to make or break someone? You bet. Lawford never again starred in another major motion picture. He was slated to co-star in the movie "Robin and the Seven Hoods", with Frank, but the role was given to Bing Crosby instead.

Frank's long reach into the depths and bowels of the

entertainment industry relegated Peter Lawford spending the rest of his career guest-starring on TV shows such as Password, Laugh-in and other game shows as a relic of a past era. Lawford struggled with alcohol and drug abuse only to get worse as his life went on. He wound up at the Betty Ford Clinic in an attempt to recover, but knowing his story I would think this guilt-ridden man may never have really wanted to recover.

In his last waning years he would write letters to the late JFK in heaven. I guess his thinking in writing those letters to JFK would buy him an introduction into heaven by JFK. His ill health as a result of long-time alcoholism brought Lawford to his end on Christmas Eve, December 24, 1984, as a result of cardiac arrest, complicated by kidney and liver failure.

10

The 60's Coming To An End

Engelbert Humperdinck

While mom was recovering from her broken shoulder and arm, I was hitting the road again. Mom's injuries came about at work at Frito-Lay company. Working as a potato chip packer my mother tripped over a pallet holding cartons of chips. She fell, and in doing so some of the cartons dropped on top of her breaking her arm and shoulder. She was 69-years old at the time. Following the injury mom was off work for quite some time. I know she was in a lot of pain during her recovery but she wouldn't let it show.

It was 1969, I was playing sax at the Riviera Hotel in Las Vegas backing the legendary Engelbert Humperdinck. He had a great show. He was a Strip headliner in the late 60s. During this engagement he was using a female backup group called The Three Degrees. They did an excellent job and complemented Humperdinck's talents. The Humpster, which a lot of musicians called him in fun, and I, are the same age. Like me, he started his singing career when he was 17 years old. Maybe that's why I enjoyed working with him when he appeared in Vegas. Being from the same era we could relate when it came to music.

Engelbert is an interesting guy. He was born in India but grew up in England. After his military service, he began singing under the stage name of Gerry Dorsey, until his new manager Gordon Mills, who also managed Tom Jones, changed his name to Humperdinck, who was actually an old-time composer. After he changed his name to Humperdinck, he had his first big hit recording, 'Release Me' in 1967. During our gig at the Riviera, a recording company recorded the live performance. To my best recollection, the company later released the Humpster's performance in a packaged album. The audience loved the guy. In fact, not unlike singer Tom Jones, women used to throw their panties at him on stage. He was really a crooner. He worked his heart out during his live performances. He's a powerhouse on stage. With his rich voice, his looks and his talents, Engelbert's a triple threat to many other entertainers. When the Humpster's engagement ended I wouldn't see him again for 36 years, in 2005. After Humperdinck's gig in 1969, I took a job, playing sax with the Ray Charles Band. Ray was a gas to work with too. I wasn't the lead saxophone player but I didn't mind because I had the chance to play music with the great Ray Charles. How good is that? Ray worked up and down the Las Vegas Strip quite often and he was a great tourist draw. He was easy to work with. He knew exactly what he wanted to do with his music and did it. It was really an experience for me.

Following Ray's engagement I returned to my home base in California and began taking music jobs with local musicians, working with duos and trios playing everything from country western, rock and roll and dinner house dance music. I also filled in my time doing music studio work. It was about this time when I decided to consider some other career beside music. I wanted to live like a regular person rather than traveling around the county like a gypsy. Stability sounded good to me. I was 33-years old now and a career change at this time in my life seemed right.

I decided to go into law enforcement. I applied for a position with the Downey, California Police Department and I lucked out and got the job. I was there going on a year when I became injured in an accident on the job. I was laid up in the Downey Community Hospital for a month. My back was injured and the doctors at the hospital advised me to have surgery on my back to correct the injury, but I refused to have surgery.

Here it was at the start of the 70s, my back was injured and the doctors at the hospital continued to advise me to have surgery, but I still refused. By now my mother was back working her job at Frito-Lay. She was still working the swing shift from 3:00 p.m. to 11:00 p.m. and I tried not to bother her with my problems. I told mom that I would be out of the hospital soon and she shouldn't worry and there was no need for her to visit me in the hospital. One day the hospital brought another person into my room that also had back problems. The man, Norman, was accompanied by his wife and son. They introduced themselves and told me that Norman was in the tub taking a bath when his back went out, and he couldn't get up out of the tub. The paramedics were called to get him out of the tub and to the hospital. The nurses gave him pain medication to knock the guy out, but a few hours later he woke up and began to cry and moan in pain again.

This went on for a few days. When his wife Louise and son Lenn Lee would come to visit, they would apologize for Norman keeping me up with his loud screams of pain. On one of the family's visits to see Norman, there was this attractive young lady with Louise and Lenn Lee. They introduced me to Linda, Lenn Lee's cousin. She was a 20-year-old secretary. She brought cookies for Norman and during one of her cookie deliveries, she offered me one. Over the next week she began showing up with Norman's family during visiting hours. His family knew I was there alone and I had nobody visiting me, so Lenn Lee and Linda began coming over to my bed to visit with me. Linda began to bring me stuffed animals, magazines, candy and cookies when they visited. Norman was going to be scheduled for back surgery, so I knew he would be my roommate for quite some time.

Engelbert Humperdinck-The King of Romance Balladeers.
Brad played sax in the band backing him in Las Vegas, NV

Engelbert Humperdinck-Ballads on the beach.

Norman and his family became very friendly. They asked me to come over for dinner when I was released from the hospital. For the month I was in the hospital, I gained the Norman family as new friends. When I was released, Louise, Lenn Lee and Linda came to the hospital and told me to follow them home and have dinner with them. They lived in Whittier, California, a few miles from the hospital and it was only a hop, skip and a jump for me, so I told them I would come over to dinner.

Dinners with Norman's family became a regular routine and Linda would come over to their house whenever she knew I was going to be there. I went with the family to the hospital when they visited Norman and was there when he was released. When I was released from the hospital, I couldn't return to the Police Department due to my back injury and I had to make money to survive, so I did what I knew best—music. I began to take jobs playing drums with local bands in Southern California.

Lake Oswego Property

Shortly after I was released from the hospital, mom received a letter from an attorney in Lake Oswego, Oregon, very near Portland. The attorney submitted an offer to buy mom's vacant lot she owned in that city. She got the lot in the early 1950's when she purchased the house in Portland, Oregon. The purchase of the house also included a 2.19-acre lot as part of the deal. Mom had been paying taxes on the lot all those years and an attorney searched the records, found mom's name and contacted her. He said he had a client that wanted the land and offered her $1,800 for it. Mom and I talked the situation over. She said she was never going to return to Oregon, so maybe she should consider selling the parcel. I contacted the attorney and told him $4,000 would be a much better offer. My client is a farmer who wants to graze his cattle on the property, he said. My offer's a fair price.

Mom and I agreed to sell the lot and told him to send the paperwork. We sold it for the $1,800. What a bonehead move though. I came to regret the decision to sell the property because a few years after we sold the acreage, I found out that Lake Oswego turned out to be one of the most desirable places to live in the Portland area. It was a magnet for people that were well off and affluent. That 2.19 acres that we let go for $1,800 could have brought us a couple hundred thousand dollars. When mom got the property back in the early 50's, it was an excellent piece because it was situated close to the center of town and it was surrounded by four paved roads. What I should have done at the time if I was thinking straight would have been to call a real estate agent in the area and have an appraisal done, or better yet I could have taken a trip to Portland and drove out to Lake Oswego and checked out the property for myself. What do they say about hindsight? I goofed up on this one. I'd had my suspicions that the attorney wanted the property for himself and used a relative or a straw buyer to get the land. Hell, 2.19 acres could have supported a shopping center, a restaurant, a nightclub or a lot of other different ventures. Somebody made out like a bandit on this deal, and you wonder why people hate attorneys.

Linda

It was 1970, Linda was 20 years-old and couldn't get into the clubs I was working at, but I would see her at Norman's and she, her cousin Lenn Lee and I would go to drive-in movies, to the beach and out to eat. One night I heard a knock on my door and to my surprise Linda was standing there when I opened it. She had a gift box in her hand. She said I know you're getting

Brad and Linda-1971
Whittier. California

ready for work and I wanted to give you a little gift to wear at work. I invited her in, opened the gift and it was a tie. I pulled my old tie off and put hers on and told her I would wear it to work that evening. She smiled and scurried out to her car and left. A few weeks later she did turn 21 years old and came back to my house again while I was getting dressed for work. She asked me to take her to the club with me that night. As we stood there in the living room, I told her I was 14 years older than her and she would probably be bored sitting around a bar and listening to music.

Age was no problem. "I like you," she said. Before I knew it she kissed me on the lips and said she wanted to go with me. I kissed her back and caressed her until she melted in my arms. I got her clothes off and caressed her naked smooth, tight young body, making her hungry for the things that were yet to come. Afterward, laying there on the living room floor, she lay there sprawled out, breathing heavy and staring at the ceiling. I lifted myself up on one elbow, running my hand over her tummy. We both lay there in silence for what seemed like a long, long time. I whispered in her ear that I had to get to work and yes, she could come with me. That was the beginning of a three-year relationship. Linda lived with her parents and brothers and sisters a few miles away in the small town of Cudahy. Her mother was from a German or Irish background and her father was Hispanic. A few months into our relationship she moved out of her parents' home and found herself an apartment in Norwalk, California that was close to her work.

Mom Retires

In 1971 mom finally retired from Frito-Lay. It was a real problem getting Frito-Lay to pay mom's retirement. She always looked 20 years younger than her real age and when she hired into Frito-Lay she fudged on her real age, and when she filed for retirement the company said they weren't going to pay her retirement benefits. To prove her real age of 71 years old, I had to contact distant relatives that were still living and obtain affidavits stating mom's real age. I also had to furnish the old family bibles because when mom was born in Hamburg, Germany in 1899, there was no such thing as birth certificates being issued.

After months of searching and contacting relatives and gathering all the documentation, I sent it to the Social Security Administration. I even hired an attorney to contact Frito-Lay with a demand to pay mom's retirement benefits. Frito-Lay still refused to pay but eventually we got a judge to act as a mediator in her case. After the judge heard all sides and reviewed the documentation from the Social Security Administration stating they were satisfied that mom's age was truly 71, he wrote a Finding of Fact stating that mom was 71 years old when she filed for her retirement and she did complete more than 10 years of service with Frito-Lay. He said Mrs. Wilson is within her legal rights to lie about her age in order to get a job. He went on to say, any woman has a right to lie about her age and women do so every day for one reason or another. If those women do it without any illegal intentions, there's no problem with it.

The fight with Frito-Lay took more than a year but I eventually got mom's retirement finalized in her favor. With the judge's Order and the Social Security Administration's verification, Frito-Lay had to pay mom her pension. Her pension benefits payable for life was $117 a month. What a rip off. Mom gave 10 years of her life and her sweat to Frito-Lay, only to receive $117 a month. At the time that was a good pension but today that amount would only buy a couple tanks of gasoline for the car.

We Buy Mom a Mobile Home

After mom retired, we bought her a brand new doublewide mobile home. We went to the mobile home factory and had one built from the ground up. It was a comfortable mobile home with all the newest appliances included. We located a nice mobile park in Orange County in the City of Stanton. However, when the mobile home people did the set up, they screwed up and didn't hook it up right. During the first two weeks mom was in the home, she was complaining of severe headaches. I had the home inspected and rechecked and found that the setup crew didn't attach the vents properly, letting carbon monoxide leak into the house, making mom ill. The company came out and corrected the problem but I was angry and I considered suing them. I even went to nearby UC Irvine Medical Center and used their medical library to read up on everything I could about carbon monoxide poisoning. I spent every day there for a period of weeks. I outlined a case with all the supporting documents and contacted an attorney and gave him everything I had.

He said, "Your mom is 71 years old and because of her age, we can't get damages. Her work life is over but if your mom had died because of the carbon monoxide poisoning, then we would have a case."

What a jerk! I wanted to punch his lights out. The case couldn't get off the ground, so the matter went nowhere. At least mom was alive. God knows what would have happened if mom didn't tell me about her headaches, dizziness and fatigue.

Mom Has Surgery

A few weeks after mom settled into her mobile home, she required surgery. She had a bad case of stomach ulcers and Dr. Levi said surgery was the only recourse, so mom went under the knife at Stanton Hospital. Things should be okay now, right? Wrong. A couple of days later following mom's operation, Linda and I took her to dinner. We were having dinner at a coffee shop about 30 miles from her home. When we sat in a booth eating, mom said she felt something warm around her waist. She put her hand underneath her blouse, and her hand came back up with blood. I looked at her waist and saw the stitches that Dr. Levi sewed mom up with had come undone. I grabbed a handful of napkins and told mom to hold them against her abdomen. I told Linda to call Stanton Hospital, tell them what happened and to get Dr. Levi back to the hospital because I was bringing mom back in. Linda sat in the backseat with mom as I drove the 30 miles like a bat out of hell breaking all speed limits.

I also knew that if we were stopped, we would probably get a police escort to the hospital, which would even make the trip faster. With tires screaming and squealing, I drove the car into the hospital emergency driveway. Dr. Levi was waiting. He immediately took mom into a room and began working on her. After treating mom, he came back out to talk to Linda and me. "You got her to the hospital in the nick of time," he said. "She lost a lot of blood and she needs a transfusion. I'll keep her overnight and monitor her. In the meantime, go home and get some sleep. Come back tomorrow morning. There's nothing more that you can do here."

The next morning Linda and I returned to the hospital and Dr. Levi told me, "We just about lost her last night, Margaret went into shock and I worked on her for about six hours to save her, now she's out of danger but I'm going to keep her in the hospital for another week."

Doctor Levi called mom Margaret. My mother, born with the first name of Mary had been using the name of Margaret Wilson ever since she ran away to New York City to get away from my abusive father in the late 1930s. Mom didn't want my dad to find her after she ran away so she began using the name of Margaret Wilson. She said the name also fit in well with her fashion modeling career. She thought the name sounded much better than Mary or Margaret Kuhns. Mom continued to use the first name of Margaret throughout her lifetime.

"Can we see mom?"

"Yes, but she's medicated and is out of it," he said.

Linda and I crept silently into mom's room and saw that she was sleeping. I asked the charge nurse on duty to give mom a message when she wakes up. I told the nurse to tell mom that I was here and I would call her later that evening. When I talked to mom later that evening on the phone, she told me she felt a little better. A week later, Linda and I checked mom out of the hospital and took her back to her place.

Mom Marries Roy Cline

Once mom was out of the hospital, she recuperated very quickly. She picked up her activities where she left off. While she was still employed at Frito-Lay, mom had been corresponding with different men through pen-pal letters. Mom belonged to pen-pal clubs for years and one of the men that she was writing to proposed marriage. The man she met was 85 years old, 14 years older than her. The man, Roy Cline, said he would buy a motel in the small town where he was living and they could work together. Mom accepted his proposal and decided to marry him, so mom was off to New Mexico just outside Albuquerque. Mom married Roy Cline in 1971. I told her I would sell her mobile home and put the money in the bank for her.

I Give the House Back to the Bank

Mom and I were trying to sell her house in Compton for

about a year without any luck. The area was going downhill fast. A few years earlier the Watts riots occurred and our house was only a few miles from Watts. Following the riots, the cities of Compton, Lynwood, Willowbrook and other nearby cities went to pot. The cities became high crime infested areas. There was a lot white flight occurring in those cities after the riots and real estate values plummeted. They dropped like a rock.

To get out from under the house payments and the neighborhood, I called the savings and loan manager and asked him to take the house back without the obligation of mom or me having to make payments on the place. The bank manager flatly refused. I told him that I was going to give his bank a choice. When he asked what that was, I said, "You can take this house back and sell it on your own or have it trashed by vandals. If your bank doesn't want to sign the papers releasing me or my mother from any future house payments, I'll walk out and disappear. You'll never find me to collect any payments and you can be sure that once I'm gone from the property, within two weeks thieves and vandals will move in and destroy the home, and possibly even burn it down."

He said, "You wouldn't do that."

"Watch me," I said, "if you reject my offer, I'm out of here within the next couple of days and your bank will have nothing except maybe scorched earth where the house once set. Let's see if you can sell it then."

The bank manager said, "Mr. Kuhns, give me two weeks to talk to the Board and I'll get back to you."

"Okay two weeks," I said. I didn't have to wait two weeks. I received a call from him within three days and he said he would send me an agreement to sign the property back over to the savings and loan, with mom and I being free and clear of any future payment obligations. I read over the agreement, signed it and within a week I was out of the house and off the property.

I Buy a Mobile Home

Once I was free from the house in Compton, I decided to buy a large doublewide 24 x 36 mobile home. It was a beauty. Linda and I went to the factory where the homes were built. We picked out a floor plan, chose the curtains, rugs and the best appliances we could find and had the homebuilder install them. I convinced Linda to move in with me. Her parents weren't too happy about that arrangement. They couldn't say too much because Linda was her own woman now. Her parents told Linda that a musician wasn't someone to get serious over because there was no security or steady job to support her. The difference in ages didn't help either. My being 14 years older than Linda just added fuel to the fire to their argument as to why she shouldn't see me. Linda moved in with me at Forest Gardens Mobile Community, which was located in Forest Hills in El Toro, California. The community was rated one of the best in Southern California.

During this time I also returned to Vegas to work the Fremont Hotel for a few nights to reunite with my friend Frankie Laine. He wanted me to back him up on a few of his shows. Since we were friends since 1953, I gladly accepted his offer. That gig with Frankie was my last gig on the road as far as I was concerned. Since I've got Linda, I wanted to stick to music jobs in our local area and stop all of the traveling roadwork. I wanted someone to come home to every night, so I concentrated on playing music around the local area in Southern California. Studio work for musicians was getting slim. It slowed down quite a bit, so I gave that up and played drums with a number of different groups, piano players and organists.

Linda and Me

Linda and I had a good arrangement and were getting along fine. She woke up in the early morning to get ready for her job and on her way out the door, she would kiss me and tell me to go back to sleep. She would then call me every day about 10:00 a.m. to make sure I was up. We'd often meet during the day on her lunch break. Once we were settled in the new mobile home, I began playing drums with a country and western group around Orange County. Our group played 50s, 60s and 70s music. Generally after Linda finished work, she would come by the club and patiently sit and wait for me to finish up.

We also had little mini getaways and places to meet before I would go to work. I remember a hotel called Rochelle's on Lakewood Boulevard near the Long Beach Airport. It had a coffee shop attached, so Linda would get off work, drive to the motel and we would have dinner there. Afterwards we would go to the motel room we had booked up earlier, and we'd spend time in the room making love until it was time for me to go to work. Other times we would go to Las Vegas for a couple days of fun and games. She and I would go to Las Vegas quite often. It got to be a weekly thing.

I recall working the Morris Steakhouse, a small steakhouse at Alhambra, California and on the weekends, she would come to the club before I finished up for the night, and after closing time we would drive to Las Vegas. We would stop for the night in Barstow at a motel we used on prior trips where we would have our love fests at 3:00 or 4:00 in the morning, grab a few hours sleep, have breakfast at a coffee shop on the way out of town and drive into Vegas. In Vegas we would lie around the pool at the Flamingo Hotel on the Strip, see a few shows and spend time gambling. These little getaways kept our relationship fresh.

Brad's number one lady in the early 1970's:, -Linda..

Chuck Norris

In 1972 everything was going pretty good. I had Linda and we had a home that was paid for. I was staying close to home with my music rather than running around the country and Linda had her secretary job to keep her busy. I thought the two of us had a pretty good life going for ourselves. I was playing drums with county singer and guitarist, Jim Kent, and Dale, a bass player. Jim was a good country singer and our trio was receiving good reviews. One afternoon our band had an audition at a club on Ventura Boulevard in the San Fernando Valley. Jim suggested we stop for lunch. After lunch we still had a little time to kill, so Jim said that a friend of his worked a couple of blocks down the street and he wanted to stop off and see him.

He told me that I'd appreciate meeting his friend because the guy had his own karate studio on the Boulevard. That's when he told me his friend's name. It was Chuck Norris. Jim told me Chuck was a world champion kickboxer and he had his own studio where he taught karate classes. At the time, Chuck wasn't the big movie star that he is today. His fame came later. The studio was a nice clean neat place. It had floor mats running from wall to wall. When we entered, I guess a bell or buzzer sounded in the back room to let someone know someone came in. Out of the back room came this man dressed in a karate gi (pronounced gee). He wasn't a tall man but he looked solid and full of muscle. Jim greeted Chuck and introduced me. We shook hands and Jim and Chuck caught up on old times. Jim told Chuck I practiced karate. "What style," he asked.

"Kempo Kung Fu," I said. He smiled and half jokingly asked me if I had time for a fast workout. Jim nodded and said go ahead. We have time before the audition. I thought you would enjoy meeting Chuck, so why not? Do it. I said okay. I removed my shoes and socks and stepped onto the mat. I bowed at

Chuck, he returned the bow and we began a workout while Jim watched.

Chuck was amazing. I could see why he was a six-time champion. He played with me like a cat with a mouse. He was pulling his kicks and punches that came a hair's width from my face and body. The guy was outstanding, super fast. He worked his arms and legs like a rapid-fire machine gun. Every move that I made, Chuck had a counter move and I couldn't lay a blow on his body. We spent about a half an hour working out. That workout was something else, I'll never forget. If I had to run up against this guy in a dark alley, Chuck would whip me in a New York minute with just a couple of his moves. I was glad he saw me as a friend. I'd hate to have him as an enemy. Following our workout, we bowed to one another and he threw me a towel to wipe away the sweat. When we were ready to leave, Chuck told me to come back anytime if I wanted another workout. I had no idea at the time that this karate instructor teaching in his own studio would eventually become a larger than life action hero and star in a number of movies and television shows. Life sure has its quirks.

As the years blew by and I saw Chuck performing in his movies and television show Texas Ranger, I often flashed back at that one time we were sparring and working out in his studio on Ventura Boulevard. That one time I met him, he came across as polite, well focused and a happy, friendly person. With his expertise in the martial arts, he was a man that didn't have to bully his way around. Just in the attitude that he exudes in movies and television roles, I would think he's still a very easy going person that can get along with most anyone. It was a real pleasure to meet the guy and especially to work out with him.

Jim Kent-Guitar and vocalist- Country singer.
Brad played drums and sang in his country group in
the early 1970's throughout Southern California..

Our Trip to Hawaii

It was the latter part of 1972, and I had a couple of weeks between jobs, I asked Linda if she would like to go to Hawaii for a vacation. We went to a travel agent and booked a two-week vacation in five-star hotels on all of the islands, which included a lot of side excursion tours. I used to tell her how beautiful Hawaii was when I worked there for four months with the Mills Brothers back in 1955, so she was really excited about seeing the islands. At the same time we also booked a 30-day tour of Europe, where we would see the U.K., France, Germany, Italy, Austria, Switzerland and a number of other countries. We were to spend two or three days at each stop throughout Europe. The European tour was set to begin a couple of months after we returned from our Hawaiian vacation.

After our vacations were booked, we went to a photographer and had our passport photos taken. A few days before our Hawaii vacation was to start, we decided to fly down to New Mexico and have a surprise visit with mom. We hadn't seen her since she left California. The plan worked out great. We flew into Albuquerque, rented a car and drove to Mountainair, New Mexico where mom's motel was located. We stayed at the motel for a few days and mom and her husband, Roy, showed us around. They took us to the old Indian ruins in the area. Linda and I then left New Mexico and flew back home and packed up for Hawaii. We had coach tickets on TWA but an ex-drummer that worked with my band years before was now working for TWA Airlines and he upgraded our tickets to First Class. That was an unexpected surprise but a nice one. Aloha, we were off to Hawaii. Our first night in Hawaii was celebrated with a lot of sex but after the first night on the islands, Linda seemed a little distant and the sex fell to a minimum throughout the rest of the trip.

My relationship with Linda had been ongoing now for a couple years but at times during the past year, it seemed strained and I couldn't put my finger on it. I was planning to ask her to marry me on our return from Hawaii, even though I knew her parents continued to hammer home that musicians were unreliable. They wanted her to get involved with someone that had a steady eight-hour a day job instead of a musician.

Mom Back in California

When Linda and I got back from Hawaii, mom called and said she was having severe back problems. She told me she had to turn the mattresses on the motel beds once a day, and that was aggravating her condition. The doctors in Albuquerque also suggested that mom had heart problems. She was also planning to divorce Roy and wanted to come back to California. I told her I would fly into Albuquerque and get a hotel room for the night, and she could drive the 30 miles from her place and meet me and we would take her car and drive back to California. She agreed.

I told Linda I would only be gone a few days and left for Albuquerque. Back in California, I took mom to Mission Viejo Hospital, which was only a mile or two from my house. The doctors there told mom that she needed back surgery. We scheduled the surgery and after her release I brought her home to stay with me and Linda until she was back on her feet. While mom was recuperating from her back surgery, I received a call from a State of California official telling me that they had arranged for me to attend a law enforcement polygraph training school. Since I was going to leave the music business, I thought this would be a good move for me and traveled to Arcadia, California to complete the training. On my graduation from the school in April 1973, Linda and mom drove to Arcadia for the occasion.

Linda Leaves Me

Following my graduation from polygraph school, Linda told me she was going to leave me. She dropped this bombshell saying she met someone else. It hit me hard but I began putting two and two together. I thought about our Hawaiian trip and thought how she became distant while we were there. Linda told me she met the man while I was working nights. She also had him over to my mobile home and had an affair with him in my house. Even when I was in New Mexico for those few days to pick up mom, she had the guy in my house staying with her.

After her revelation, she moved out of our home and went back to live with her parents. A few days later she called and said that she would like to come by with her sister and her brother to pick up her things from the house. Okay I said, but before you do I would like to have one more conversation with you. She swung by one evening after she got off work and we drove to the South Coast Shopping Plaza to sit down in a public place to have our discussion. Over coffee I told her again that I loved her. "Honey," I said, "if my earning a living in music was the problem, you don't have to worry about that. I'm going to work in law enforcement. It will be a whole new career." I also suggested that if she had any feelings for me, we could drive over to Las Vegas right then and there and get married.

She listened but insisted that she'd found a new love and that's what she wanted. I could see there was no reason for me to press the point any further. It was clear she had her mind made up to leave and start over with someone else. She said she would like to come over in the next two days when I was home so that she could gather up her belongings. Sure enough, right on the appointed time, she and her brother and sister came by, picked up her things and were out of the house in about 15 minutes. They all left without saying a word to me. There were no goodbyes. They just drove off, so for me another serious relationship comes to an end. I guess I couldn't be too upset though because in my lifetime of fooling around, I've broken up a lot of marriages.

What really bothered me about this breakup was that she carried on the affair under my roof. I think I would have had more respect for Linda if she would have come to me early on and said she met someone else and was going to leave me and then go live with him.

I Quit the Music Business

After Linda left me, I officially quit the music business and chose another career. I had a great 20-year run in music. I had the opportunity to work with people that I would never have met under any other circumstances. The music business treated me very well and I made a good living at it, but everything has to come to an end at one time or another. It looks like it's time to move on to a new chapter in my life.

The first thing I did after making my decision to leave the music business was to sell all of my music equipment. I then put my mobile home on the market. I asked one of the neighbor residents living in the park that if he and his wife would keep an eye on the home and show it to prospective buyers, I would let him have a few hundred dollars worth of liquor in my wet bar and give them commission from the sale of my home. He agreed. My home was only about a year and a half old and it was located in an adult only park in one of the most desirable locations for some of the affluent well-off people in Orange County.

I was hoping it would be a fast sale. The home was custom made with a sunken living room, the best grade of carpets and drapes one can buy and the best major appliances that were available for homes at the time. I furnished it with a full seven-foot square glass and chrome dining room set with high back chairs. It also had a large hutch area for displaying chinaware. I also had a small office area and red leather Captain chairs that sat next to the breakfast bar. It had a wet bar installed that had all of the chrome sinks and fridge and mirrored shelf lit up back bar. Even though I didn't drink alcohol myself, a lot of my friends in the entertainment business and music business did, so the wet bar was a must in my home.

I personally made the decision not to drink alcohol when I was only 9-years old. After hearing the many stories that were told to me by my mother, Aunt Tres, and my half-sister, Grace about how my drunken father beat and abused my mother and how out of control my father got when he drank, it scared the hell out of me. In the back of my mind I always had the feeling that if I ever consumed alcohol I would turn out like him, a murderer. Was it in the genes? I didn't want to take the chance so I became a teetotaler. I don't think I missed anything making that decision. I could have as much fun at a party, bar or nightclub sucking down orange juice. It's funny, I have been around hard booze all my life. The clubs, casinos, my mother's taverns and restaurants and I cared less about tasting it. Maybe that was a good thing.

When I sold the home, I included everything in the house as part of the sale. I didn't even take the silverware or the bed sheets off the bed. All I left with was my clothes and nothing more. All the little decorations, pictures on the wall and knick-knacks went with the place. I continued to pay the rent on the lot each month but the place sold in less than six months. That was some good news for me because I was hoping I wouldn't have to pay a month's rent on my old home and pay my current apartment rent for an extended time. I was working my new job in Stockton, California as a criminal investigator when I received a call from my old neighbor telling me he had an offer from a buyer. It was a low offer but I accepted it to get out from under the house. Boy, the buyer made out on this deal. All he and his wife had to do was pick up the keys and start playing house. Everything else was there. Talk about a turnkey operation. This was it.

I took a big loss on the home but that's life. I couldn't afford to keep paying two rents, so I signed the papers and it was a done deal. I sent my old neighbor his commission and closed another chapter in my life. What do they say about hindsight? Had I been using my noggin, I would have contacted a real estate agent in the area before I left and had him or her represent me, instead of my neighbors. The agent could have held onto the keys to the place and shown it to all prospective buyers. If I did that, I may have gotten more money back or maybe broken even.

I also wondered if the neighbor I asked to watch the place only took the liquor from the back bar as agreed. Did he and his wife take anything else from my home for themselves? Did they take the heavy glass dining room table, the leather Captain chairs and office equipment, any small appliances like crockpots and pans and bedding? I'll never know but I always wondered about what the buyers received for their money. I often thought maybe that's why the selling price was so low. Was the place stripped? I was over 800 miles away so there was no way of knowing what the neighbors did. Over time I wiped the sale of the home from my mind because I didn't want to cry over spilt milk. I couldn't change what happened. If there's ever a next time, I'll first consult with real estate professionals for appraisals and representation before I go into the deal blind.

Law Enforcement Jobs

After leaving the music business in 1973, I worked in Northern California as a criminal investigator with a county agency. I then worked as Director of Security for a major clothing store retail chain. I gave that job up when I saw too many retail operations fold. I immediately went back into law enforcement and worked for different major police departments in California over a number of years. The last police department I worked with was the respected and elite Los Angeles Police Department. I joined their ranks in 1981, I was 45-years old. I loved it. There's no one in the world that doesn't know about the work the Los Angeles Police Department has done, and I enjoyed putting the bad guys away. The City of Los Angeles has always investigated some of the most horrendous crimes in the annals of history dating back to such grisly murders as the Black Dahlia murder case. Being at the epicenter of the movie and entertainment industry, the Los Angeles Police Department has seen its share of celebrity crimes over the decades and will always be in the forefront solving tough, unimaginable crimes.

Back to School

While with the Los Angeles Police Department, I returned to school and received two professional graduate degrees, one in clinical psychology and the other in the healthcare field. The Department allowed its employees to work at other jobs for a few hours a week if it didn't interfere with police business, so I received permission to work part time with my marriage family therapy counseling practice. In the late 1980's I eventually retired from the Los Angeles Police Department and acted as a consultant to law enforcement anywhere in the nation. I would consult with federal, state, county and the municipal agencies on polygraph (lie-detection) and forensic hypnosis matters. There were many times an agency would want me to use my hypnosis skills to elicit valuable information during a criminal investigation. I also continued to concentrate on alternative medicine and healthcare matters.

Back in Music

My life made a full circle so to speak. In the early 90s I again got involved in the music business. I was retired from law enforcement and looking for something to do. I relocated to Las Vegas, my old stomping grounds where I had such a good life working with name entertainers. Once music is in your blood, it's there for a lifetime. I bought a custom-made music keyboard that had all of the sounds that you could find in an orchestra and made the decision to work alone as a single musician. After being out of the music business for 20 years, I found that it had drastically changed. Instead of musicians working at the casinos on the Strip and in the hotel lounges and being paid a good union wage, some musicians were working for $10 an hour for a three-hour job. That didn't set right with me.

The live musician was replaced with recorded music and the live music acts that used to perform were replaced with magic acts and big production circus shows. I saw musicians in Las Vegas wanting to get a start in the business so bad that they worked for free meals at the club just for the chance to be heard. I told some of them that they were nuts. I wouldn't unpack my instruments for less than a few hundred dollars a night for a three-hour gig. I told some of those hungry musicians that if they had any talent, someone would pay to hire them and urged them not to work for free. It was sad.

Then there was the scam by the club owners to let musicians audition for a promise of a steady job. The musician works for free auditioning while the club owner packs the place with customers that can hear the free music and at the end of the day the club owner doesn't hire the musicians. I sold myself as a one-man band and I hired out for a specific amount of money to play VIP casino executive parties, appear at dinner houses and restaurants and play fashion shows and dances for all occasions. There was only me and my trusty keyboard. If the club didn't want to meet my price, too bad, I'd play elsewhere. Playing as a solo artist, I didn't have to worry about trying to keep four or five musicians working. I could play my keyboard by myself and sound like a trio, a quartet, a quintet or even a 20-piece big band. I had an edge.

A club, casino or dance hall could hire me and pay me, only one person, and have their customers listening and dancing to music that would have been played by a five, six, or seven-piece band. It saved the club a lot of money and they liked that. From the late 90s through 2008, I was appearing all over Las Vegas doing my one-man band thing while recording some albums. During this time I reconnected with some fellow entertainers that I hadn't seen for over 30 years. In June, 2003, I was 67 years-old and I was doing my one-man band routine in Las Vegas at a small Hungarian dinner house and at the same time Wayne Newton was appearing at the Stardust Hotel/Casino and the Righteous Brothers were doing their great show at the Orleans Hotel/Casino. The local newspaper, the Las Vegas Review Journal, thought it was worth mentioning and they put all three of our photos on the same entertain pages. It reminded me of the old days in the 50s, 60s and 70s when all of us were in Las Vegas performing at the same time.

Two years later, in 2005, I was entertaining for a number of casino VIP parties in town and lo and behold, I ran into two more entertainer friends that I hadn't seen in 36 years. The first was Engelbert Humperdinck, who I had last worked with in 1969, on the Las Vegas strip at the Riviera Hotel/Casino. He was now appearing at the Orleans Hotel/Casino, a small local casino off the strip. He was still going strong at 69-years old. As always, the ladies loved the guy. A few weeks later after seeing the Humpster, I returned to the Orleans casino to see Burt Reynolds. I had only met Burt two or three times at a few

Hollywood parties that I played at in the 1960s and 70s. Each time I met Burt, he was always congenial, funny and polite. Everybody I knew in the entertainment business who knew Burt always had good things to say about him. He's only 12 days younger than me and at 69-years old, like Engelbert and me, he too was still going strong. I guess 2005 was a good year for all three of us. We were still working in the entertainment business. Burt Reynolds, appearing in Las Vegas? It sure peeked my interest and caught my curiosity.

Since Burt wasn't a professional musician or singer, no one would expect to see famed actor Burt Reynolds appearing in a Las Vega showroom as a solo performer, but believe it or not, Burt had himself a nice, small, put together act. It wasn't a song or dance, or a stand-up comedy act but instead, he was doing a small intimate show which consisted of him sitting in front of the audience telling stories about his life, sprinkled with a few jokes. Burt would also invite the audience to ask him questions they might have about his life. His show wasn't an extravaganza or glitzy production but I thought he had an act that was interesting and different from the run of the mill Las Vegas venues. He should do it more often. The circle closes. What goes around comes around. I began my career in music and after the many changes throughout my life, I'm doing it again.

Some Reflections On My Life

The music business was good to me but as I reflect back on those days as a musician I can appreciate the good things about the life while at the same time, see the down-side. The up-side was meeting and working with some of the greatest entertainers in the world. As a result, I had the chance to form some lifelong friendships with many of them. Another plus was the free-wheeling life style music provided me with as a single man. I had my pick of many ladies as I bounced around the country. Then there were the parties and great food. I was constantly living in a never ending adult Disneyland. Some of the down-side of the music business was that I didn't have the chance to establish a grounded, secure, family life. My constant traveling didn't allow me to provide for family and children. I've found that most women look for a man that has a steady job and can provide security. Being a musician, my rag tag life didn't offer that. Over the many years working as a musician I was reminded of that fact many times over. There were those who thought all musicians were bums, or drug addicts and could not offer a future to their daughters. One of my biggest regrets was missing out on the house, the white picket fence, marriage and kids.

Throughout my music career and my entire life my mother was my hero. She was indeed an amazing woman. Here was a lady who only had a third grade education, a woman who was used and abused early on in her life by my father. As a single, divorced woman my mother struggled to support my sister and me by working two and three jobs just to put food on the table. My mother taught us kids, the benefits of hard work, fortitude, family values, morals and much more. My mom was a gracious, loving, caring person. Even though she was working multiple jobs she found the time to go to the hospitals in New York City and read books and magazines to the wounded veterans returning from the war. For those vets that were blind or their disability prevented them from writing home she would write the letters that the vet dictated to their loved ones. She worked as a professional hotel chef, fashion model and was an entrepreneur owning and operating her own restaurants and taverns.

Mom and I were close all of our lives. She was the one

person that provided for me as I grew up. After my mother got out of the abusive relationship with my father, I think she was searching for a good solid loving relationship with a man throughout the rest of her life and I believe that accounted for her multiple marriages. I don't think mom's multiple marriages had any significant impact on how I related to the women in my life. Personally, I have always treated all of my ladies with love, respect and courtesy. One of my pet peeves was to see a man disrespectful to his significant other. I couldn't abide seeing a man using foul language or verbally and physically abusing his woman. There is no excuse in the world the guy could offer that would make it right.

In all the years I was in the entertainment business I lost track of all my relatives. I left Pennsylvania when I was 15 years old. That was the last time I saw my Aunt Tres, Uncle Louis, my cousins, my half-sister Grace and her daughter Lana. I had no contact with them again until 1977, when my mother received a card asking her if she wanted to return to Pennsylvania for a family reunion. Since mom and I had not seen our relatives in over 30 years we decided to fly out to Pittsburg, Pennsylvania, where we were met by my mother's daughter Grace, who is my half-sister, and Grace's daughter Lana. We stayed at Grace's house in Belle Vernon and visited the relatives we hadn't seen in all those decades. Grace and Lana drove us to Pitt Gas, Pennsylvania where we visited with Aunt Tres and Uncle Louis. It was nice to see relatives that I hadn't seen for years. It was an experience.

That would be the last time I would see my half-sister, Grace. In 1981, my mother received a telephone call telling her that Grace was in the hospital and did not have long to live. Apparently Grace collapsed at work and when she was taken to the hospital she was diagnosed with a serious heart condition and possible cancer. I put mom on a plane to Pittsburg so she could see Grace. Lana, Grace's daughter, picked my mom up at the airport and drove her directly to the hospital. At the hospital mom was able to see Grace only minutes before she passed on. At least mom got there before Grace took her final breath. I could just imagine how my mother felt losing her first born. I don't think a child should go before their parents. It could only be a devastating experience. Once mom returned to California I could see she was grieving over the loss so I didn't say too much about Grace's death. I wanted mom's grieving process to run its course.

Since the reconnection with relatives at the reunion in 1977, I would occasionally receive a birthday or Christmas card from my half-niece Lana, who was living in Cleveland, Ohio. She even came out to California on occasion to visit me off and on, for a few days. On those visits I would take her to Las Vegas. She loved the city. Lana was the only relative that kept in touch. We would send each other a card on the holidays and I would send here clipping out of the newspaper letting her know what was happening in Las Vegas. I even tried to talk her into relocating to Vegas and start a new chapter of her life here but that suggestion never materialized. The cards and visits became less and less and there were long periods of time when I wouldn't here from her for years at a time. There was even one four year period where I had no word from Lana. We hardly communicate at the present time. A Christmas or birthday card, maybe.

It was 1989 when my mother's life was coming to a close. Between 1985 and 1989 mom had two small strokes. The second left mom unable to move her left arm but she could get around on a walker. Through 1988 mom had to use a wheelchair to get around. 1988 would be my last Christmas with mom. In 1989, the third stroke put mom in the hospital and during that episode my mother lost the ability to speak. She was transferred to a convalescent home for 24 hour care. I visited her every day, sometimes two and three times a day. I would just sit by her bedside and talk to her even though she could not respond. On November 25, 1989, about 3:30 in the morning I received a call from the head nurse at the convalescent home. She said," Mr. Kuhns, you asked me to call you if there was any change in your mother's condition. I would urge you to get here as quickly as possible. Your mother is not responding, I don't think she has much time left." I jumped out of bed, threw on my pants and a shirt and headed to her bedside. On the drive to mom I prayed to God and talked to mom in a loud voice, asking her to hang on until I got there. When I got to her room I saw her lying there covered in sweat. I tried to arouse her, yelling, "Mom, Mom, it's me, Brad." There was no response. I sat at her bedside, holding her hand, praying to God, and talking to momma from 3:40 in the morning until 12:25 that afternoon of November 25th. When mom's time came for her to cross over into heaven her eyes suddenly burst wide open, she looked up to the left, toward the ceiling, only for about a second, and then her eyes closed. She was gone. I lost my beloved mother 17 days before her 90th birthday. My regret was that I could not communicate with mom for those many weeks before her death. I wondered if she heard me all those days I sat and talked with her about our lives.

The only other relative I did stay in contact with on an intermittent basis was my sister, Ramona. We were never that close. I couldn't get along with her dysfunctional family. Ramona had two boys from her previous marriage while she was living in New York and a third child, Robyn, with her common-law husband, Ronnie. Mona abandoned her two sons in New York when she came out to California in 1957. I disowned Mona's family for good about the time her daughter, Robyn attended high school. Robyn became involved in drugs and thefts, and spent time in jail for the crimes. As the years passed, Robyn continued to hang out with the wrong crowd, who were all a bunch of losers. I told Ramona I didn't want to be involved with relatives like that and I refused to associate with her family. At one point in time there was a period of 20 years that I did not see Ramona's family. In the 1980's Mona married her common-law husband, Ronnie. The two decided to make their union legal after 30 years. They were living in Ontario, California when in 1995, Ronnie died of lung cancer. After Ronnie's death Ramona reconnected with me and would occasionally take the Greyhound bus to visit me in Las Vegas for two or three days, mostly on the holidays, either over Christmas or Thanksgiving. Ramona never learned to drive a car so the bus was her mode of transportation. She would stay at my apartment and I would take her out to dinner and around town so she could play the slot machines, she liked that. When she and I would meet we were always courteous to one another, but only because we were family. Between 2005 and 2008 Mona became closer and closer with me and visited me more often. She was becoming more estranged from her daughter Robyn and her grand-children. Some of the visits to my place were only to complain about the relationship between Ramona and her daughter. In 2005, Mona began to have heart problems. Those problems resulted in her having to wear a pacemaker. Her health began to deteriorate quickly. She eventually had to give up on her visits to my place in Las Vegas because she had trouble walking. It wasn't long after that she had to use a wheel chair. In the last few weeks of November, 2008, Ramona called me and asked me to visit her in California. On my arrival at her house she told me she wanted me to act as executor of her trust. Mona said she didn't trust her daughter Robyn, or Christopher, the one son she had contact with, who lived in Florida, to handle the matter for her. I told her I would rather not take on the job but she pleaded and begged me to take on the task. Seeing her sitting there in her wheelchair with her frail body trembling I relented and told her I would do as she asked. She was family and I couldn't say no. On November 21ˢᵗ, I called her attorney who came to Ramona's house to memorialize the agreement. I then returned to Las Vegas and a day later I received a call from Robyn, Ramona's daughter, telling me Mona had passed. I lost my sister on November 22, 2008.

Everyone in my immediate family is now gone, Grace, my half-sister, my mother, and my sister, Ramona. Where do I go from here? Only time will tell.

"End"

From left to right: Brad, in center- T.V. shows
host, 2nd. from right-Chuck Miller organist and
on the right-T.V. shows producer. T.V. studios in
Hollywood, California. Brad is being interviewed
regarding his charity work, with his band, the
"Encores."-1971.

Brad (2nd. from Left), being interviewed for his
Bands, the "Encores" charity work, TV studio in
Hollywood appearing on the Hobo Kelly show-1971

Brad, on drums during a T.V. show in Hollywood, California-1971

Billy Eckstine-A fantastic voice. In his later years he sang with Brad a few times at some private parties in Las Vegas, Nevada.. Billy was from Pittsburg, Pennsylvania, close to where Brad grew up. They remained friends until his death in 1993.